I0759503

FORWARD PROGRESS

FORWARD PROGRESS

The **DEFINITIVE GUIDE** to the **FUTURE** of **COLLEGE FOOTBALL**

BILL CONNELLY

Library of Congress Cataloging-in-Publication Data available upon request.

This book is available in quantity at special discounts for your group or organization. For further information, contact:

Triumph Books LLC
814 North Franklin Street
Chicago, Illinois 60610
(312) 337-0747
www.triumphbooks.com

Printed in U.S.A.
ISBN: 978-1-63727-870-3
Editorial production and design by Alex Lubertozzi

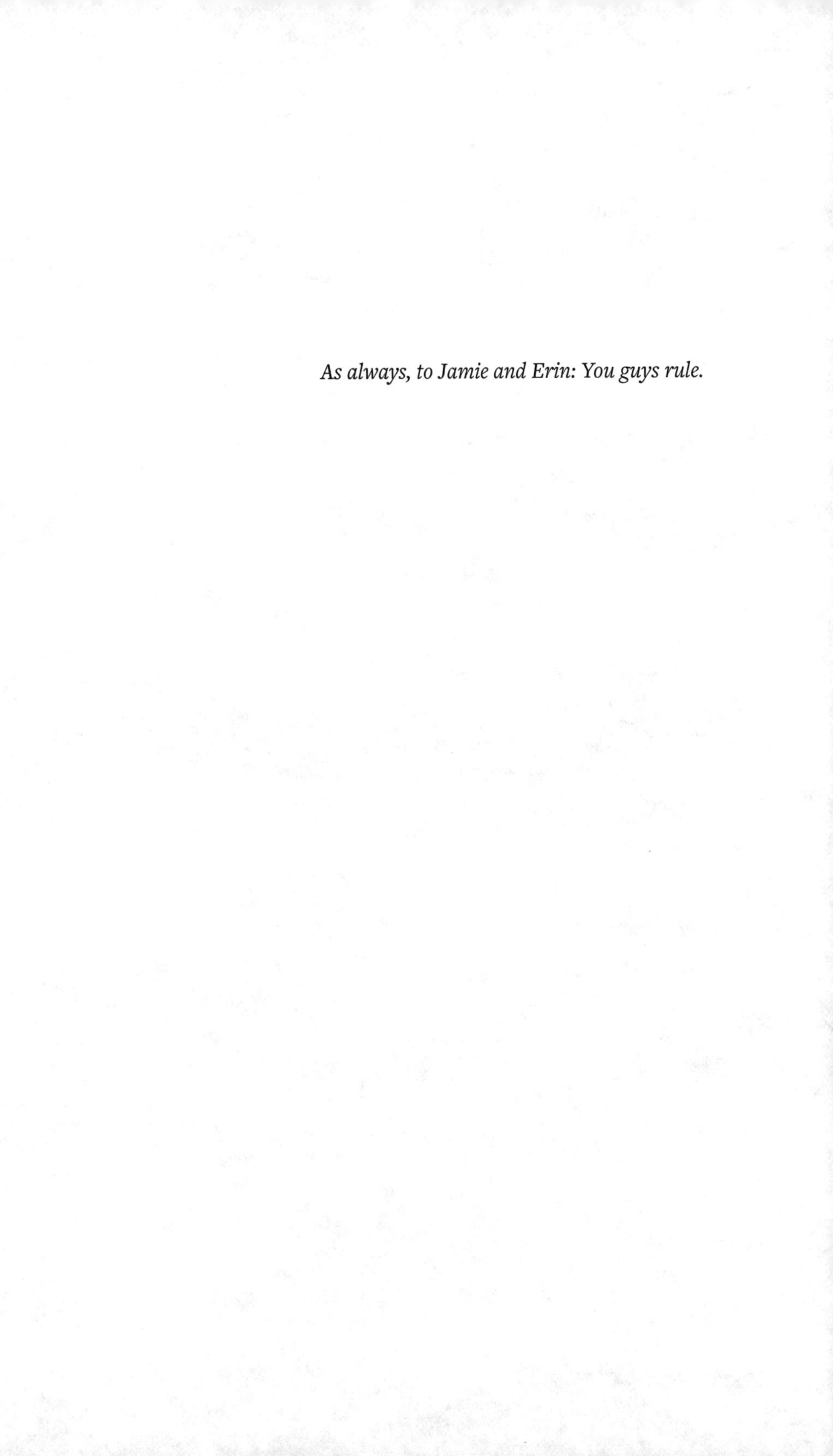

As always, to Jamie and Erin: You guys rule.

Contents

A Mission Statement

"Charles Thompson was framed!" an uncle of mine insisted in the late 1980s, speaking of the Oklahoma quarterback who was videotaped selling cocaine to an undercover FBI agent, got sent to prison for 17 months, won an NAIA national title after his release as a running back for legendary HBCU head coach Billy Joe at Central State (Ohio), became a motivational speaker and father of future college quarterbacks, and was almost certainly not framed. Before I had even attended my first major college football game—a blowout win for 2–2–1 Missouri over 0–5 Oklahoma State in 1991 that might not have survived a rigorous test of what qualifies as "major"—I got it. I had a pretty good understanding of what makes college football so unique, and my entire ethos as a fan was in place.

Simply living in Oklahoma and interacting with my obsessive OU friends and family, with all of their conspiracy theories and grievances, taught me what I needed to know about the blind fury of college fandom. Life on the Internet has since reinforced this lesson a thousand times over; this intensity exists at so many schools at so many levels, and it is at all times the sport's greatest asset and biggest liability.

Television had shown me Doug Flutie's Hail Mary and Barry Sanders and Brian Bosworth and Oklahoma-Nebraska and the 1987 Fiesta Bowl and Rocket Ismail and the glories of the triple option. I was obsessed with virtually any sport I could consume, but college football produced the wildest moments and the most sheer personality and passion of anything I had come across. And simply being able to watch a lot of games on TV, a relatively new thing at the time, was a game-changer. My college football universe centered around the Big 8, but I only needed to watch one Backyard Brawl between West Virginia and Pitt on cable to understand that *everyone* was obsessed with this thing. (One game was also all it took for me to understand how perfect Pitt's script helmets were.)

Attending random Southwestern Oklahoma State games in my hometown of Weatherford had exposed me to fight songs—SWOSU shares its "Stand Up and Cheer" song with Ohio; Western Kentucky; Montana State; Orchard Farm High School in St. Charles, Missouri; and loads of other schools—and mascots. (SWOSU has had a Duke the Bulldog and a Brandy the Bulldog, though I've always been more of a Brandy guy.) It also reinforced that college football really is everywhere, even when it's not on TV. In 1996, I watched SWOSU win the NAIA national title in Weatherford, topping the mighty Montana Tech Orediggers 33–31 after kicker Jeff Steindorf, who had missed two PATs on the day, pinned Tech at the 1 with a brilliant punt, setting up a game-winning safety with four minutes left. If I hadn't already known that this sport is as or more silly and delightful at the smaller-school level, I certainly did after that. (Of course, in my freshman year at Mizzou, I watched Nebraska beat the Tigers in part because of the Flea Kicker, an intentionally and illegally kicked ball from Shevin Wiggins' feet into Matt Davison's arms. This sport's pretty silly at the top, too.).

This sport is forever maddening and forever incredible. And in 2025 it is digesting the effects of a spectacular amount of change in a short amount of time: from unpaid "student-athletes" to properly paid football players; from a smattering of self-interested bowl games to a full-on, tournament-style playoff; from smaller, geographically convenient conferences to genuinely national leagues; from rampant inequality to, well, whatever's a few steps beyond "rampant."

Some of this sport's shift is a course correction of sorts, a genuine evolution. Athletes actually have some semblance of rights now! They can actually make money! And the playoff at the highest level of the sport is actually inclusive! But this evolution is threatened by the deleterious effects of conference realignment and the hoarding of revenue and power by an increasingly small group of schools and commissioners.

It's as easy as ever to be both cynical and hopeful at the same time. (Cynics, after all, are nothing if not constantly disappointed optimists.) There's a chance that, no matter what happens and no matter how much changes, we will continue to watch, attend, and obsess. But a sport never knows it's gone too far away from what its fans most genuinely value until it's too late to do something about it. Just ask NASCAR. Or boxing. If there's a negative tipping point for college football, we'll find it in the next few years. Or maybe we'll find that Saturdays are just too perfect for the sport to ever fall off course.

FORWARD PROGRESS

1.

Rewatching Texas-USC 2005 (Everything Has Changed)

"We're gonna play football. Yippee!"

Announcer Keith Jackson, for whom the word "venerable" could have been invented, immediately set a delightful tone for what would be the final college football game of his legendary broadcasting career. The game itself would follow his lead.

It was January 4, 2006, the end of college football's 137th season—if you count two 1869 games between Rutgers and Princeton and some football-ish 1871 games between Princeton and the Princeton Theological Seminary as "seasons," anyway (and you should)—and unbeaten Texas was meeting unbeaten USC for the BCS Championship. The Georgia-born Jackson, whose perfect drawl had defined the sport for decades, intended to retire following the 1998 season, but fate had evidently required him to stick around for a few more years so he could call this specific game.

Jackson called his first game in 1952 at age 23 as a Washington State undergrad. (Stanford beat Wazzu 14–13 after the Cougars botched an extra-point attempt.) As with seemingly every other industry in America, college football had changed significantly over the course of the more than half-century since. It was an intensely regional sport at that time. Michigan State and Georgia Tech finished 1952 unbeaten and claimed shares of the national title. Michigan State, with its integrated roster, played only one team from further south than Bloomington, Indiana.

Georgia Tech, still segregated, played one team from north of Nashville. The NCAA, college sports' governing body, had only recently acquired the ability to actually govern *anything*, really, and its members were still very split on how best to compensate athletes for their efforts. For decades, an intense debate raged between supporters of options as diverse as "a little" and "not at all."

In the late-nineteenth and early-twentieth centuries, football had arrived as a gift to regions throughout the country, and everywhere you looked there was a team that thought it could be the best at it. If you finished your season unbeaten, you likely figured out a way to claim a national title. As the 1900s advanced, the sport became more nationalized, and the number of places that could genuinely claim to have a shot at being the best shrank considerably. Prominent coaches and newspaper columnists began calling for a national playoff as early as the 1960s, and after a momentous Supreme Court case ruled that the NCAA couldn't control and limit television contracts in the early 1980s, more and more games began popping up on television. Media rights contracts eventually exploded in terms of both size and significance. So did conferences: in 1992, the Southeastern Conference expanded to 12 teams and added a championship game. The Big 8 and half the Southwest Conference merged and became the Big 12 in 1996.

An arms race had begun. To prove you were serious about competing for titles and big-time recruits, you needed more money, bigger and fancier facilities, and a larger coaching staff. Meanwhile, after countless split national titles and only 19 games between No. 1 and No. 2 teams in the 44 seasons between 1947 and 1990, those who controlled the sport—to the extent that anyone has *ever* controlled this sport—grew increasingly hungry to create something resembling an actual national title game. The Rose Bowl, with its ties to the Big Ten and Pac-10 conferences, held out as they were long wont to do, but other major conferences formed the Bowl Coalition in 1992 with these intentions. It became the Bowl Alliance in 1995 and, eventually, with the Rose Bowl and its tied-in conferences in tow, the Bowl Championship Series (BCS).

Mind you, Jackson, who had started calling games nationally for ABC Sports in 1966, didn't love all the changes coming to the sport. And he seemed frustrated by the constant cries for a playoff. "I think the hue and cry for the playoff comes more from the media and the public than it does from the people who play the game," he told journalist Jerry Crowe in 1995. "I think that the presidents of the collegiate community have to sit down and make up their mind one way or the other and put the issue to rest—either we're going to do it or we're not going to do it—and stop letting the harangue go on endlessly." In college football fashion, they did it, but only after nearly two more decades of harangue.

In 2005, however, we didn't need a playoff to know who the two best teams were. Everyone was ready to watch them duke it out.

USC was college football's gold standard. Since a triple-overtime defeat at California in 2003, Pete Carroll's Trojans had won 34 straight games and two straight national titles (the first shared and the second later vacated). They split the 2003 title with Nick Saban's LSU after a 12–1 campaign—not even the BCS could get the Trojans and Tigers on the same field—and in 2004 they romped to 13 wins and another ring, issuing a 55–19 BCS Championship Game humiliation to unbeaten Oklahoma in the Orange Bowl. USC players had won three Heismans in four seasons: Carson Palmer in 2002; Matt Leinart in 2004; and Reggie Bush, who topped Texas's Vince Young, in 2005. Now, with 93,986 in attendance and more than 35 million watching on television, they were one win from a third straight title.

After years of battling "off-season national champion" ridicule because of their inability to turn top-ranked recruiting classes into top-ranked finishes, Mack Brown's Texas Longhorns seemed ready. They began the 2005 season ranked behind only USC in the AP poll and faced only one real test all year: they scored nine points in the final three minutes to beat No. 4 Ohio State 25–22 in Columbus in Week 2. From there all other challengers fell by the wayside. In the Big 12 Championship, Young and company made an example of North division champion Colorado. The 'Horns led 42–3 at halftime, then scored twice in 90 seconds early in the third quarter. They could have chosen whatever they wanted for the final score; they went with 70–3.

The table was set for the biggest college football game in years. Carroll and Brown had crafted rosters overflowing with future pros, and after a number of controversies, college football had given the BCS formula a result it could actually work with. Born in 1998 after three split national titles in eight years, the BCS had at least assured us of a No. 1 vs. No. 2 battle at the end of the season, but choosing only two teams proved difficult. We got controversial selections in 2000 and 2001, plus the aforementioned split title in 2003. Even more controversy followed—Florida getting picked over Michigan in 2006, Oklahoma over Texas (despite a head-to-head win for UT) in 2008, Alabama over Oklahoma State in 2011—and every instance seemed to further galvanize support for an eventual College Football Playoff. And after we finally got a CFP in 2014, we got an even bigger one in 2024.

The BCS's biggest problem indeed tended to be that it couldn't fit three teams on the same field. (That, and every time the humans disagreed with the computer portion of the BCS formula, they ended up tweaking/neutering the computers, which ruined the whole point of the exercise.) But USC and Texas were by far the two best teams of 2005. And they produced a game so good and so perfectly timed that it would in many ways define two eras at once.

On one hand, USC-Texas is a clear relic of an era further and further in the rearview mirror. Keith Jackson's presence itself makes it a product of history, just as his absence would help to define the era that followed; after more than 50 seasons of work, he would retire soon after the 2005 season. "I'm 77 and I feel it," he would tell the *New York Times* the following spring. He was making an increasing number of errors on air, and while they were almost all minor and took nothing away from the experience, "I hate it," he said.

Jackson was the voice of college football's nationalization. If something memorable happened in the sport between the late 1970s and mid-2000s, be it in California, Florida, or anywhere in between, it's likely that either Jackson or another veteran announcer, Brent Musberger, called it. Jackson was there when Ohio State head coach Woody Hayes committed career suicide by punching Clemson's Charlie Bauman on the sideline in the 1978 Gator Bowl. A few days later, he was there for the goal-line stand that won Alabama the 1978 national championship over Penn State in the Sugar Bowl. He was there when Bo Jackson dove over the top to win the Iron Bowl for Auburn over Alabama in 1982. He was there when another Keith Jackson, Oklahoma's impossibly athletic tight end, took a reverse 88 yards for a touchdown against Nebraska in one of the defining moments of the Sooners' 1985 national title run. He was also in Lincoln the next year, when Jackson's one-handed grab set up a game-winning field goal and locked up another Orange Bowl bid for the Sooners.

He was there for Wide Right I in 1991, the first of a series of missed field goals that befell Florida State against Miami. He was there for Wide Right II, as well. He proclaimed, "Hello, Heisman!" when Michigan's Desmond Howard struck the Heisman pose after scoring on a glorious punt return against Ohio State in 1991. He was there when Peyton Manning made his collegiate debut in 1994; a few weeks later, his voice actually cracked in surprise when Colorado's Kordell Stewart and Michael Westbrook connected on a Hail Mary heave to beat Michigan. He was there for the delayed pass-interference flag that gave Ohio State one last chance in 2002's BCS Championship against Miami.

Jackson added to the lexicon of the sport in a permanent way with phrases like "big uglies" and "donnybrook," and, of course, "Whoa, Nellie." He called the Rose Bowl "the granddaddy of them all." His absolute Southernness was always on display, but he was also a Washington State grad and openly reminded everyone of his love for his alma mater; he claimed a bond with the hard-nosed Penn State program for which he called so many games; he was all of college football. The Rose Bowl announcer booth has a plaque in it dedicated to Jackson, featuring a call from USC-Texas: "This has to go down as an all-time all-timer."

There were plenty of other aspects of this game that make it feel like an historical artifact. USC had won or shared four straight conference titles in the *Pac*-10, after all, and Texas was celebrating its first Big 12 title in nearly a decade. Both schools famously landed in new conferences in 2024—Texas in the SEC, USC in the Big Ten—as the Pac-10, which had become the Pac-12 during an early 2010s round of conference realignment, slowly lost almost all its members. Plus, though stars like Reggie Bush and Vince Young brought ridiculous athleticism to the table, the offensive systems in which they operated have long since grown outdated. There were fullbacks in this game. Fullbacks!

At the same time, however, you can watch a USC-Texas replay in high definition. It's not quite 4K, but it's crystal clear on a big TV, something you can't say about games from just a few years earlier. Instant replay was becoming a huge part of the game, too. Plus, seeing so many relevant coaches—Carroll went on to win a Super Bowl with the Seattle Seahawks, with whom he remained until 2023 (at 73, he's starting with the Las Vegas Raiders in 2025); Brown coached at North Carolina until the end of 2024; USC assistants Lane Kiffin and Steve Sarkisian got screen time and mentions during the broadcast, too, and have since gone on to produce important and successful head coaching careers—certainly helps to connect past and future.

Neither past nor future mattered on the evening of January 4, 2006. It was all about the present. USC was a seven-point favorite. The weather was perfect, as it always seems to be in Pasadena. It was time to play football. Yippee, indeed.

USC quickly went three-and-out on the first drive of the game, but on the ensuing punt, the Trojans' Scott Ware rocked Aaron Ross, and the ball popped loose. Kaluka Maiava, USC's special teams player of the year, recovered. In the present day, the hit on Ross might have drawn a targeting review; regardless, it was USC's ball.

The first big offensive play of the game came from a fullback, fittingly enough. After a Bush first down, Leinart lobbed a 23-yard pass to 230-pound David Kirtman on a wheel route. A hard hit from corner Cedric Griffin knocked Kirtman's helmet off and knocked Kirtman out of the game. Jackson expressed surprise that there wasn't a flag for a helmet-to-helmet hit; we'd have *definitely* gotten a targeting review for this one. But it was first-and-goal, and one play later, big running back LenDale White scored from four yards out. It was his school-record 55th career touchdown. Just 2:33 into the game, it was 7–0 USC.

Texas got its first chunk play from a player about to have the game of his life: tight end David Thomas. His 18-yard catch brought Texas to the 43-yard line, but after Vince Young was stopped short on a third-down faux-option, five Trojans stuffed running back Selvin Young on fourth-and-1. USC got the ball in Texas territory for the second time. Bush moved the chains with a run out of the I formation—"vintage USC football," according to color commentator Dan Fouts—but the Trojans soon faced a fourth-and-1. Bush went in motion as a decoy, while Carroll attempted to call a timeout, presumably because he didn't like the look of things; and Texas stood up USC's offensive line, as Leinart lost his footing attempting a quarterback sneak. Another turnover on downs.

Neither of these teams had played since December 3, and it seemed both had some rust to kick off in the early going. Those long breaks are a relic now, too. In a 12-team playoff like what we saw in 2024, with a minimum of five conference champions in the field and byes going to the top four champs, then with current conference memberships, we'd have had a playoff that started in mid-December and might have looked something like this:

HYPOTHETICAL 12-TEAM 2005 COLLEGE FOOTBALL PLAYOFF

First round (mid-December):

No. 9 seed Georgia at No. 8 Notre Dame

No. 12 Tulsa (AAC champion) at No. 5 Penn State

No. 11 Auburn at No. 6 Ohio State

No. 10 Miami at No. 7 Oregon

Quarterfinals (around January 1):

No. 1 USC (Big Ten champion) vs. Notre Dame in the Fiesta Bowl

No. 4 Florida State (ACC champion) vs. Penn State in the Orange Bowl

No. 3 West Virginia (Big 12 champion) vs. Ohio State in the Peach Bowl

No. 2 Texas (SEC champion) vs. Miami in the Sugar Bowl

Semifinals (about a week later):

USC vs. Penn State in the Rose Bowl

Texas vs. Ohio State in the Cotton Bowl

Finals (mid-January):

USC vs. Texas in somewhere like Tampa or Atlanta

To be sure, this playoff would have packed all sorts of storylines and star turns. A USC–Notre Dame quarterfinal would have given us a rematch of the famous "Bush Push" game, a 34–31 Trojans win decided by a Matt Leinart quarterback sneak in the closing seconds. (Bush gave him an extra push into the end zone, which would have been legal in 2025 but really wasn't in 2005.) An Ohio State–West Virginia quarterfinal would have pitted Buckeyes quarterback and future Heisman winner Troy Smith against WVU's dynamic backfield of Pat White and Steve Slaton. Another Texas–Ohio State game in the semis would have been a treat for the eyes, and, hey, Penn State and Florida State really did meet in the Orange Bowl that year, and the game went to triple overtime.

Odds would have still favored a USC-Texas title game no matter what, but everything else about this path would have been dramatically different. Both teams would have had to take down their stiffest 2005 opponents—Notre Dame for USC, Ohio State for Texas—for a second time, and while rust wouldn't have been an issue, injuries and wear-and-tear might have been. And with all due respect to Tampa, well, Raymond James Stadium isn't the Rose Bowl, even if it does have a pirate ship.

These rosters were also put together in manners that feel awfully dated in 2025. While in recent years college coaches have had to maneuver through a landscape that features nationalized recruiting, expanded freedom of player movement (translation: infinitely more transfers), and the legal payment of players through NIL rights, both Texas and USC were incredibly *local*.

Thirty-seven of the teams' 44 combined offensive and defensive starters in the Rose Bowl were playing for their home-state schools—20 for Texas, 17 for USC. Both Vince and Selvin Young (no relation) were from Houston, as was star defensive tackle Rodrique Wright. Fifth-year left tackle Jonathan Scott and defensive tackle Frank Okam were from Dallas. Cornerback Cedric Griffin was from San Antonio. Safety Michael Griffin hailed from Austin. Others were from small Texas towns like Mart (receiver Quan Cosby), Splendora (defensive end Brian Robison), and Wolfforth (David Thomas).

While Carroll won some national recruiting battles for stars like White, receiver Dwayne Jarrett, and linebacker Brian Cushing, the vast majority of the team was Californian, from Leinart (Santa Ana) and Bush (La Mesa) in the offensive backfield to defensive standouts like ends Lawrence Jackson (Inglewood) and Frostee Rucker (Moreno Valley) and safety Darnell Bing (Long Beach). The only transfer in either starting lineup only sort of counted as one: USC left guard Deuce Lutui hailed from Mesa, Arizona, and, after initially signing with USC, played in junior college for a couple of years after failing to qualify, then arrived in Los Angeles.

Player movement was still rather restricted in 2005, too. Fourteen of Texas's starters were in their fourth or fifth year in Austin, and 16 of USC's were in at least their third year in L.A. When Texas reached the College Football Playoff for the first time in 2023, the 'Horns were one of the most local-heavy and transfer-light elite teams, but they still started transfers at quarterback (Quinn Ewers) and receiver (Adonai Mitchell). Only six of their CFP starters were in at least their fourth season at UT. When they returned to the semifinals in 2024, they were up to four transfers in the starting lineup but also up to nine fourth- or fifth-years. (USC's 2023 starting lineup was made up of nearly 70 percent transfers, far too many in retrospect.)

▻

On the second play of the second quarter, with the score still 7–0—it was the first time all season that Texas had been shut out over the first 15 minutes—Bush got loose. He fielded a screen with blockers in front of him, one of those moments that made college football fans lean forward in their respective seats in 2005, and exploded into the open field for 37 yards. But he wanted more. As he got hemmed in by Texas defenders, he saw teammate Brad Walker running nearby and attempted to pitch the ball to him. Two problems: Walker wasn't ready for the lateral, and it wasn't a very good one. If the ball had hit him in stride, the play likely would have become a spectacular touchdown; instead it hit the ground, and Texas safety Michael Huff fell on it.

The Longhorns' defense had bought the offense some time—with help from Bush's ill-advised improvisation—and Young and company finally got on track a bit. David Pino's 46-yard field goal made it 7–3. USC quickly moved inside the Texas 30 in response, but Leinart put too much air under an end zone pass for Steve Smith, and Michael Griffin swooped in to make an acrobatic interception. The refs didn't seem to believe he could possibly have gotten his foot down in bounds while flying toward the sideline at full speed, but replay confirmed the incredible play. With 6:50 left in the half, USC had created four scoring opportunities but scored only once. That'll kill you in a big game.

To take advantage of the frustrated Trojans, Texas offensive coordinator Greg Davis decided to go no-huddle, bringing a bit of tempo to the table and keeping USC's defense from substituting. Texas ripped off gains of seven, 10, nine, eight, nine, and 15 yards. Then, from the 22, Young gained 10 yards on a keeper. As he was getting tackled, he pitched to Selvin Young, who took the ball in for a touchdown. Inexplicably, there was no replay review; if there had been one, it would have clearly shown that the former Young had his knee on the ground when he pitched it to the latter Young.

Years later, this still irked Jackson. "The replay official didn't have the picture of it—they weren't plugged into the right place," he told Wazzu site CougFan.com in 2014. "We had it on our cameras—why not just open the door and ask to see it? The replay booth was really the first fumble of that game." Texas hurried to attempt the PAT, perhaps in case a replay stoppage was on the way, and Pino's kick sailed wide. Ball don't lie, as they say, but Texas led 9–7 with 4:57 left in the half. A discombobulated USC quickly went three-and-out thanks to a pair of penalties, and after a nice Ross punt return and another first-down catch for David Thomas, Taylor took a handoff off left guard and—with help from some incredible downfield blocking from receiver Limas Sweed—cut outside for a 30-yard touchdown: 16–7.

Bush and Jarrett moved the chains for USC, but the Longhorns defensive front then asserted itself. Leinart had to escape pressure and took a big hit from Tarell Brown and Ross at the end of a 14-yard scramble; USC called timeout with 49 seconds left in the half and Leinart wincing. After a checkdown to Bush gained 12 yards, Okam sacked Leinart. After another USC timeout, Okam charged into the backfield again; Leinart escaped but slipped down for another sack. The Trojans settled for a 43-yard Mario Danelo field goal and a 16–10 halftime deficit.

As Jackson noted on the broadcast, this was the eighth time the Trojans trailed at half during their 34-game winning streak. That included an

11-point deficit against Stanford in 2004 (they eventually won 31–28) and a 21–3 deficit against Arizona State earlier in 2005 (final: 38–28). Sometimes it took them a while to hit the accelerator, but typically when they hit it, the game ended soon after.

Fun fact: USC was once in the same conference as the ACC's Stanford and the Big 12's Arizona State! Crazy, right? There might be nothing more quaint about rewatching this game than the fact that USC actually played in a conference based in the Pacific Time Zone. With schools and conferences in an unending hunt for television riches—and with no commissioner figure atop the sport to provide a vision and prevent "everyone for themselves" maneuvering—conference realignment has, over time, broken geography and thoroughly scrambled the idea of what a conference is supposed to be. Thoughts of a nationwide conference first emerged as far back as the 1950s, but it took until the 2010s and 2020s to officially bring it to fruition. The 18-team Big Ten now stretches from Southern California to New Jersey; the 16-team Big 12 from Arizona to West Virginia to Orlando; and the 17-team ACC from San Francisco to Boston to Miami. At one point in the Great Realignment Wars of the early 2010s, as the Pac-10 was attempting to cannibalize the Big 12, it looked as if USC and Texas might become conference mates. A decade later, the Big 12 took part in cannibalizing the Pac-12. The SEC is still *reasonably* southeastern, but only because it found the big-name programs it needed closer to home.

Realignment has broken rivalries, too. Oregon and Oregon State aren't conference rivals anymore, but Oregon and Rutgers are. From 2012 to 2024, Missouri and South Carolina, located in Columbias about 875 miles apart, played 13 times as conference rivals while Missouri never played its historic border rival, Kansas. (The Tigers and Jayhawks will finally play again in 2025.) Oklahoma vs. Nebraska defined the sport for most of two decades; the Sooners and Cornhuskers have played twice since 2010. It felt like a win when Oregon and Oregon State agreed to keep playing as September non-conference foes; Oklahoma and Oklahoma State did not. In terms of ratings or attendance, these developments have not damaged the sport in any concrete way, but you never know where the lines are before you cross them.

It's the ultimate paradox: College football holds all the power in college sports, but no one is actually in charge of college football. Indeed, with no centralized leadership for the sport, the leaders of the most powerful conferences have filled the void, and any development that could be considered positive or progressive for players has simply threatened to expand the gap between the sport's haves and have-nots. Player rights increased exponentially in the 2010s and 2020s, with freer transfer possibilities and legal compensation available. Taking care of your athletes and paying them more has rarely made a sport less popular, but the SEC and Big Ten have tilted the playing field dramatically in their favor, both in terms of the size of their media rights contracts and their share of future College Football Playoff money. As we enter an era in which athletes receive a share of the overall revenue pie, schools within these conferences will be far better equipped to pay well and thrive. Most of college football's most successful brands reside in these conferences, and they're the most likely to thrive in any system, but it's awfully difficult to figure out how such inequality is good for the sport, especially if it results in proud and sizable fan bases from schools outside of the Power Two disengaging to some degree.

▻

Texas went three-and-out to start the second half. It felt like a statement by a fired-up USC defense, but it was fleeting—the second half would belong to the offenses. Leinart completed passes to fullback Brandon Hancock and Jarrett, then handed to White, who stiff-armed Huff, cut outside, and rumbled to the Texas 3. On the next play, White scored up the middle, and USC had the lead again, 17–16.

Texas responded by going no-huddle once more. A couple of zone reads gained a combined 22 yards, and after a quick pass to Sweed for six—this Texas offense was so good at just stealing quick yards and keeping defenses winded and on their collective heels—Vince Young gained 18 yards on a quarterback draw. After another pass to Sweed and a run by Jamaal Charles, Young raced to the right pylon on another QB keeper. His 14-yard touchdown made it 23–17 Texas.

By 2005, the media rights explosion was well underway, accompanied by the requisite rising budgets, and the idea of schools getting left behind in the process was already a familiar one. Less than a decade earlier, Texas had become one of four schools—along with Texas A&M, Texas Tech and, by a nose, Baylor—to leave the Southwest Conference and join the Big 8's schools in forming the Big 12. It was the second major super-conference—with 12 teams, divisions, and a conference title game—to form at the top level of the sport, and it forced four other SWC programs (Houston, Rice, SMU, and TCU) to scramble for new, lesser homes.

Realignment had already been a common conversation topic for a while by 2005, too. It had been only 15 years since the Great Realignment Wars of 1990, and moves were still trickling. A year after severely wounding the Big East by plucking away Miami and Virginia Tech, the ACC had recently taken Boston College as its 12th team, breaking into divisions and debuting a conference title game in 2005. It had created yet another domino effect—and food chain—with the Big East plucking from Conference USA, CUSA stealing from the MAC and WAC, and the WAC taking from the Sun Belt.

Back and forth we went. Leinart rolled left and hit big tight end Dominique Byrd for 12 yards, then found Jarrett, Steve Smith, and Fred Davis with consecutive completions. Then it was Jarrett again, up the seam for 24. Texas was able to force a fourth-and-1, but with Bush on the sideline, White followed his fullback up the middle for an easy 12-yard score. USC led again, 24–23, with 4:07 left in the third quarter.

After a short pass to Sweed and another well-covered keeper for Young, Thomas lost his footing on a pivotal third-and-3 pass but made a diving catch to move the chains. Then it was time for more Young magic: he dropped back to pass but immediately noticed USC's linebackers turned in the wrong direction, leaving acres of space down the left sideline, and rumbled for 45 yards to the USC 20. It put him over 150 rushing yards for the day and 1,000 for the season. Taylor got stuffed for a big loss by Frostee Rucker, however, and on third down, Pinkard brought down Thomas for no gain. On the first play of the fourth quarter, Pino missed a pretty easy kick—this time a 31-yard field goal—wide right for the second time of the evening.

USC quickly expanded its lead. Leinart hit Jarrett and Byrd for nice gains, then the Trojans went back to the run game: White, then Bush, then White, then White up the middle for 15. With White properly fulfilling the role of Mr. Inside, it was time for Bush, Mr. Outside, to do his thing. He took a hand-off, cut right, hit the corner, and flew down the sideline. His Superman somersault into the end zone capped a 26-yard touchdown. On the call, Jackson could only say, "Wow." Fouts, a father of four who had obviously read some Harry Potter in his time, said, "It's a game of Quidditch for Reggie Bush! Where's his broom? I don't see his broom!" (Jackson didn't respond to this. I'd love to know how immersed in the Potterverse the legendary announcer might or might not have been.)

On an end zone replay of Bush's amazing score, you can see Carroll in the background making his way onto the field and raising his arms in triumph before Bush even dived. In a game with a different ending, this could have been the defining memory.

In June 2010, four and a half years after USC-Texas and four years into Bush's solid but surprisingly unspectacular NFL career, the NCAA's Committee on Infractions issued a report accusing USC's football, men's basketball, and women's tennis programs of a number of major violations. Among them: Bush and his family allegedly received cash, free travel, and rent-free access to a home in the San Diego area from an aspiring sports agency, one that eventually leaked these violations to the NCAA after it failed to earn his business when he went pro. While even the Olympics had moved on from strict amateurism two decades earlier—with little to no impact on its overall popularity or perceived integrity—the NCAA had not only resisted such a move but grown even more punitive in its enforcement. USC was forced to vacate 14 wins stemming from late 2004 to 2005, forfeit 30 future scholarships and forgo bowl bids in both 2010 and 2011. And in a particularly mean touch, though the school had already disassociated with Bush (and Bush had already given back his Heisman), the NCAA required a disassociation period of at least 10 more years and told the school to justify "why it should not be penalized further if it fails to permanently disassociate." And despite a lack of definitive evidence, the NCAA also slapped forceful—and what a Los Angeles Superior Court judge would later call "malicious"—sanctions on Todd McNair, USC's former running backs coach, on the grounds that he "knew or should have known" about these violations. McNair would not coach in college again; he filed suit against the NCAA in 2011, and with the NCAA refusing to back down, it took a decade for the two parties to settle the suit through mediation.

Carroll had already left for the Seattle Seahawks following the 2009 season, but while his successor, Kiffin, brought his own inconsistencies and incongruities to the table, the iffy depth created by the sanctions certainly contributed to Kiffin's merely decent 28–15 record over parts of four seasons. After a run of seven straight AP top-four finishes from 2002 to 2008, USC has managed only one in the 16 seasons since.

Sagas like this and another involving Ohio State players trading memorabilia for free tattoos (which resulted in suspensions for star players and, eventually, title-winning head coach Jim Tressel's resignation) feel almost quaint in the 2020s. While the NCAA seemed to have public sentiment on its side in the 1980s as it attempted to investigate and eliminate illegal benefits—SMU famously received the death penalty in the late 1980s after an endless run of violations—that had shifted by the 2010s. The organization's overreach and frequently cruel treatment of the athletes it swore it was protecting contributed to this shift, but in addition, television revenue was also exploding. Because schools couldn't provide benefits directly to the athletes, that money was instead going toward skyrocketing coach salaries and facilities that were becoming nicer than those in the pros. Combined with a generally pro-athlete shift in sentiment that was occurring even at the professional level, the push for athlete compensation grew. And in 2021, following a unanimous Supreme Court ruling declaring that the NCAA couldn't prevent schools from offering additional benefits, the NIL era began. Nearly 70 years after the NCAA so cynically crafted the concept of the "student-athlete" in an attempt to avoid paying workers' compensation (or anything else), athletes were allowed to make money off of their names, images, and likenesses. The type of benefits that Bush received in the 2000s became in many ways both legal and commonplace. And the shifts eventually made their way to Bush, too: in 2024, he got his Heisman back.

▻

USC almost caught another break to start Texas's next drive. Charles was stripped of the ball after a brief catch, but the pass was ruled incomplete. It was a modern-day replay paradox: watching in real time, it looks obviously incomplete; in slow motion, it looks like a fumble. The call stood after a lengthy replay review—probably the right call—and Pittman quickly caught passes of 12 and 23 yards before coming off with a twisted ankle. But USC's defense stiffened again and forced another field goal. Pino's 34-yarder cut the lead to five, but the Trojans were ready to take control. Kirtman took a short pass for 33 yards, with a roughing-the-passer penalty tacking on another 15. White then gained nine to set up a play-action strike to Jarrett—"Six-foot-five and made outta old leather and hay string," per Keith Jackson—for the score. Griffin and Tarell Brown had hit Jarrett at the 2 from different directions, but they both fell, and Jarrett lunged into the end zone. (I guess the hay string made the difference.) Brown and Griffin stayed on the ground for a while, and Brown ended up with his arm in a sling. Texas's defense was getting thinner and thinner and had given up touchdowns on all four of USC's second-half possessions. Sideline reporter Holly Rowe said Texas defenders' heads were down, "dejected" on the sideline. USC led 38–26 with just 6:42 left. Young had led five fourth-quarter comebacks in his career, but now he needed a masterpiece.

USC's defense played a bit soft on Texas's ensuing drive, trying to force the Longhorns to eat clock. Young completed passes of seven, nine, and 16 yards, but from the USC 37 the Trojans blitzed, and Young made a bad decision. He threw against his body, across the field to the right, and safety Ryan Ting had a shot at a game-clinching pick. But he seemingly elected to bat the ball down instead. Or maybe he just did a very poor job of trying to catch it. Regardless, the incompletion gave Young one too many lifelines. He ran for eight yards, then found Thomas for six on yet another third-down completion. Young stole another six yards to Sweed on a blitz; on the next play, he rolled left, found no one open, and scrambled back right into space. Lots of space. His 17-yard touchdown cut the USC lead to 38–33 with 4:03 left. The first-ever quarterback to throw for

3,000 yards and rush for 1,000 in the same season still had a shot at pulling this off. Fouts: "I've never seen anyone like him in my life." Twenty years later, that might still be true.

After a nice Bush kick return, White gained four yards, then Leinart rolled right to find Jarrett for a tough catch, his eighth of the second half, along the sideline. It was a first down, but the clock stopped with 3:08 left. In today's game, thanks to a rule change, the clock would restart once the ball was spotted, allowing USC to eat up more clock. That rule wasn't in place in 2005. White rushed for three more yards, and on second-and-7, a Drew Kelson blitz forced an inaccurate throw from Leinart to Hancock out of the backfield. The clock stopped again—sub-optimal—but with 2:22 left, one more first down would still just about finish the job. Out of the I formation, White took a handoff up the middle and nearly spun for a first down before the ball slipped out. Teammate Steve Smith pounced, but it was fourth-and-2. Texas called its first timeout of the half.

You probably know what happened next. With Bush again on the sideline for a fourth down, White took a handoff and ran left. But Texas's defensive front surged, and White went down about six inches short of the first down. Texas had two minutes and nine seconds to drive 56 yards for the title.

The 'Horns went backward at first. A screen to Taylor lost two yards, then a pressured Young fired short and incomplete to Sweed. On third-and-12, Young threw a short pass to Quan Cosby for seven yards, but a five-yard, incidental face-mask penalty from Darnell Bing gave UT a first down. A slant to Brian Carter gained nine yards, and on a QB draw, Young stepped through a tackle and raced out of bounds. First down at the USC 30, 53 seconds left.

Carter took a short cross and raced 17 yards, again out of bounds. A jump ball to Sweed fell incomplete, then Young was gang-tackled again on a five-yard QB draw. Timeout Texas, 30 seconds left. A dangerous, well-covered slant to Sweed fell incomplete, setting up a fourth-and-5. Young's moment. The pocket almost immediately opened up on the right side, and for anyone who had watched a Texas football game in 2005, it was clear what was about to happen. Young again outraced every defender to the right pylon, ran into a swarm of media just off the field, and looked up into the stands surrounded by teammates, the aforementioned media, and Texas's mascot. (The costumed one, not the actual steer.) USC had to use its final timeout before Texas's two-point conversion, and the Longhorns converted it anyway when Young plowed straight ahead on yet another draw. Young finished the evening with 267 passing yards, 200 rushing yards, three scores, and the two-pointer. It was 41–38 Texas with 18 seconds left.

The game wasn't over. Leinart chest-passed a ball to Bush, who raced 27 yards and got out of bounds at the Texas 42 with eight seconds left. USC needed one more completion to get into field-goal range, but Leinart spent too much time scrambling and fired incomplete to Jarrett along the sideline. That was it. Cue the famous shots of a) Young looking up into the crowd with confetti all around him and b) actor and Texas fan Matthew McConaughey joyously wandering around the field.

Eleven years later, at age 88, Jackson attended his first game since USC-Texas. Naturally, it was the Rose Bowl, an epic 52–49 USC win over Penn State and maybe the best USC game since 2005's classic title game. In the third quarter, he made one last trip up to the TV booth to chat for a bit with announcers Chris Fowler and Kirk Herbstreit. His voice was diminished, and his attention span waxed and waned, but he was still Keith Jackson. And he was able to connect over a century of the sport's history with a single Amos Alonzo Stagg anecdote. Stagg won more than 300 games as a head coach at Springfield College, the University of Chicago, and the University of the Pacific in a career that spanned from—and this is not a typo—1890 to 1958, even longer than Jackson's career in the booth. After a Wazzu win over Pacific, Stagg told Jackson, "Big, fast people beat little, fast people." Nearly 60 years later, Jackson said the same thing to a modern, national audience and the current day's most prominent announcing team. If an 80-year-old Herbstreit tells this story to the announcers of the 2050 Rose Bowl—a semifinal of a 32-team playoff, probably, and quite possibly another USC-Texas game—and then they pass it on as well, we could keep this anecdote going into the 22nd century!

By the time of USC–Penn State, we were into the third year of the College Football Playoff era. Both the Trojans and Nittany Lions had narrowly missed out on a CFP bid because of early season miscues, though both would have made it into a 12-team playoff field. We weren't yet to the point where players would begin opting out of non-playoff bowls, and it would be a few more years until use of the transfer portal would so comprehensively change the basics of roster building, but it was noticeable how much the sport had already changed between Jackson's last two television appearances. You could tell this was on his mind to some degree; he at one point ignored a question from Fowler to ask the broadcast duo about their thoughts on the new college football schedule, though he didn't expound further.

Jackson passed away on January 12, 2018, just a few days after yet another classic Rose Bowl: Georgia's 54–48 overtime victory over Oklahoma. It might still be the greatest College Football Playoff game to date. He was around for when the new era kicked into overdrive, with the game itself proving as capable as ever of brilliance, even as tectonic plates were beginning to shift even more dramatically than usual. We're still trying to figure out where this era will take us and whether we'll like it. Let's use the rest of this book's pages to talk about how we got here, where we might be going, and what should (and shouldn't) happen to keep this game as healthy as possible into the 22nd century.

2.

A Brief(ish) History of Conference Realignment

Our story begins where so many college football tales do: in a hotel ballroom.

From what was once Atlanta's Equitable Building to the Mercedes-Benz Stadium, home of the annual SEC Championship and a mostly disappointing NFL franchise, it's about a 20-minute walk. Maybe it's a hair longer if you sojourn up into the Centennial Olympic Park and by the Olympic Rings. Longer than that, even, if you stop at the requisite Waffle House across the street. Regardless, not too bad a jaunt.

The building itself isn't all that memorable, especially now that the semi-iconic EQUITABLE sign is gone from the top, but maybe you can still feel a bit of a college football glow, an aura, if you walk by it slowly enough. Because on that spot once stood the Piedmont Hotel, where, in February 1921, representatives from 14 schools—Alabama, Auburn (then Alabama Polytechnic), Clemson, Georgia, Georgia Tech, Kentucky, Maryland, Mississippi State (then Mississippi A&M), North Carolina, NC State, Tennessee, Virginia, Virginia Tech (then Virginia Polytechnic), and Washington & Lee—met to form what would become the Southern Conference. Within a few years, Duke, Florida, Louisiana State, Ole Miss, Sewanee, South Carolina, Tulane, Vanderbilt, and Virginia Military Institute (VMI) had come aboard, too.

From the massive SoCon sprang two of college football's most storied and powerful conferences. Well, one in particular.

In 1932, Knoxville's Farragut was the hotel of choice for another momentous meeting, this one determining that 13 of the SoCon's more football-obsessed schools—Alabama, Auburn, Florida, Georgia, Georgia Tech, Kentucky, LSU, Mississippi State, Ole Miss, Sewanee, Tennessee, Tulane, and Vanderbilt—would separate and form the Southeastern Conference (SEC). In May 1953, the Sedgefield Country Club of Greensboro, North Carolina, was the site of the next relative mutiny, when, as the Associated Press reported, "seven schools, representing most of the actual athletic prowess of the circuit, pulled out in a momentous session." Clemson, Duke, Maryland, NC State, North Carolina, South Carolina, and Wake Forest broke off to form the Atlantic Coast Conference (ACC). Virginia would join a year later, selected over Virginia Tech and West Virginia.

The SoCon continues to chug away outside of college football's elite level, but only VMI remains from those initial batches of arrivals. While we're at it, the Piedmont's gone, and the Farragut is now a Hyatt Place. Change doesn't stop for anyone. Neither does conference realignment.

When it comes to conference membership and general school alliances, loyalty has never been a thing, even if we sometimes like to pretend otherwise. The Big Ten, then known as the Western Conference, voted Michigan out in 1907 because, among other crimes, UM chose not to limit itself to games against conference mates. Idaho and Montana were benevolently allowed into the Pacific Coast Conference in the 1920s, but the conference's California schools—California, Stanford, UCLA, USC—barely ever actually agreed to play them and *definitely* didn't deign to play them much on the road. Similarly, though Michigan has been a continuous conference mate of Indiana's since it rejoined the Big Ten in 1917, the Wolverines only agreed to play at Indiana twice before 1968. Conference membership has always been as much about geographic convenience and scheduling ease as anything, and there's always been a hierarchy within and among groups.

From this lens, the predatory conference moves of the 21st century begin to make a lot more sense. Money and ease of travel made geography less of a factor in major college football, and breaking long-played rivalries in the name of status moves and increased revenue became a more realistic option in the process. The schools that could take advantage of that, did so.

Still, things have just gotten *weird* at this point. The pull of (and revenue from) college football has created strange, unwieldy conferences, and since football is still tied to the rest of college athletics, despite the NCAA's minimal governance over the sport, this unwieldiness has been inflicted on volleyball and track and field and all the lower-revenue sports, too.

The NCAA runs the championships for the lower levels of football, but for the top level it has long existed primarily to sanction rule-breakers. Without a governing body or commissioner figure, there has been no one to express a vision for the sport as a whole to follow. That means conference commissioners or, even worse, university presidents who have minimal knowledge and/or concern about how college sports operate, have become de facto leaders for college football even though their actions have been and will always be made from extreme self-interest. (And for any fiendish traits I assign to conference commissioners in this book's remaining pages, remember that they are to some degree just reflecting desires of and assignments from their presidents.) The sport goes wherever the most powerful programs and conferences take it, and that might not work out so well for anyone outside of that power group. But before we can talk about the present, let's dive into the past.

We'll pick up this tale in 1935, in the aftermath of the SoCon-SEC split, as the sport's nationalization truly began. The first Heisman Trophy was awarded that year, to Chicago's Jay Berwanger, and the Associated Press began a national poll ranking the next season. There were millions of moves before then, but this is as good a place as any to start.

1935–45

Following the SEC's separation, it was mostly minor moves for a while. And obviously there were no major moves during World War II. The SoCon added a number of minor programs like Furman, The Citadel, and William & Mary. The Rocky Mountain Conference experienced a SoCon-esque split, with its more ambitious programs—BYU, Colorado, Colorado State (then Colorado A&M), Denver, Utah, Utah State, and

Wyoming—separating from the Colorado Colleges and Colorado Mines of the world to form the Mountain States Conference (eventually the Skyline Conference). Meanwhile, the come-one, come-all Missouri Valley Conference added various and sundry programs like Tulsa, Saint Louis, and Grinnell, and poor Sewanee, quickly realizing it had bitten off more than it could chew, left the SEC after 1939 and left top-division football altogether after 1941. In 36 total games against SEC foes, the Tigers had gone 0–36 with 26 shutout losses and a combined scoring margin of 1,143–84. Only two of their losses were by single digits: 7–0 versus Kentucky in 1933 and 10–6 versus Florida in 1938.

1946–59

In 1953, Michigan State, chosen over candidates like Pitt and the Big 7's Nebraska and Iowa State (who would have ditched their conference mates in a heartbeat for a shot in a grander conference), officially began life in the Big Ten; the Spartans were the conference's last addition for nearly 40 years. Meanwhile, the breakaway ACC officially formed, and West Virginia joined the SoCon. Colorado joined the Big 6, turning it into the Big 7—in those days, conferences actually aimed for numerical accuracy—and the Missouri Valley continued to add and subtract. And to the eventual delight of 21st-century college football fans looking for something to watch on Tuesday nights in November, the Mid-American Conference (MAC) formed with inaugural members Butler, Cincinnati, Miami (Ohio), Ohio, Western Michigan, and Western Reserve University, part of what is now Case Western Reserve.

Over the back half of the 1950s, things were mostly stable, aside from the brief waft of a rumored "superconference" consisting of major eastern independents (Army, Navy, Pitt, Penn State) and maybe powers like Oklahoma and Michigan State—nothing came of it, obviously—and the ever-revolving door in the Missouri Valley. The conference would at least briefly house everyone from Oklahoma State to Detroit to Louisville to Washburn to New Mexico State at some point. From its creation in 1907 into the 1980s, not including the World War II years, it never went more than six years without adding a new program. It almost never went more than six years without losing a program either.

Storms were brewing out West, however. In 1959, the Pacific Coast Conference fell apart. It was a long time coming. After a player mutiny against Washington coach—and future state lieutenant governor—John Cherberg, the PCC uncovered evidence of a slush fund for paying UW players. Then it found evidence of similar activities at UCLA, then USC, then Cal, to a degree (though that one was more "faux-work program" than "slush fund"). After a few years of mud-slinging, the outlaw programs and Stanford broke off to form the Athletic Association of Western Universities (AAWU), with its champion (Washington, in 1959) taking the West Coast's Rose Bowl slot. Idaho, Oregon, Oregon State, and Washington State were initially relegated to independent status. The idea of Washington ditching its Apple Cup rival for a better opportunity: not a new one.

In the coming years, first Wazzu, then Oregon and Oregon State would rejoin the crew, which would rebrand as the Pacific-8. But in the meantime, we almost saw the queen mother of all realignment developments: the Airplane Conference. Pitt athletic director Tom Hamilton, looking to go big in an attempt to assure strong schedules for his school, among others, attempted to put together a genuine, coast-to-coast superconference. In 1959! The five AAWU schools would theoretically join Air Force to form a western division, while powerful independents Notre Dame, Penn State, Syracuse, Army, Navy and, of course, Pitt could form the eastern division. The winners of each division would meet in a conference championship game. At one point, quite a few other schools were rumored to be involved in discussions—Duke, Georgia Tech, Miami, Penn, West Virginia, even an Oklahoma program that had perhaps grown a bit bored of laying waste to the Big 7.

Sports Illustrated wrote about this gambit in early 1959, and for a couple of years it seemed almost an inevitability that it would come together. But that dastardly Pentagon got in the way, dragging its feet on thc inclusion of Army in particular. By 1962 the idea had died on the vine.

The Airplane Conference is the ultimate rabbit hole, and in a couple of different ways. First, just think of how *good* this conference would have been. Here are the initial proposed Airplane Conference teams that finished in the AP top 10 in the 25 seasons from 1960 to 1984:

1960 No. 4 Navy, No. 6 Washington
1961 *None*
1962 No. 1 USC, No. 9 Penn State
1963 No. 2 Navy
1964 No. 3 Notre Dame, No. 10 USC
1965 No. 4 UCLA, No. 9 Notre Dame, No. 10 USC
1966 No. 1 Notre Dame, No. 5 UCLA
1967 No. 1 USC, No. 5 Notre Dame, No. 10 Penn State
1968 No. 2 Penn State, No. 4 USC, No. 5 Notre Dame
1969 No. 2 Penn State, No. 3 USC, No. 5 Notre Dame
1970 No. 2 Notre Dame, No. 8 Stanford
1971 No. 5 Penn State, No. 10 Stanford
1972 No. 1 USC, No. 10 Penn State
1973 No. 1 Notre Dame, No. 5 Penn State, No. 8 USC
1974 No. 2 USC, No. 6 Notre Dame, No. 7 Penn State
1975 No. 5 UCLA, No. 10 Penn State
1976 No. 1 Pitt, No. 2 USC
1977 No. 1 Notre Dame, No. 5 Penn State, No. 8 Pitt, No. 10 Washington
1978 No. 2 USC, No. 4 Penn State, No. 7 Notre Dame
1979 No. 2 USC, No. 7 Pitt
1980 No. 2 Pitt, No. 8 Penn State, No. 9 Notre Dame
1981 No. 3 Penn State, No. 4 Pitt, No. 10 Washington
1982 No. 1 Penn State, No. 5 UCLA, No. 7 Washington, No. 10 Pitt
1983 *None*
1984 No. 2 Washington, No. 9 UCLA, No. 10 USC

That's eight national champions, 36 top-five finishers, and 59 top-10s, more than two per season. Even with Army and Navy soon bottoming out from a football perspective and Syracuse doing very little in this period, this is a ridiculously deep and high-level collection of teams. And considering what it would have done for Penn State's perceived strength of schedule, it's possible that Joe Paterno might not have had to wait until 1982 to score his first title.

Then there's the other series of what-ifs: What the heck would *other* conferences have done in response? One assumes the odds of some sort of merger between the Southwest Conference and what would become the Big 8 (when Oklahoma State joined in 1960) are pretty high. Or perhaps it might have been the SWC and SEC, since neither conference was integrated yet? Maybe the other reasonably solid and interesting independents of the day (Boston College, Florida State, Miami, Pacific), plus sturdy programs from what qualified as mid-majors (Arizona State, Cincinnati, Clemson, Duke, Houston, Utah, UTEP, West Virginia, Wyoming) would have become prime commodities for other conferences suddenly looking for expansion and an increase in big games?

Regardless, this would have been utterly seismic. But it ultimately didn't happen.

1960–75

The Big 7 indeed became the Big 8 by adding Oklahoma State, while the SWC also moved to eight programs by adding Texas Tech. The Western Athletic Conference (WAC) formed from members of both the Border (Arizona and Arizona State) and Skyline Conferences (BYU, New Mexico, Utah, Wyoming), leaving behind programs like the Skyline's Colorado State, Denver (which dropped football), Montana, and Utah State. Montana would join Idaho, Idaho State, Montana State, and Weber State to form the Big Sky.

Some of the biggest moves in this time were actually contractions. In a massive move for the time, Georgia Tech left the SEC in 1964, striking out for independence. It's long been theorized that a feud between legendary Tech head coach Bobby Dodd and Alabama's Bear Bryant was the cause of this departure: as the story goes, when Alabama's Darwin Holt elbowed Tech's Chick Graning in the face on a punt in 1961, fracturing basically his entire face, knocking out teeth and giving him a major concussion, he wasn't penalized on the field, and Dodd was infuriated when Bryant didn't punish him after the game either. That supposedly fractured what had been a friendly relationship. The more official reason cited, however, was that in 1964 the SEC introduced what it called the "140 rule," which limited teams to a combined 140 players in football and basketball. Dodd wasn't in favor of the rule—he thought it would result in coaches running off less talented athletes (and therefore impeding their ability to get an education)—but it passed at least in part because Alabama voted in favor of it after Bryant said he would lobby against it. It's hearsay of hearsay at this point, but what we know is that Tech struck out on its own. Two years later, Tulane followed suit for a different reason: the Green Wave just couldn't keep up as investment levels increased and academics became a secondary concern for many. A power program in the 1930s and 1940s, they had averaged just 1.9 wins per year from 1957 to 1965.

For most of the next decade, moves were limited to the mid-major universe: South Carolina (ACC) and West Virginia (SoCon) each went independent, the Pacific Coast Athletic Association (PCAA) formed out west with schools like San Diego State and Long Beach State, and both the WAC and MAC expanded. And, of course, the Missouri Valley continued to add and subtract.

1976–82

After a run of big seasons from Bill Yeoman's Houston, the SWC finally added the Cougars in 1976. They tied for first place with Texas Tech and Texas A&M in their very first year. Elsewhere, the Pac-8 became the Pac-10 by adding the WAC's Arizona and Arizona State at USC's behest in 1978, and the WAC responded by bringing in Hawaii and Air Force. And as always, the SoCon and Missouri Valley rosters continued to shift.

The major-conference ranks had been pretty stable for a while, but the entire top level of the sport was going through a bit of an identity crisis. "More than ever, the NCAA is deeply divided and headed toward a crisis that could result in its destruction," the *Washington Post*'s Paul Attner wrote in January 1977. "And no one seems to know how to patch the cracks before they get too wide. Now NCAA executive director Walter Byers, who once laughed off talk of his organization splitting apart, is speaking of 'convulsions' and 'disruptions' within the group he has served for the last 25 years. That is how serious and open the wounds in the NCAA have become. Byers is presiding over an organization that has football powers warring with college presidents and small colleges fearing they are being run over by everyone. There is resentment and pessimism in all quarters and not even Byers has a way to put things at ease."

For a while, larger schools had been pushing for the creation of a football-schools-only top division within the NCAA, which created resentment from schools like Georgetown, with major basketball programs but no football program (or at least no *major* football program). It didn't pass. Meanwhile, university presidents and smaller or more academics-oriented schools were pushing need-based legislation—giving aid only to student-athletes with financial need (like what currently exists in Division III)—which also failed after threats of NCAA secession from football powers in conferences like the SEC, SWC, and Big 8.

By 1978, there was some level of detente in the form of a Division I split into subdivisions called I-A and I-AA—a "division of apples and oranges," as Notre Dame president Father Edmund Joyce put it. If you played at least 60 percent of your games against other I-A teams and boasted either a) a 30,000-seat stadium and average home attendance of 17,000 for one of the last four seasons, or b) a straight average of 17,000 over the last four seasons, you qualified to play in I-A as long as your school played at least eight total sports. If you failed in either *a* or *b*, you needed to offer at least 12 sports to qualify.

The initial hope was that this would create two subdivisions of about 80–90 schools each, but that 12-sport bar was pretty low, and the draw of (and potential money from) top-division life remained too strong. In the inaugural I-AA season, only 43 teams competed—teams from the Big Sky, MEAC, Ohio Valley, SWAC and Yankee Conference, plus a handful of independents—while 137 competed in I-A. The 1978 I-AA season ended with a four-team playoff featuring the best team from the East (UMass), West (Nevada), and South (Jackson State), plus an at-large (Florida A&M). The at-large won it: FAMU took down JSU 15–10, then topped UMass 35–28 in the final. In the proceeding years, Eastern Kentucky emerged as an early power, reaching four straight title games and winning two, while western teams also fared well: Boise State won the title in 1980, then Idaho State did it with its "Throwin' Idahoans" offense in 1981.

By 1982, the Ivy League, MAC, SoCon, and Southland had also been forced to reclassify as I-AA, as had most of the Missouri Valley, sans Tulsa, New Mexico State, and Wichita State, which would drop football altogether in a few years. The Missouri Valley would eventually make a move that might create a model for the current era: it ceased offering football in 1985 after its conference got caught on both sides of the I-AA dividing line, but it eventually formed a football-only conference—the Missouri Valley *Football* Conference, which houses schools that are in either the Missouri Valley, Summit League, or Horizon League for other sports. (It probably would have been pretty convenient for Oregon, UCLA, USC, and Washington to have joined the Big Ten *Football* Conference while keeping its other sports in a western-based power league, yeah?)

1983–89

On the surface, not much changed in the 1980s from a realignment perspective. After joining the ACC in all other sports in the late 1970s, Georgia Tech officially started playing ACC football in 1983. The MAC jumped back up to I-A, too. But while the balance of power was shifting dramatically atop the sport—college football saw five straight first-time AP national champions from 1980 to 1984 (Georgia, Clemson, Penn State, Miami, and BYU); and both Miami and Florida State, schools with almost no track record of major success before the 1980s, had emerged as the sport's shining lights by the end of the decade—conference rosters remained mostly the same.

Beneath the surface, however, the rumbling was endless. By the early 1980s, Penn State's Joe Paterno had become convinced that his Nittany Lions needed to belong to a conference and pushed publicly for it. In the summer of 1981, representatives from Penn State and other eastern football independents Boston College, Rutgers, Syracuse, Temple, and West Virginia met to discuss the formation of an Eastern Seaboard Conference with eyes toward inviting Pitt, Army, and/or Navy. But BC and Syracuse, original members of the non-football Big East, a basketball powerhouse, were happy with life there, and Pitt was voted into the Big East late in 1981. Penn State applied to join the Big East instead but was voted down 5–3. The school had talks with the Big Ten as well, but nothing came to fruition (yet).

The Big East lived a wonderful basketball life. Within a decade of its formation, six of its first eight members had reached at least one Final Four, including three in 1985 alone, and both Georgetown and Villanova had won national titles. But football's dominance of college athletics would only continue to grow. Mike Tranghese, who served as conference commissioner from 1990 to 2009 (and as a staffer before that), said this to the *New York Times* in 2009: "I think we made one major mistake. We had a chance to take Penn State in 1982 and we didn't. You look back on it and the whole face of college athletics would be changed now. If we had taken Penn State in 1982, we may still have football independents. The idea wasn't to take Penn State and start a football league. It was to give Penn State a place. And then they would have been aligned with Syracuse and Boston College. We probably would have brought Pitt in, too, and the four of them probably would have agreed to play and continue as independents. I think the whole face of college football would have changed. I don't think Florida State would have moved and Miami would have moved. All of it came about when Penn State made the decision to go to the Big Ten."

Is that actually true? It's hard to say. Tranghese has always had a bit of a dramatic streak—"My people are fighting for their lives!" he said to the media when talking about negative realignment rumors in 2003—and the financial pull of joining a football conference in the 1990s would still prove to be immense. But, if nothing else, adding Penn State in 1982 would have given the Big East both a head start and a trump card for the epic round of realignment that would come in the 1990s.

1990–95

Sports message boards would have thrived in 1990. Realignment rumors were unceasing. The era of superconferences was approaching, but no one had any idea what it would look like. Everything was believable, and anything seemed possible. Mergers! Scheduling alliances! A mega-Metro Conference! Something called the Mighty Midwest! The change we got seemed almost lackluster compared to the rumors that flew, but a lot still changed in a short amount of time.

The wave of realignment actually began in December 1989, when the Big Ten officially invited Penn State to become its 11th member. Commissioner Jim Delany, in his first year on the job, had to navigate tricky politics when word of the likely invitation leaked and school presidents within the conference clammed up, but he and the conference got the invitation over the line, and the school accepted.

Soon after the Penn State announcement, and perhaps in response to rumors that some of its programs might be plucked away, the Metro Conference announced that it was looking to expand. The Metro was another basketball-centric conference, and while all of its members—Cincinnati, Florida State, Louisville, Memphis, South Carolina, Southern Miss, Tulane, and Virginia Tech—played I-A football, they were all independents. That didn't seem sustainable, so the Metro Conference hired regional broadcaster Raycom, its basketball carrier, to prepare a report on expansion candidates and potential revenue opportunities.

In February came another bombshell: Notre Dame left the College Football Association. Helmed by former Big 8 commissioner Chuck Neinas, the CFA was effectively a lobbying agency for many Division I-A conferences and major independents. It negotiated television contracts for its batch of teams and established a platform for which it could air other NCAA-related grievances. From the start, the CFA was on borrowed time because the Big Ten and Pac-10 had never come aboard; when the Supreme Court ruled that conferences could negotiate their own media deals in the 1980s, the Big Ten and Pac-10 crafted their own deals separate from the CFA.

The CFA had the other major conferences, but in the 1990s, when money increased but primary rights holder ABC elected to regionalize a lot of its coverage to get more games on the air, Notre Dame became as concerned about national coverage as television money. NBC offered the school its own deal—one that continues more than 30 years later—and despite former school vice president Father Edmund Joyce having served as one of the CFA's chief cheerleaders (and having turned down many lucrative media rights offers in the past), the school accepted it. That struck a dramatic blow to both the CFA's relevance and its ability to strike big-money TV deals.

That spring, amid rumors that Texas, Texas A&M, and Arkansas might be lured away by an expansion-curious SEC, the SWC attempted to go on the offensive, discussing its own expansion plans with programs like LSU and Oklahoma. Those went nowhere. The Pac-10 hinted at potential expansion into television markets like Denver (near Colorado and Air Force), Dallas (SMU and TCU), and Houston (Houston and Rice), but nothing came of that either. DePaul athletic director Bill Bradshaw attempted to leverage the Metro Conference's uncertainty by discussing the thought of a "Mighty Midwest" basketball conference featuring metropolitan schools like DePaul, Marquette, St. Louis, and the Metro's Cincinnati, Louisville, and Memphis.

On May 31, the SEC, its presidents having just agreed to move forward on expansion plans for the first time in its nearly 60-year history, officially adopted a bylaw that would require 75 percent approval from its membership to invite new members. (It would soon pull a Notre Dame and sign its own huge TV deal outside of the CFA, leveraging CBS's desperation over losing NFL rights.) Within a couple of weeks, Arkansas, Florida State, and Miami were rumored to be under serious consideration, but FSU head coach Bobby Bowden was allegedly unsure about his path to a national title in a loaded conference. Plus, the school was unsure about revenue distribution and wanted to hear about Raycom's study. And, man, was it a doozy. Submitted in mid-July, it didn't just prescribe expansion, it recommended the Metro Conference *double in size.*

"The result of the study," the presentation said, "is the formation of a major, 16-team, *Super Conference* [italics theirs] encompassing over 35 to 43 percent of the nation's television households. It would be the largest collegiate football conference in America. The plan also includes a powerful, two-division, 12-team basketball conference that includes more television households than the Atlantic Coast, Southwest, Big 8, Pac-10, Western Athletic, or Southeastern Conferences."

To satisfy the heavyweights in the league (namely, burgeoning powerhouse Florida State), the plan also included allowing members to retain 90 percent of their athletic income while sharing a mere 10 percent with other members. The league would negotiate its own television contract "should the College Football Association television plan cease to exist."

How would a 16-team conference work, in Raycom's eyes? With pods! The two divisions would be divided into four groupings: Boston College, Rutgers, Syracuse, and Temple in Group 1; East Carolina, Miami, South Carolina, and Virginia Tech in Group 2; Florida State, Memphis,

Southern Miss, and Tulane in Group 3; and Cincinnati, Louisville, Pitt, and West Virginia in Group 4. The groups would be paired together in rotating divisions—Groups 1 & 2 and Groups 3 & 4 one year, Groups 1 & 3 and Groups 2 & 4 the next, et cetera. The winners of each division could meet at season's end in a conference championship.

At one point in the presentation, Raycom began brainstorming. "We foresee a time when the superconference concept that we have introduced in these reports could be applied to all major college athletic conferences in the nation. The Southwest Conference could merge with the Big 8 Conference, the Atlantic Coast Conference could merge with the Southeastern Conference, the Pac-10 could move farther east and south and include the WAC, and the Big Ten could expand east and include the Big East. Metro schools could become part of the Big Ten and ACC/SEC. In effect, there could be four superconferences with each having two divisions. Each division could consist of as many as 12 teams. Each division winner would play each other and the superconference winner from the East would play the superconference winner from the West. The North and South superconferences would do the same. The two winners would play for the national championship. The superconferences could include as many as 96 major college football teams with a chance to be national champions."

I've been playing around in spreadsheets and writing realignment-related what-if fantasies on the Internet for quite a while now, and I've never come up with something quite *that* wild. It makes the initial proposal of a single, 16-team conference seem almost restrained. And while this mega-Metro wouldn't have been *Airplane Conference*–level awesome, it would have been awfully strong. Over the 15 seasons from 1990 to 2004, this group of 16 would produce four national titles (two each from Florida State and Miami), 19 top-five finishes and 27 top-10s. Obviously, FSU and Miami carried most of the weight here, but Virginia Tech enjoyed a big run of success in that span, and East Carolina, Syracuse, Tulane, and West Virginia all registered at least one top-10 finish, too.

It obviously didn't take shape, left to become another historical what-if. Arkansas agreed to join the SEC that August, though Texas and Texas A&M stayed with the rest of the SWC because of political pressure.

(The state legislature wasn't big on the idea of its two flagship schools leaving others in the dust, though it would evidently soften that stance in the future.) Florida State paired up with the ACC, and with the Big East deciding to sponsor football—a few years too late, perhaps—Miami, Virginia Tech, Rutgers, Temple, and West Virginia joined Syracuse, Pitt, and Boston College in the league's first foray in 1991. Thanks to Miami's prowess, the Big East got to celebrate an immediate national title. After missing out on some bigger rumored names, the SEC added South Carolina to get to 12 programs.

The Mighty Midwest had its day, too, forming instead as the more restrained *Great* Midwest in 1991 and roping in the Metro's Cincinnati and Memphis as basketball members with DePaul, Marquette, Saint Louis, and the not-so-Midwest Alabama-Birmingham. It would last only a few years before becoming part of Conference USA. Elsewhere, after renaming itself the Big West, the former PCAA expanded with the addition of both western (Nevada) and very much non-western, football-only programs (Arkansas State, Louisiana Tech, what is now Louisiana and, for some reason, Northern Illinois).

1996–2003

The SEC ended up serving as a test case of sorts when, having expanded to 12 teams in 1992, it broke into divisions—Florida, Georgia, Kentucky, South Carolina, Tennessee, and Vanderbilt in the East; Alabama, Arkansas, Auburn, LSU, Mississippi State, and Ole Miss in the West—and created the first conference championship game at the I-A level. It was almost a costly gambit: without a conference title game in 1992, 11–0 Alabama would have been assured of a shot at the national title against Miami in the Sugar Bowl. Instead, Gene Stallings' Crimson Tide were first forced to take down East champion Florida in the inaugural SEC Championship. They led 21–7 late in the third quarter, but the Gators charged back to tie the game before Antonio Langham's 27-yard pick-six sealed the title for the Tide. They would go on to upset Miami in New Orleans to win their first post–Bear Bryant national title.

Once that bullet was dodged, only one thing mattered: the SEC Championship Game was a damn *goldmine*. It generated nearly $40 million in its first five years, and viewership was so strong that the league's television rights fees skyrocketed in a short amount of time. The formation of more 12-team conferences was inevitable, and in 1996 the Big 12 joined the party. Formed from a combination of the Big 8 and half the SWC—Texas, Texas A&M, Texas Tech, and, after significant political influence, Baylor (both Governor Ann Richards and Lieutenant Governor Bob Bullock were BU grads)—the new conference split into a North division (Colorado, Iowa State, Kansas, Kansas State, Missouri, and Nebraska) and a South division (Baylor, Oklahoma, Oklahoma State, Texas, Texas A&M, and Texas Tech) and became the second major superconference. It wasn't quite as lucky as the SEC, however: in three of its first six seasons, a national title contender lost in the Big 12 Championship and fell out of contention: Nebraska (to Texas) in 1996, Kansas State (to Texas A&M) in 1998, and Texas (to Colorado) in 2001.

One conference didn't stop at 12 teams. Following a lot of Raycom's blueprint, the WAC expanded to 16 (with pods!), adding former SWC programs Rice, SMU, and TCU, plus the Big West's San Jose State and UNLV and independent Tulsa. BYU won a 28–25 thriller in the inaugural WAC Championship in 1996 on its way to another innovation of sorts: a 15-game season. The Cougars played the customary 11-game slate, plus the preseason Pigskin Classic against Texas A&M and the bonus nonconference game that programs were granted to offset costs when playing at Hawaii. Throw in the WAC Championship and a Cotton Bowl win over Kansas State, and you had a unique and dominant 14–1 campaign. We wouldn't see another 15-game schedule until the College Football Playoff days.

As it turned out, we weren't yet ready for 16-team superconferences. Craig Thompson certainly wasn't. The Sun Belt's commissioner at the time, Thompson interviewed for the WAC commissioner job in 1994, and it became pretty clear what answers the conference was looking for. "Nobody's a clairvoyant, nobody's a soothsayer, but I'll never forget that interview," Thompson said. "They were at 10 [schools], and they said, 'We want to add a couple of schools. Who would you add?' I go, Hmm, boy, let me think. I'd add UNLV because of the [Las Vegas Bowl] and because of the market. And the basketball tournament's there. That's a good one. 'Then who would you add?' Boy, I don't know. But that was, like, for teams 11 and 12. 'Okay, let's add two more.' Two more! At that point, I said, 'I am not your guy. I think you're barking up the wrong tree here.' They hired Karl [Benson] instead. I just didn't believe in 16 schools. You can say all you want about being in four time zones, and San Jose State being part of the Bay Area and the fourth-largest market in the country or whatever. I'm not knocking San Jose State, but my point was, this is not going to make sense. And it didn't."

Indeed, the 16-team WAC wasn't long for this world. Frustrated in part by fewer rivalry games against each other, eight of the WAC's more powerful and/or well-located programs—Air Force, BYU, Colorado State, New Mexico, San Diego State, UNLV, Utah, and Wyoming—broke off to form the Mountain West, and the mega-WAC only ended up with a three-year run. The WAC did, however, still snag Boise State, Louisiana Tech, and Nevada from the Big West, which was struggling to maintain relevance after Arkansas State, Louisiana, Louisiana Tech, and NIU opted (briefly) for independence and Pacific dropped football. The Big West stopped offering football after the 2000 season.

Meanwhile, Conference USA formed from SWC remnant Houston and football independents Cincinnati, Louisville, Memphis, Tulane, and UAB in 1996 (RIP, Great Midwest); the MAC added I-AA power Marshall—which immediately won five of six conference titles—plus Northern Illinois, Buffalo, and strangely, Central Florida; and the Sun Belt Conference began sponsoring football. It formed quite the large belt, spanning from Louisiana-Monroe to Idaho. North Texas won the first four titles.

2004–09

As documented in the ESPN *30-for-30* film, "Requiem for the Big East," once it began offering football, the Big East found itself with dueling identities. It was still a basketball powerhouse to a degree—four national champions, 10 Final Four teams, and more than one Elite Eight team per season from 1989 to 2013 (plus nine national titles and 23 Final Four teams in that span on the women's side, thanks primarily to UConn)—but after initially forming a powerful northeastern identity, it drifted from its base. By the late 1990s, it stretched as far south as Miami and, thanks to the vital but not-very-eastern addition of Notre Dame in all non-football sports, nearly as far west as Chicago. There were two camps of schools, one for football and one not, and it produced awkward votes. West Virginia and Rutgers, added for football in 1991, weren't voted in as full members until 1995, Virginia Tech wasn't full until 2000, and Temple was never given full membership.

"I was never a Big East guy," said The Athletic's Ralph Russo, a New York native and longtime college football writer for the Associated Press. "I was a Big East *basketball* guy—that's what the Big East was. I understood that the Big East played football and had some pretty good football teams, but I didn't root for Miami because they were in the Big East like I might have rooted for almost any Big East team in 1988 in the NCAA Tournament. It was just my reflex—'Seton Hall's on? I'm going to root for Seton Hall!' But having been around that league, I don't think we appreciated what [the addition of football] meant—that the league was going to get torn apart." Dissatisfaction and division quickly grew, and eventually the ACC pounced, nabbing Miami and Virginia Tech in 2004 and Boston College in 2005. This brought the ACC's membership total to 12 teams, so it could do the divisions-and-title-game thing; instead of splitting its divisions geographically, however, it overthought things dramatically, creating divisions called the Atlantic (Boston College, Clemson, Florida State, Maryland, NC State, Wake Forest) and Coastal (Duke, Georgia Tech, Miami, North Carolina, Virginia, Virginia Tech). It was clear there was a vision of endless Miami-FSU ACC Championship Games. Two decades after the move, there have been zero Miami-FSU ACC Championship Games.

In response to this attrition, the Big East did a very Big East thing, raiding Conference USA to add three more schools with football teams (Cincinnati, Louisville, and USF) and two without (DePaul and Marquette). None of them were particularly northeastern, but Louisville would win a basketball national title in 2013, at least. The conference also used the occasion to incorporate UConn's independent football program and boot Temple for general football ineptitude; in 14 years in the conference, the Owls averaged 2.1 wins per season. After a couple of bleak seasons of independence, they would find their footing in the MAC.

Elsewhere, Conference USA underwent one of its many regenerations, not only losing five schools to the Big East but also losing TCU (Mountain West) and Army (independence). It reached down the ladder to claim six WAC programs, while the WAC reached down to take three from the Sun Belt, and the Sun Belt added a trio of programs from Division I-AA, which was now called the Football Championship Subdivision (FCS). Division I-A had become the Football Bowl Subdivision (FBS), because FBS and FCS designations are apparently clearer and more understandable than I-A and I-AA?

2010–19

It began with an incredibly mundane statement from the Big Ten Council of Presidents/Chancellors (COP/C, maybe the worst acronym in the history of acronyms) on December 15, 2009.

"Penn State joined the Big Ten Conference in June of 1990," the statement read, "and its addition has been an unqualified success. In 1993, 1998, and 2003 the COP/C, in coordination with the commissioner's office, reviewed the issue of conference structure and expansion. The COP/C believes that the timing is right for the conference to once again conduct a thorough evaluation of options for conference structure and expansion. As a result, the commissioner was asked to provide recommendations for consideration by the COP/C over the next 12 to 18 months."

And with that, a million Internet rumors ignited. Missouri fans and officials, long fascinated by a potential Big Ten move and annoyed by the Big 12's Texas influence and unequal media revenue distribution, were all over the idea. The university had supposedly hired a public relations firm to promote itself to the Big Ten in the 1990s, and this time even Missouri governor Jay Nixon got in on the act, telling the Associated Press, "I'm not going to say anything bad about the Big 12, but when you compare Oklahoma State to Northwestern, when you compare Texas Tech to Wisconsin, you begin looking at educational possibilities that are worth looking at." (That's the academic version of Ricky Bobby saying, "With all due respect, and remember, I'm saying *with all due respect...*")

The speculation continued through the spring, with the Big 12's Missouri and Nebraska; the Big East's Pitt, Rutgers, and Syracuse; and the ACC's Maryland all drawing mention. Meanwhile, the Pac-10, led by aggressive new commissioner Larry Scott and looking for a smash-hit conference network to compete with the money-printing machine that the nascent Big Ten Network was becoming, started hinting at a big swing, hoping to reel in half the Big 12: Colorado, Oklahoma, Oklahoma State, Texas, Texas A&M, and Texas Tech. Texas A&M was linked to both the Pac-10 and SEC. Notre Dame was rumored to be maybe kinda sorta actually open to a Big Ten invitation after decades of ignoring interest. Every football columnist in the country, give or take, wrote about the impending world of four 16-team superconferences. The Big East and Mountain West both prepared to pounce on whatever leftovers were produced when the Big 12 inevitably fell apart. By June, the information seemed to change by the day. The likelihood of the Big Ten adding both Nebraska and Missouri, plus at least one eastern program, seemed high. The Pac-16 seemed like a done deal.

On June 10, Colorado officially announced it was heading to the Pac-10; on June 11, Nebraska regents voted unanimously to join the Big Ten. Here came the domino effect! But then...nothing. The Big Ten stopped at 12 programs—they also did the most pretentious thing in the history of organized sports, eschewing geography in favor of specifically curated divisions named Leaders and Legends—and Texas announced on June 14 that it was remaining in the Big 12. Conference commissioner Dan Beebe had presented assurances of improved television revenue for all conference members and pointed out to Texas that it would be able to start its *own* network by remaining in the Big 12. That wouldn't be an option in the Pac-16.

That slowed the rumor train down considerably. The Mountain West would soon lose three schools—Utah to what would become the Pac-12, BYU to independence, and starting in 2012, TCU to the Big East—and add the WAC's Boise State, Fresno State, Nevada, and Hawaii, but moves ceased at the major-conference level. We all made jokes about the Big 12 having 10 schools and the Big Ten having 12, but otherwise things calmed down. For a few months.

In July 2011, the long-rumored Longhorn Network was officially announced. With Beebe's encouragement, Texas had linked up with ESPN to create its own network, allowing it to make a significantly higher amount in media rights revenue than its conference colleagues. That was evidently the last straw for Texas A&M, which started making phone calls; on August 31, the Aggies were officially announced as the 13th SEC program. About two months later, Missouri joined them. Scrambling for safety once again, the Big 12 added West Virginia and TCU, which left the Big East, and paid an exit fee, without ever actually playing in it. (Craig Thompson relayed a quote from TCU's then–athletic director Chris Del Conte: "I spent $5 million to go to one Big East meeting.")

The Big East's long-term cracks were suddenly becoming fissures. Syracuse and Pitt also announced they were leaving for the ACC, and in response the conference scooped up every decent mid-major program it could find, taking Conference USA's UCF, Houston, and SMU, and the *decidedly* non-east Boise State and San Diego State. It reinvited Temple's suddenly perky football program, too. Meanwhile, to fend off further plucking, the Mountain West and Conference USA agreed to form an alliance of sorts, a giant league—first football-only, then all sports—featuring whatever programs they had left after this round of raids. "I'm now going to be a hypocrite," Thompson said. "In 1994, I didn't believe in that model. But jump forward almost two decades, and [CUSA commissioner] Britton Banowsky and I were talking about coming up with a big, ol' 24[-team] deal! But our model was like the AFC and NFC in the NFL—like, you'd have your own deal, and we'd have one big tournament, the top however many teams. But you really wouldn't play those guys much. It was two separate divisions."

By the spring of 2012, this arrangement was said to feature most or all WAC schools, too. But alliances never actually stick in realignment; by May, the MWC announced it was adding the WAC's San Jose State and Utah State, and Conference USA plundered schools from the dying WAC (Louisiana Tech, Texas-San Antonio) and the Sun Belt (Florida International, North Texas) and added new Charlotte and Old Dominion football programs, as well. By the summer, the idea of an alliance or merger had quietly fizzled. "We were misguided in thinking somehow we'd be awarded two automatic bids in all those sports," Thompson said. "That wasn't going to happen. It would have been a fun deal, but consolidation was the point. We'd gone down the road a little bit and basically realized we weren't making a lot in TV revenue—if you put a couple halves together, do you get a complete whole? Maybe, maybe not."

The steady trickle continued in the fall of 2012. In September, Notre Dame announced it would be moving its non-football programs from the increasingly wobbly Big East to the increasingly sturdy ACC. In November, the Big Ten leaned heavily into the "adding media markets for your television network" thing, adding Rutgers (near New York City) and Maryland (near Washington, D.C.); both teams had seen reasonable football success of late, but the intention of these moves was obvious. In response, the ACC again raided the Big East, this time for Louisville. That one hurt. A couple of weeks later, the Big East's non-football schools, colloquially known as the Catholic 7, split to form their own conference, one that would be called...the Big East. The remaining schools would form the American Athletic Conference (AAC). It would no longer be recognized as a power conference. Boise State and San Diego State backed out and decided to remain in the Mountain West.

When the dust settled, we still didn't have four 16-team power conferences, but the landscape was set for a bit. The ACC, Big 12, Big Ten, Pac-12, and SEC became known informally as the Power Five, and with the WAC falling apart, there were five mid-major conferences we called the Group of Five. By 2013, three of these power conferences (Big Ten, Pac-12, SEC) had their own networks, and the ACC would join that party in 2019. Four of the five had conference title games, with the Big 12 having dropped its own after dropping to 10 teams. But feeling left out—okay, it wanted the money—it got a "you don't need 12 teams and divisions to have a title game" waiver and reinstated the title game in 2017.

Rosters continued to churn at the G5 level: the AAC added Navy for football (and then Army in the 2020s), the MAC and ill-fitting UMass parted ways in 2015 (and then reunited in 2025), and the Sun Belt dropped ill-fitting Idaho (which fell to FCS) and NMSU (independence) and added FCS call-ups Appalachian State, Coastal Carolina, Georgia

Southern, and Georgia State. But for a brief time, at least, we had both relative symmetry and stability at the top of the sport.

2020–Present

There was a time in the 2000s and 2010s when Internet sleuths could occasionally out-journalist journalists. To hell with your well-established sources and proper fact-checking protocol—we've got Flight Aware! We've got friends of friends of friends within the athletic department! Our spouses have friends who are real estate agents who showed Bobby Petrino's wife around some houses in [insert your city here]! There was nothing more exhilarating than hopping on Flight Aware and finding a special flight from a particularly interesting city to a particularly interesting regional airport and jumping to conclusions. (Especially when those conclusions turned out to be right about 2 percent of the time.)

By the 2020s, athletic departments had gotten too smart for that. Search firms allowed athletic directors or conference commissioners to meet prospective coaches or school officials without much of a proverbial paper trail; that, or they would meet said coaches or officials on a neutral site, so to speak, a larger city that wouldn't draw suspicion. As it turned out, journalists' sources weren't quite as talkative, either. And while realignment rumors never completely fell silent, two of the biggest moves in the history of realignment came with almost no warning whatsoever. On July 21, 2021, seemingly out of the blue, the *Houston Chronicle* reported that the Big 12's Texas and Oklahoma had reached out to the SEC about joining the league. Within a week, it was official. On June 30, 2022, word broke that USC and UCLA were leaving the Pac-12 for the Big Ten. It was official that very afternoon.

There are only a certain number of genuine *brands* in college football, schools that can serve as anchors for a successful and lucrative conference. For decades, they were pretty well-distributed. You had Oklahoma and Nebraska in the Big 8 and Texas and Texas A&M in the SWC; that quartet then anchored the Big 12. Michigan and Ohio State have always lorded over the rest of the Big Ten, and Penn State joined the ruling class in the 1990s. Alabama has been the most successful program in the sport for the last century, though the SEC has long benefited from having a number of huge fan bases in particularly high-capacity stadiums (Tennessee, LSU, Georgia, Florida, Auburn). And while the balance of power shifted occasionally out west, the Pac-12 always had its Big Bad in USC. The Trojans were always the team other conference members would get up for. These programs didn't need to be good to command eyeballs—and some of them frequently weren't—but they were still heavyweights.

All told, there are 22 programs that currently play in stadiums with a capacity of 75,000 people or higher. In 2004, the SEC housed eight of them, while the Big Ten had five, the Big 12 four, the Pac-10 two, and the ACC two. (Notre Dame, the other team, was and somehow remains independent.) The SEC and Big Ten led the way, but they had only 62 percent of the non–Notre Dame programs between them, and every power conference was represented.

In 2025, 19 live in either the SEC (11) or Big Ten (eight). The Big 12 has lost all four of its guiding lights, and the ACC might or might not hold onto its two (Clemson and Florida State) for much longer, due primarily to disparity in media rights revenues: Big Ten and SEC schools will approach $80–100 million per school per year in the coming years, while the Big 12 and ACC are more in the $30–40 million range.

Walk through realignment's history, and you'll see that there's really nothing new under the sun. Programs that consider themselves particularly serious have always tried to align with other serious programs. USC was willing to choose Penn State and Notre Dame over Oregon State and Washington State as far back as the 1950s, and schools deemed less serious than their peers, from Montana to Colorado College to much of the SoCon, have been getting left behind for a century. But for one reason or another—geography, the promise of the Longhorn Network, the Pentagon—the biggest moves never quite happened, and the anchor programs remained reasonably well-distributed. As with seemingly every other industry in America, however, consolidation officially found college football in the 2020s.

"It's the consolidation of the brands and big powers. I don't think that's healthy for the sport," Ralph Russo said. "We do love the what-if game, but what if Texas does join the Pac-12? That would have been, 'RIP,

Big 12,' and maybe that's not the kindest way to treat Iowa State and Kansas and Kansas State. But I could sort of see a path here where the country stays a little more balanced. If the states of Texas and California are now sort of aligned in their power, that lifts up that conference, and you have the traditional Southeast still sort of pouring into [the SEC and ACC], and then the Midwest is strong, as well. We talk about making it a national sport, but we blew up the balance."

We also blew up a bunch of longtime series. "I had a chart on my desk at one point," Thompson said. "There were like 70 series, contests between schools, that aren't played anymore. Pitt–West Virginia. Oklahoma-Nebraska at Thanksgiving. We just lost a lot of that. Now, times change. I get it. But that was probably the greatest single marketing tool college football had."

The Big 12, wobbly as it may have been, remained unkillable. In the fall of 2021, after talks of a raid from or merger with the Pac-12—an idea many suggest was shut down by USC, which might or might not have already been engaging in conversations with the Big Ten at the time—the Big 12 instead plucked Cincinnati, Houston, and UCF from the AAC and added independent BYU. The AAC then reached down the totem pole and grabbed a sextet of Conference USA teams (Charlotte, FAU, North Texas, Rice, UAB, and UTSA), a true quantity-over-quality addition. Sensing vulnerability, the Sun Belt pounced on CUSA just as CUSA had done to the Sun Belt a decade earlier, adding Marshall, Old Dominion, and Southern Miss, and outdueling its rival for the services of FCS powerhouse James Madison. Down to just five programs, CUSA quickly added two independents (Liberty and New Mexico State) and two FCS programs (Jacksonville State and Sam Houston). For good measure, it announced the addition of more FCS programs (Kennesaw State, Delaware, and Missouri State) in the following years. In 2025, FBS's membership stands at 136 teams. At one point or another in its existence, CUSA has housed nearly one-quarter of them. It is the Ellis Island of conferences.

While the Big 12 was decisive in 2021, the Pac-12 took *forever*. It wanted to both expand (likely with San Diego State and SMU) and somehow secure a TV contract superior to the Big 12's, but that contract didn't exist. All of 2022 came and went without either expansion or rights renegotiation, and by July 2023, the mood was so uncertain that Colorado, after just over a decade in the conference, bailed to rejoin the Big 12. A week later, Washington and Oregon opted for junior membership and reduced revenue in the Big Ten; and Arizona, Arizona State, and Utah frantically jumped to the Big 12, too. On September 1, California and Stanford further made a mockery of geography by joining the ACC—when you think "Atlantic Coast," you obviously think "Bay Area"—along with an SMU program so desperate for upgraded conference status that it volunteered to forego media rights revenue for years to make the move. But geography, broken as it may have been, still managed to screw Oregon State and Washington State, who had boasted better football programs than any of Arizona, Arizona State, Colorado, Cal, and Stanford in recent years but were left without a major-conference home. They formed a brief scheduling arrangement with the Mountain West, then elected to use the Pac-12's branding to plunder the conference for Boise State, Fresno State, San Diego State, Colorado State, and Utah State (plus basketball power Gonzaga of the West Coast Conference). The MWC scrambled to add UTEP, Hawaii for all sports (it had been a football-only member), and in a callback to the 1990s Big West, Northern Illinois (football-only). At press time, the dance continues. We no longer have a Western power conference, and we've basically got two Mountain Wests.

The Airplane Conference. The Eastern Seaboard Conference. Four perfectly symmetrical 16-team superconferences. So many things we assumed would happen, didn't. Others, like "Arkansas, Texas, and Texas A&M to the SEC?" and "Washington and Penn State, conference mates?" took decades longer than imagined, and one of the most impactful (and destructive) moves we've seen, USC and UCLA to the Big Ten, seemed to come completely out of the blue. You can find plenty of people who think they know where things are headed—see: all the "Super League?" references in coming chapters—but as it turns out, we're usually wrong about all this stuff. Indeed, nothing is predestined. Even the health of college football.

3.

How Sports Fall from Grace

The annual American Football Coaches Association (AFCA) convention is...a lot. Timed to coincide with the end of the football season, it has lately rotated between a trio of convention-friendly cities (Charlotte, Nashville, and the convention city of all convention cities, San Antonio). Though attendance has fallen as the football recruiting calendar has gotten more and more cluttered, thousands of coaches still convene for what is at once a trade show, a seminar series, and a year-end party.

According to the AFCA's mission statement, the association's goal is "to maintain the highest possible standards in football and the profession of coaching football; to provide a forum for the discussion and study of all matters pertaining to football and coaching; to make the game as safe and entertaining as possible through the rules of play; to have a strong voice in intercollegiate legislation affecting football programs; to exchange freely information on coaching methods and techniques, and to promote good fellowship and social contacts within the Association." Within the convention there are meetings and talks and an exhibition floor with vendors for basically everything you would need if you were starting a football program tomorrow—helmets, playbooks of varying degrees of fanciness, practice equipment, video and scouting services, and everything else. At the end of the convention, all FBS (Football Bowl Subdivision) coaches meet for a few hours to vent and complain and make recommendations that the executive director, typically a former FBS head coach, then shares with the media.

Rob Ash served as AFCA president while he was Montana State's head coach in the early 2010s. A long-respected, smaller-school coach who graduated from a Division III school (Cornell College in Iowa), Ash's first head-coaching job came at D-3's Juniata College in Pennsylvania before he moved on to Drake for 18 seasons and to MSU for another nine. Now retired, he serves as director of coaching development for Championship Analytics, the data service mostly famous for the fourth-down decisions book that a majority of FBS schools (plus lower-level schools, high schools, and at least one NFL team) have signed up for. Ash has an army of former assistants who would follow him into hell, and I have gotten to know him during my time socializing on the convention floor (and in suite parties during national title games). He is the kind of coach AFCA was made for. "I started out as a volunteer in meeting rooms and committees," Ash said. "We checked badges at the door to make sure guys who came into the lectures had registered. I was chair of the meeting rooms committee, and then I was an FCS [Football Championship Subdivision] representative, eventually got on the board and so forth. And just to be able to understand all of the different pressure points and all the different impacts that were going on across the country with our game, to me it was fascinating. I really enjoyed the meetings and the fraternity with the other coaches. To have everybody's voice in the room about what's going on with the game, what issues we need to be aware of, how we're going to address those? I thought it was fantastic to be able to be there and hear that and understand what was going on."

AFCA leaders make recommendations to the NCAA, but they have no control over whether those recommendations are actually followed. "The frustrating part about AFCA was that, at the end of the day, you walked out of the room without having done anything," Ash said. "I mean, there was a discussion, there were many different viewpoints, but there was no vote to do anything and no power to be able to put something out there." (Case in point: the 2025 convention ended with FBS head coaches, after a four-hour discussion/venting session, recommending the two transfer windows currently in existence be cut to one in early January. Mere hours later at the NCAA Convention, NCAA president Charlie Baker politely shot that down, citing enrollment timing issues and saying simply, "I get the fact that it's a challenging calendar as it is, and I fully expect that that will get thoroughly vetted as it should, by the appropriate committees.")

"The AFCA is really a powerless organization," said Ash, who loves AFCA more than anyone. "It has no legislative power. We don't make the rules of the game. We just take a straw vote on this and a straw vote on that, how do we feel about this and that. Then we walk out of the room and go back to our business again. So that was pretty frustrating. But it was real."

It's also real *big*. While the more big-name coaches don't arrive until later in the convention, if at all, if you walk around the convention centers and their surrounding areas on the first day of the show, when it's mostly NAIA and D-3 guys, you'll see quarter-zips and pullovers with logos and names you've never heard of. There are nearly 350 football schools in Division III and NAIA alone, more than 160 in Division II, and more than 260 in Division I.

The worst team in college football in 2024, according to the SP+ ratings I record for every level, was Dean College of Franklin, Massachusetts. The Bulldogs were outscored 366–28 in nine games at the Division III level. They listed more than 60 players and seven coaches on their 2024 football roster. Other schools near the bottom listed over 80 players with double-digit coaches. Add in the folks in the press box, the medical staff, the bus drivers...it takes so many damn people to field even an ineffective football team. There are damn near 800 teams out there. And I didn't even count junior colleges.

This sport is almost immeasurably huge, in other words. Its sheer size and omnipresence—no matter how hard (and low-paying) you make the job of college coaching, you'll find someone willing to do it, and no matter how bad the team, you'll find guys willing to play on it—makes college football unkillable. Which is funny, considering we think basically any tiny change is going to kill college football.

I was obsessed with this sport for about 25 years before I started getting paid to write about it, so when I talk about college football fans, know that I still very much consider myself one of them. And we're *nuts*. We're just so *dramatic* about everything. The only thing we enjoy as much as college football is predicting college football's demise. A small playoff will destroy college football. A big playoff will *definitely* destroy college football. A super league, in which the top programs in the sport separate into a new entity, will obliterate college football. Of course, not allowing the top programs to earn as much as they deserve will *also* destroy college football. Head injuries are going to destroy all of football, not just college; targeting penalties and other efforts to decrease head injuries? They're going to destroy football, too. Television has been slowly destroying college football since about 1952. Paying players? Making them employees?? Hoo boy, college football will be dead before the ink dries on the first employment contract.

We think everything that doesn't reflect our proper vision of the sport will end the sport. But despite the seemingly countless Armageddon scenarios facing college football at the moment—we all have our own list of them—good luck finding a sign that the sport is actually in any sort of trouble. Television ratings are excellent. Attendance levels are strong at both the largest (well over 105,000 for Ohio State vs. Michigan) and smallest ends (22,000 for a random Wisconsin-Whitewater conference game) of the sport's long tail. People plan their entire fall around home Saturdays, and they're planning around *game days*, not games. The sport is personal for so many, which means it only matters so much who your team is playing or what it's playing for.

It does still matter, though. We've seen both attendance and ratings concerns in the past, and even the most loyal customers have a limit to how much change they will tolerate, even if they don't know where that line is in advance. It's worth reminding ourselves that people have plenty of other ways to spend their entertainment dollars if they aren't getting what they love the most.

Just ask those in charge of NASCAR.

▻

"I worked at NASCAR's television production division 20 years ago," ESPN's Ryan McGee said. "I would sit in the meetings—and oh, by the way, Brett Yormark was there, too." The current Big 12 commissioner was NASCAR's director of corporate marketing from 1998 to 2005. "You're seduced by the boom. You're making so much money that you make bad decisions, but you don't realize it because you're making so much money. You end up making decisions that ultimately feed into the same sin: forgetting where you came from."

In the mid-2000s, NASCAR reached absurd levels of popularity. In 2005, NBC, TNT, and Fox were all enjoying record television ratings for their NASCAR telecasts, and the pop culture impact was pretty evident through movies like Pixar's *Cars* (my daughter's favorite movie when she was three) and Will Ferrell's *Talladega Nights: The Ballad of Ricky Bobby* (my daughter's favorite movie when she was 12). Executives made changes to cater to a larger audience—incorporating more races outside of the South, building new tracks that were spiffy but a little more generic in nature—and the numbers kept going up. Assuming their loyal fans would watch no matter what, they kept forcing the issue in catering to the casuals.

Within 15 years of those 2005 record highs, both attendance numbers and TV ratings had plummeted to record lows. Safety measures put into place following the death of Dale Earnhardt at the 2001 Daytona 500, including the unveiling of the much-reviled "Car of Tomorrow," were justifiable but unpopular, and both the loss of advertiser money following the economic crisis of the late 2000s and the retirement of a number of huge stars—Jeff Gordon, Tony Stewart, and Carl Edwards in 2016; Dale Earnhardt Jr. in 2017—did serious damage. Those things were out of NASCAR's control, but while you may not need the hardcore fans as much when everything's going well, you'll lean on them when everything isn't. And after chasing the casuals and television money, NASCAR found it had alienated its base. They left North Carolina's North Wilkesboro Speedway in 1996 and Rockingham Speedway in 2004 and moved their famed Labor Day race at Darlington Raceway in South Carolina to Los Angeles in 2003. To gin up more interest in the points race and continue standing out in the fall when the NFL dominates, they introduced the Chase for the Cup in 2004, but the rules were confusing, convoluted, and ever-changing.

"They made changes that probably needed to be made in a lot of cases," McGee said, "but they made so many changes all at once, and they made a couple of key, roots-ripping-out decisions that pissed off the fan base. The leadership of NASCAR—and this is a quote—they would stand in the room, and they would say, 'This is what we're gonna do with the schedule next year,' and they would literally say, 'and don't worry about the core fans. They're never gonna go anywhere.' That's Brian France, third-generation chairman of NASCAR. His grandfather founded the sport, his father ran it forever, and Brian would say all the time, 'Don't worry about the core fans. They aren't going anywhere.'

"All these changes happened, and then the market crashed in 2008," McGee continued. "It forced all the sponsors who were paying for everything to look at the business model and go, 'Why the hell am I writing a check for $25 million to sponsor Kevin Harvick's car?' The teams' entire business models were based on sponsors writing ridiculous checks—not unlike the business model college football is based on: television writing ridiculous checks. One day those checks might stop coming for some reason. But when you're making so much money, you make horrible choices."

As it turns out, if you are messing with the stalwarts on your calendar and making your title race impossible to follow or trust, even your most dedicated followers might become disillusioned. And they might find other ways to spend their money.

"Darlington is the all-time example," McGee said. "Darlington was the original NASCAR speedway. They decided they were going to pull the Labor Day weekend date from Darlington, and they were going to send it to the brand-new track out in Southern California. It has been 20 years since they did that, and they fixed it 10 years ago, but people are still pissed off about it."

Of course, at least Darlington still kept a race. Other tracks, like North Wilkesboro Speedway north of Charlotte, weren't so lucky. It had hosted NASCAR races since 1949 but grew outdated and got taken off the calendar. "There's all this beautiful, rich history around North Wilkesboro," said Andrew Carter of the *Charlotte News & Observer*, "and then all of a sudden in 1996, it's their last race. You had people all around there being like, 'What the heck is going on? We helped this thing grow and become a national phenomenon, and you took it away from us.'"

"You can make all the changes you want, and you can grow all you want, and you can expand all you want," McGee said. "You can do all those things. But the DNA of who you are still has to be there. NASCAR finally started correcting. The last five years have corrected a lot of the mistakes they made 20 years ago, and it's helped. But they're never gonna get back to where they were. They're never gonna get close! You start messing with the fabric of the schedule, that's when you're gonna lose them. And that doesn't mean you have to just race on racetracks in the Southeast—just like it doesn't mean you have to keep the Big 8 together. But you can't get so far away from the people who got you there that they feel like you've left them behind in search of the next dollar, in search of the next revenue stream."

Television has driven nearly every major decision the sport has seen for 40 years. While that has paid off handsomely, the meter isn't guaranteed to forever rise when it comes to media rights, and you might not find out just how much you've alienated the core fans until the money train slows down.

You also might find out that core fans don't make up as large a piece of your audience as you think.

▻

In November 2021, researchers Daniel A. Rascher (University of San Francisco), Kenneth Cortsen (University College Nordjylland), Mark S. Nagel (University of South Carolina), and Tiffany Richardson (Seattle University) published "Who Are Our Fans: An Application of Principal Component–Cluster Technique Analysis to Market Segmentation of College Football Fans." It was an attempt to separate fans—not including students—into buckets and figure out just how big each bucket might be. They found that 20 percent of fans qualify as "core football fans," the middle-aged, mid- to high-income folks (mostly male) who buy season tickets, join booster clubs, attend tons of games, buy tons of gear, and don't care about things like customer service or how fancy the new scoreboard might be.

On one hand, 20 percent is a big number. When Michigan's Big House is full, it is housing about 90,000 non-students among its 110,000 or so. That means about 18,000 people in that stadium are hardcores who will put up with just about everything. But that also means about 72,000 aren't.

The authors of "Who Are Our Fans" found that about 28 percent of fans are "older experiential seekers" whose income isn't quite as high, who don't have a direct relation to the school, and whose interest and willingness to attend games is heavily dictated by the quality of concessions, merchandise, and entertainment options (like the bands). A solid 20 percent are "high-income critics" who aren't impressed with the concessions on offer, who don't enjoy crowds, whose family status influences their decision-making, and who are "most likely to contribute to booster clubs to get better seats." They want nice things. Meanwhile, 16 percent are "single-game, middle-income critics" in their thirties and forties who don't enjoy the experience all that much but will attend big events, and 14 percent are "price-sensitive, health-conscious fun seekers"—younger people (often women) far more involved on social media who attend a game or two and aren't receptive to marketing materials.

That's a pretty diverse crowd right there. And a large portion of it, maybe more than we think, seems pretty fickle.

We should probably treat college football's current level of popularity, then, as something that isn't guaranteed, no matter how big the sport may be and no matter how many hungry coaches attend AFCA conventions. And we should probably see what lessons we can draw from other sports that have found themselves facing downturns in popularity. Starting with NASCAR's lessons, let's make a What Not to Do list:

1. ***Don't take your core fans for granted.*** This applies to absolutely every sport. You can put your hardcores through hell, but you probably shouldn't change what's most important to them, even if it means sacrificing some short-term growth. And you won't find out if you've driven them away until the casuals have ditched you and you need them more than ever.

2. ***Don't change too much at once.*** Make sure fans still know what to expect from a given week, month, or season. Make sure they still recognize what they're looking for. College football has changed a *lot* of late, from the playoff structure to the conference rosters to how rosters are put together (and how compensated their players are). A lot

of that was necessary, and aside from the fact that we get USC-Minnesota and Louisville-Stanford games now, which is never going to feel normal, the product still looks about the same on TV. So maybe this isn't an issue yet.

3. Keep your product where your audience can see it. Perhaps no sport has seen its stock diminish more over the last 40 years than boxing. There are still big names and big fights that can draw a big audience—and the big fights can still feel like enormous events—but everything outside of the very top layer of the sport has diminished significantly.

The early days of television were kind to boxing. NBC's *Gillette Cavalcade of Sports* ran from 1946 to 1960, and ABC's *Wide World of Sports* debuted in 1961. *Cavalcade* regularly broadcast fights live from Madison Square Garden, and while *Wide World of Sports* rarely aired live fights, it exposed a large base of viewers to many of the bigger fights of the era. In 1964, it aired heavyweight champion Sonny Liston's mammoth upset loss to a young Muhammad Ali (then Cassius Clay) a few weeks after the fact, as the sports world was still buzzing about it, and it aired a series of Ali's title defenses in the years that followed. When Ali was stripped of his title after refusing to be drafted into the military, it aired Joe Frazier's 1970 knockout of Jimmy Ellis to win the vacant title. It aired some of Ali's comeback fights in the early 1970s, too, and it gave us Howard Cosell's "Down goes Frazier! Down goes Frazier!" call during George Foreman's title winning knockout of the champ. It aired two of the three Ali-Frazier fights and gave us Ali's famous rope-a-dope upset of Foreman in the Rumble in the Jungle. In the late 1970s, as the big-name heavyweights were beginning to age, it helped to make Olympic gold medalist and eventual four-division champion Sugar Ray Leonard a household name by airing his second professional fight in 1977, plus big matches against Roberto Duran in 1980 and Thomas Hearns in 1981.

In terms of cost and scope, this was an easy, television-friendly sport to air. You didn't need countless cameras, and you knew that even a 15-round fight would end within about an hour. But as with NASCAR, boxing's popularity made decision-makers seek larger and larger profits. By the mid- to late 1980s, virtually every big fight in the sport was either on burgeoning subscriber network HBO or closed-circuit pay-per-view. In the short-term, this was great for the bank accounts of big fighters and promoters, but it also took boxing off of network television and decreased the raw number of viewers for other fights. As we've learned for everything from sports to websites, when you go to a pay (or subscriber) model, you are essentially declaring that you're done growing and you're now in the business of milking money from your known fans. That threatens to make you more of a niche product.

College football has its own version of this issue. If you want access to every FBS game this fall, you're going to need not only a cable package that features the major networks plus ESPN, ESPN2, ESPNU, FS1, FS2, CBS Sports Network, the SEC Network, the Big Ten Network, the ACC Network, and The CW (plus probably five other channels I'm forgetting); you'll also need, at minimum, a subscription to ESPN+ and Peacock. AppleTV+ has been toeing the waters, too—Apple was a major player in the Pac-12's 2023 saga: The conference worked out a decent-if-unspectacular deal with them, but schools were justifiably hesitant to move most of their inventory away from linear television—and Amazon Prime has already gotten involved with the NFL. That's a lot to keep track of (and pay for), and this list is more likely to grow than shrink moving forward.

Sometimes forcing your viewers to pay to watch your product can work out just fine. The English Premier League certainly didn't regret selling its rights to the subscription network Sky Sports in the early 1990s, after all, even if raw viewership numbers were far lower than they otherwise could have been. But even some hardcore Ohio State or Notre Dame fans likely resisted the urge to subscribe to Peacock when one of their teams' lesser games aired there in recent years, and anytime a hardcore voluntarily decides not to watch a game (potentially finding out that he or she was fine without it), that should ring an alarm bell or two.

4. Keep the participants (as) healthy (as possible). When your product is both harder to watch and *harder to watch*, it can be troublesome. On

November 13, 1982, WBA lightweight champion Ray "Boom Boom" Mancini and No. 1 contender Kim Duk-koo put on a fierce fight, live on CBS, that ended with a 14th-round TKO victory for the champ. Kim collapsed and fell into a coma after the match, and he died five days later due to a subdural hematoma in his skull. On November 26, not even two weeks later, WBC heavyweight champion Larry Holmes pummeled outmanned contender (and future *Raising Arizona* villain) Randall "Tex" Cobb for 15 rounds; Cobb continued to answer the bell and take more punishment, but he lost every round of the fight, and Cosell, one of the defining voices of the sport, declared, "This is as brutal a mismatch as I think I've ever seen." With Kim's death almost certainly still lingering in his head, Cosell stopped calling boxing afterward. Combine that with the fact that networks had an increasing number of sports they could air that *wouldn't* make you worry about on-screen fatalities, and it wasn't just the draw of pay-per-view that took boxing off of network television.

This is always going to be a potential obstacle for football in general because it is, by nature, a violent sport played mostly by very large human beings. But it seems we're seeing a bit of progress in college football when it comes to the rule changes designed to lower the number of head injuries, and the NCAA took a nice step in offering post-eligibility injury insurance (for up to two years after players' careers end) beginning in 2024. Two years isn't much, but it's a start. Granted, with an expanded playoff we're also asking the best players to play more games, which has its own health consequences. But at least we're paying them to do so now, I guess.

5. *Don't make your title race too hard to follow.* Granted, it's a lot easier to fall into this trap in individual sports where points systems are involved. But things can get dicey anytime individuals are ranking contenders, too. (You know, like the College Football Playoff committee does.) In boxing, instead of NASCAR's convoluted points race problem, the proliferation of organizations that sanctioned bouts and named champions—the World Boxing Association (WBA) formed in 1962, followed by the World Boxing Council (WBC) in 1963, and they were joined by the International Boxing Federation (IBF) in 1983 and the World Boxing Organization (WBO) in 1988—has made it virtually impossible to figure out who the sport's real champions are. They all have their own rankings and rankings criteria, they all have their own laundry lists of corruption issues, and they sometimes even name their weight classes different things (example: "junior lightweight" vs. "super featherweight"). They can all declare their titles vacant for any number of reasons, too.

Granted, it's sometimes cool when someone reaches "undisputed champion" status by winning the WBA, WBC, and IBF titles at the same times—especially when that someone was Mike Tyson in 1987—but for the most part it just creates confusion. The casual fan would simply like to know who the best fighter in the world is. We're seeing similar themes with men's golf at the moment: The creation of LIV Golf and its competition with the PGA Tour has split the sport and actively limited the number of opportunities fans get to watch all of the sport's best players in the same tournament. That dynamic helps no one, as evidenced by the travails of IndyCar, which experienced a split of one tour into two in the late 1990s and suffered.

6. Fans hate fights over money. With revenue sharing beginning in 2025—and most likely followed in coming years by fights over the amount of revenue sharing—this lesson might soon apply to college football (and college sports in general). But for now this remains unexplored territory.

Baseball has explored this territory enough for everybody. Called America's pastime since basically the Civil War, baseball was the most popular sport in the nation well into the 20th century. It's still a lucrative industry, to be sure; Major League Baseball reported a record $12.1 billion in revenue in 2024, and players were paid over $5 billion in salary that season (it only *felt* like all of that went to Shohei Ohtani). But television ratings have eroded for decades, and in fan preference surveys, baseball lags behind professional football, college football, and professional basketball in terms of overall popularity.

Baseball was at the forefront of the owners-versus-players battles that seemingly every professional sport in America has dealt with at some point since. And in the 1970s, that fight seemed to earn headlines on a yearly basis. "I am a baseball fan in good standing, and my first reaction on regarding the enormous and unsavory dog's breakfast that was plunked down before me on the morning of this new season was simply to push back from the table and walk away," famed baseball columnist Roger Angell wrote in 1976, following a lockout that closed a large portion of spring training and threatened to advance into the season. It was the third lockout or strike in five seasons—perhaps not coincidentally, football officially passed baseball in Gallup's "What is your favorite sport to watch?" survey during this run of stoppages in 1972—and there would be two more within the next five years, as well. It was still nearly two decades before the 1994 strike that canceled the postseason altogether, but it was already wearing on fans even as loyal as Angell. "A lot of fans, I suspect, may be on the point of leaving the game," he wrote. "Professional sports now form a noisy and substantial, if irrelevant and distracting, part of that world, and it seems as if baseball games taken entire—off the field as well as on it, in the courts and in the front offices as well as down on the diamonds—may now tell us more about ourselves than they ever did before."

Angell was, like so many of us in the college football universe, rather fatalistic about the potential downfall of his sport. (Honestly, he was in so many ways the first sports blogger. I read *The Roger Angell Baseball Collection*, an enormous compilation of his columns, after his death in 2022, and while I can only aspire to the quality of his actual writing, I recognized and related to so much of his writing *voice*.) He predicted that fans might walk away, but while per-game attendance dropped by 3.7 percent in 1972 when Opening Day was postponed until April 15 by a brief player strike (86 games were canceled), attendance actually rose in both 1973 and 1976 following lockouts. Still, weariness would kick in. In 1980, there was another brief strike, and attendance fell by 1.5 percent. In 1981, a big strike caused the cancellation of more than 700 games, and average attendance fell by 6.8 percent. And in

1995, of course, following the cancellation of 938 games and the entire 1994 postseason, attendance plummeted by *19.9 percent*.

Now, attendance also rebounded each time. From 1976 through 1998, it rose in all but three seasons that didn't include a lockout or a strike. It even surpassed 1994 averages from 2006 to 2008. But it's fallen below that mark for 16 years and counting, and in 2022, when Opening Day was again postponed, this time by a lockout, attendance fell by 5.8 percent compared to the pre-COVID season of 2019. Recent rule changes designed to speed up games has produced another uptick—2024's attendance average of 29,373 per game was the league's highest since 2017—but the league is still 10 percent off of its historic high.

Work stoppages might have even wounded the country's ever-growing NFL obsession. In 1981, NFL attendance hit an all-time high of 60,745 per game; but in 1982, following a nearly two-month player strike, that figure fell by 3.9 percent to 58,472. It was 54,315 in 1987, when the season was impacted by a month-long strike, and the league didn't top its 1981 averages again until 1997.

7. Too much inequality sucks (or at least, it doesn't help). Major League Baseball has also dealt with some pretty significant problems when it comes to a tilted playing field.

"Baseball fans in Kansas City want to be heard. They need to be heard. The game is broken, it's tilted, and baseball fans here want to hope again. They want to dream again. The way the money rolls now, with some teams spending and making so much more than others, well, it's awfully hard to dream baseball in a little ol' town like Kansas City." That's what famed *Kansas City Star* columnist Joe Posnanski wrote on May 1, 1999, after Royals fans and local radio personalities engineered a walk-out protesting Major League Baseball's exploding inequality. (I still have the "Kansas City Loves the Royals. Share the Wealth." shirt in my closet, though it's practically disintegrating at this point.) The New York Yankees had just won their second World Series in three seasons, and their payroll in 1999 was 4.9 times higher than the league's lowest and was more than the four lowest payrolls combined. And this was actually an improvement: their payroll had been 5.8 times higher than the lowest in 1997 and 6.8 in 1998. (They would win the World Series in 1999 and 2000, too.)

Super Bowl aside, TV ratings for even the biggest sporting events have mostly trickled downward through the years as television viewing options have increased. But they plummeted in a short amount of time in baseball. In 18 seasons from 1975 to 1992, the World Series averaged at least 30 million viewers 15 times, dropping below that mark only for blowouts in 1983, 1984, and 1989. But starting in 1991, the average fell in five of the next six postseasons. From 35.7 million in 1991, the average had been nearly cut in half, to just 18.1 million, by 2000. Even with a big brand leading the way, even with the buzz created by 1998's famous home run race between Mark McGwire and Sammy Sosa, and even with a luxury tax (enforced if you spend over a certain salary threshold) increasing in strength, ratings just kept going down, perking up only for a classic seven-game series between the Yankees and Arizona in 2001 (24.5 million), the Boston Red Sox' first World Series win in 86 years in 2004 (25.4 million), and the Chicago Cubs' first World Series in 108 years in 2016 (22.8 million). In the seven seasons after the Cubs' magical run, the average fell five more times. It was just 9.1 million for Texas's easy five-game win over Arizona in 2023, and it rebounded only to 15.8 million for 2024's blue-blood showcase between the Dodgers and Yankees.

There are plenty of factors here, from increased viewing options to longer games to a number of noncompetitive World Series. But at the very least, allowing the Yankees and other giant-market baseball teams like the New York Mets (who began 2025 with a payroll 4.8 times higher than the Miami Marlins) and Los Angeles Dodgers (4.7 times higher) to spend whatever they want while smaller-market clubs lag further and further behind doesn't seem to help matters.

8. You don't have as much control over everything as you think. NASCAR certainly learned this one as 2008's economic difficulties dramatically altered its sponsorship-earning potential. But men's college basketball also comes with its own set of warning signs in this regard. It was never as big as college football on average, but its title game routinely drew more of a television audience than college football's biggest bowls in the early 1990s, and in most years, the NCAA Tournament still packs in all the Cinderella-loving chaos you could ever hope for. But the sport's popularity has waned. As with the World Series, viewership for the men's basketball national championship routinely went over 30 million in the 1980s; it topped 32 million for three consecutive years from 1992 to 1994, too. (This actually scared the hell out of college football higher-ups and likely drove some of the increased motivation to create more relevant bowl games and No. 1 vs. No. 2 matchups.) But after an initial slip, to 27.1 million on average from 1995 to 1999, the numbers plummeted in the 2000s. The title game averaged just 20.2 million viewers in the decade of the 2000s; and after a bit of a rebound—an average of 22.9 million from 2010 to 2015, peaking with 28.3 million for a much-anticipated Duke-Wisconsin finale in 2015—came another fall. Only an average of 17.5 million viewers have watched the last eight title games. That number fell below 15 million in both 2023 and 2024, and for the first time ever, the ratings for the women's Final Four trumped those of the men's in 2024.

I refer to TV numbers because that's what we have available. It's easy to lose sight of context by focusing on only this, though; after all, you can easily make a case that college football itself is on wobbly ground itself if you average things out just right: the average audience for college football's title game was 26.8 million for the last 11 years of the BCS, for instance, but only 24.7 million for the first 11 years of the CFP. That's a far softer fall than what we've seen in other sports, but it's still technically a fall. Still, poor TV numbers contributed to overall poor vibes for college basketball as a whole, something a decrease in scoring seemed to also exacerbate. Of course, it's tough to blame *college basketball* for whatever problems college basketball may have been dealing with in recent years.

Neither college football nor the NBA have done college basketball many favors. Nearly every conference realignment decision of the last 30 years has been driven by football concerns. This has created a particular amount of absurdity in the east, where Syracuse and UConn, two schools so prominently linked to Big East basketball, at least briefly ended up conference mates with schools like Georgia Tech and USF, respectively, instead of Georgetown and St. John's. Now realignment has replaced USC-Arizona and UCLA-Cal basketball games with UCLA-Nebraska and USC-Rutgers, too.

The NBA, meanwhile, has screwed with the player pool on multiple occasions. First, it introduced the one-and-done rule in 2006, which prevented players from entering the NBA Draft until a year after their high school graduation. Future NBA stars like Kevin Durant (Texas) and Anthony Davis (Kentucky) made the most of their single collegiate seasons, but a lot of the sport's biggest brands ended up annually replacing five-star freshmen with five-star freshmen and rarely felt like a finished product. Baseball may have taught us that power imbalance can be a bad thing, but we've almost learned the opposite lesson in college hoops: from 2019 to 2024, only one team, UConn, made multiple Final Fours, and programs like Texas Tech, San Diego State, and Florida Atlantic each made more (one) than Kentucky (zero). Power imbalance may be bad, but almost no one having any power isn't any better.

In 2020, meanwhile, the NBA began to use its G League as an alternative to college basketball altogether, creating "G League Ignite," a team of developmental prospects with no affiliation to an NBA team. From 2021 to 2024 it employed six players who would be selected in the top 11 of the draft, including three top-five picks. Overtime Elite, an Atlanta-based league for 16- to 20-year-old prospects, produced a pair of direct-to-the-NBA top-five picks in 2023, as well. This all meant fewer one-and-dones, but it also meant less talent in the college pool. There's a balance somewhere in there, and college hoops struggled to find it.

Ironically, however, more factors outside of the sport's control—namely, NIL rights and player movement—may have contributed to a college hoops rebound. With schools splashing around solid NIL cash for both freshmen like Duke's Cooper Flagg and high-level veteran transfers like Auburn's Johni Broome (from Morehead State) and Florida's Walter Clayton Jr. (Iona), the highest level of college hoops began to feel more high-level again in 2024–25. And after weeks of buzz, TV ratings boomed during Championship Week (viewership for the SEC's conference tournament final improved by 74 percent over the previous season), and the first weekend of the NCAA Tournament produced the highest viewership numbers in more than 30 years. The national title game topped 18 million viewers for the first time in six years, too.

In 2023, Will Leitch wrote in *New York Magazine* that, "In an age of constant realignment and dramatically shifting priorities for universities and television networks, the sport...seems to be fading more in relevance by the year." Just two years later in the *Washington Post*, he said, "College basketball has stumbled across a formula for sustainability that augurs a new era of excitement for the sport. The irony? It's the result of the tumult caused by paying players for their name, image, and likeness rights as well as the roster chaos wrought by the transfer portal—the very changes that many thought would be the game's death knells." Scoring did rise in recent seasons: 29 teams averaged at least 80 points per game in 2024–25, compared to just six in 2021–22. That can't hurt when it comes to crafting an enjoyable product that people want to watch. But thanks primarily to factors outside of its control, the sport has over the last decade alone both suffered a downfall and potentially enjoyed a renaissance.

9. Understand your roots. Whether it's Darlington on Labor Day, or Syracuse-Georgetown basketball games in the winter, or anything else, understanding what's at the heart of your brand is important for every sport in the world. College football still fields important games in the Rose Bowl every year, and Alabama and Tennessee still play every year on the Third Saturday in October. But conference realignment has unquestionably removed a few roots, so to speak.

"Realignment's been awful," said another longtime ESPN writer, Adam Rittenberg. "I honestly have a hard time finding too many good realignment moves versus ones that either haven't worked out or have severely damaged the sport." There have certainly been a number of hidden costs to recent moves; you indeed might have to subscribe to quite a few different streaming services to catch the games you want, and the breaking of geography in conference rosters means that not only do teams of all sports have to travel far more miles on average, but so do their fans—you're much more likely to be hosting teams whose fans can't easily drive to and attend road games, and your own home atmosphere could sometimes suffer as a result.

There are plenty of less-than-hidden costs, too. "My entry to college football was growing up in California and going to Cal games," Rittenberg said. "Before we moved there, we lived in the Boston area, and I didn't know anything about college football. But my dad took me to the Cal-Stanford game in 1992. I'll never forget it. That was my first rivalry game, and it was a Pac-10 game, and I was hooked. For [the conference] to be taken away because of greed and panic and all these things that are human but show up too often in this sport, it's really sad." But on the bright side, I guess, Rittenberg can now watch Cal and Boston College play as ACC rivals. Call it the "Rittenberg Rivalry."

"Even Nebraska to the Big Ten," he continued, "it made sense to a degree at the time, but it has not worked out well for Nebraska other than financially. I just struggle to see the benefits of any of this. And it keeps happening and happening, to the point where a conference I grew up watching was destroyed. Realignment has easily been the worst thing of the last 20 years."

Granted, fans of schools like Utah or TCU might disagree with that sentiment; the Utes and Horned Frogs both moved from the mid-major level to power conferences in 2012, and they have won or shared three conference titles since. TCU reached the CFP Championship in 2022. Both Missouri and Texas A&M have enjoyed a pair of top-10 finishes since moving up to the SEC, too. But the sport as a whole lost defining, annual rivalry games like Oklahoma-Nebraska, Texas–Texas A&M (restored when Texas moved to the SEC in 2024), West Virginia–Pitt, Oklahoma–Oklahoma State, and Missouri-Kansas in the process. Texas and Baylor have played 113 times, Cal and USC 109 times, Missouri and Iowa State 104 times, Stanford and USC 101 times. Cal and UCLA played every year from 1934 to 2023. That's a lot of roots. These connective-tissue series are finished for the present, at least as annual get-togethers.

For another obvious cost, just look to the Northwest. Wazzu and Oregon State aren't the first schools to get left behind in the realignment process. Houston, Rice, SMU, and TCU were left scrambling for mid-major homes when the Southwest Conference dissolved in the mid-1990s. And when the Big East's leftovers—primarily Cincinnati, Temple, UConn, and USF (and, ever so briefly, Louisville and Rutgers)—became part of the American Athletic Conference in the early 2010s, as college football was moving from the BCS system to the College Football Playoff, they lost their power conference designation. The SWC's leftovers had all struggled mightily in the years leading up to their abandonment, but this was definitely cruel for a Cincy team that had come achingly close to a BCS Championship bid in 2009 and won at least nine games all but one year from 2007 to 2014.

Oregon State and Washington State were members of a power conference for more than half a century, and unlike the SWC's leftovers, both had enjoyed success in recent seasons. OSU won 10 games in 2022, the year before the moves that caused the Pac-12 to fall apart, and Wazzu had enjoyed a top-10 finish in 2018 and bowled in seven of eight seasons from 2015 to 2022. But now, even as they piece together a new Pac-12, they're looking at making tens of millions of dollars less than their former rivals with each year. Granted, that probably made it feel extra sweet for Wazzu when the Cougs beat Washington with a goal-line stand in the (nonconference) Apple Cup early in a 2024 season in which they finished 8–5. But obviously losing ground financially is a good way to lose more frequently on the field, too. After losing more than 25 players, including quarterback Cam Ward (who would move to Miami and finish fourth in the 2024 Heisman voting), to the transfer portal after the 2023 season, they lost head coach Jake Dickert and more than 35 transfers, including star quarterback John Mateer (to Oklahoma), after 2024. Even with a seemingly great replacement hire—South Dakota State's FCS title–winning Jimmy Rogers, who brought a healthy number of Jackrabbit players with him—the Cougs will be completely starting from scratch in 2025.

Back in 2008, the Apple Cup gave us one of the most remarkable examples of how a rivalry game can change, or downright salvage, the tenor of a season. Washington State's Martin Stadium was at 98 percent capacity for a game between 0–11 Washington and a 1–11 Wazzu team that had beaten only FCS's Portland State. After a dire battle of attrition for most of 59 minutes, Wazzu pulled off a miraculous last-minute, field-goal drive to force overtime; another field goal earned the Cougs a 16–13 win, prompted a field rush from Wazzu fans, and somehow salvaged a smidgen of joy from an otherwise wretched season.

Rivalry games have offered salvation through the years. When you don't have them, your season simply becomes all about how good you were. If you're awesome and winning a bunch of games, great—it might not matter who you're playing. But rivalry wins have provided silver linings for otherwise poor seasons, just as rivalry losses have given great seasons nagging regrets, for more than a century. These rivalries might sometimes be simple marriages of geographic convenience, but losing them (or, in the case of the Apple Cup, moving it to the beginning of the season with lower stakes), still leaves a hole.

For all of these losses, however, seemingly nothing has impacted the sport's overall popularity. In July 2023, just as the Pac-12 was veering toward collapse, The Athletic published a survey of college football fans about their general attitude toward the sport. People were as wary as possible regarding impending conference realignment moves—on a scale of 1 (hate it) to 10 (love it), 43 percent of respondents gave the upcoming realignment moves a score between 1 and 3, nearly doubling the votes in the 8–10 range (22 percent).

Doom on the horizon, then? Not so much. When asked, "What is your attitude toward the future of college football?" with a scale of 1 (very concerned) to 10 (very excited), 53 percent of respondents voted between 7 and 10; meanwhile, "How does your enjoyment of consuming college football now compare to 10 years ago?" ended up with half the responses between a 4 and 6—no change. In another survey, administered by Sportico and the Harris Poll in August 2023, 68 percent of respondents agreed that conference realignment was a "problem in college sports," but it was apparently *someone else's* problem: 55 percent said it hadn't impacted their enjoyment. Television ratings in 2023 were the highest in years, too, and they would be excellent again in 2024. It was like those national opinion polls where everyone agrees that America is moving rapidly in the wrong direction, but *they're* doing just fine.

College football's decision-makers really do seem to have it pretty easy. They know we're all going to bitch and moan about everything, but they have no evidence that we're ever going to actually leave. Still, NASCAR's tale reminds us of what could happen if they simply assume we won't. "You can't assume that the guys who have always sat in Section Whatever at Neyland Stadium, or at the L.A. Coliseum, or at the Horseshoe or whatever, you can't just assume they're gonna keep coming because they've always come," Ryan McGee said. "And oh, by the way, they pay for everything. And they're already pissed because they lost their paper tickets, and they don't know how to get into the stadium"—many schools use electronic tickets stored on cell phones now—"and now you're handing them a schedule they don't want to play. You have to take care of those people. You can't rip your roots out of the ground. You can pull on them, and you can grow, but you cannot rip your roots out of the ground."

▻

We've got a pretty good case study for this, fittingly enough, in NASCAR country, where one of the sport's mightiest underdogs made some iffy decisions, stopped playing the teams it likes to play, and watched nearly 30 percent of its fan base disappear.

There aren't many cities in the country that reflect a community's commitment to football like Greenville, North Carolina. It's a city of about 89,000 people, the 12th-largest in the state. But Dowdy-Ficklen Stadium, home of the East Carolina Pirates, holds 50,000, and it's stuffed to the gills when it has a reason to be. There is an alternate universe in which the proposed Metro Conference takes shape in the early 1990s and East Carolina becomes a mid- to upper-tier player in a power conference.

In our reality, however, the Pirates have struggled to find a proper home for their ambition.

This has always been a program capable of not only knocking off the big boys but occasionally embarrassing them. In 1975, led by future Auburn head coach Pat Dye, the Pirates stomped North Carolina 38–17 in Chapel Hill, then left an even bigger mark with their celebrations. After spray-painting Rameses, the UNC mascot, in purple and gold before the game, ECU fans rushed the field and threatened to tear down the goal posts afterward. Two weeks later, they embarrassed Virginia 61–10 in Charlottesville. The Cavaliers were led by former ECU coach Sonny Randle, who had, in Greenville, taken on the habit of saying things like "compare apples to apples" after his Pirates would get thumped by bigger schools. ECU rushed for more than 600 yards on Randle's Cavaliers, and as the story goes, ECU fans threw apples onto the field to rub it in.

About a decade later, the increasingly noisy neighbors got a little too noisy. ECU stomped NC State 32–14 to start the 1987 season, and according to the *Charlotte Observer*, "Anything of NC State's that didn't get run past, around, or through by East Carolina's football team Saturday night got trampled, mangled, or disfigured by Pirate fans." They tore down goal posts, trampled shrubs, and "danced and pranced.... A half-hour after the game ended, there still were fights breaking out." In response, NC State discontinued the teams' annual series. But the joke was on the Wolfpack: the teams were paired together just a few years later in the 1992 Peach Bowl, and in front of 59,322 in Atlanta's Fulton County Stadium, quarterback Jeff Blake and ECU overcame a 34–17 deficit with under nine minutes remaining and won 37–34. The celebrations were pretty raucous after that one, too, but the bar was low enough to clear. "The north end-zone area erupted in a celebration that made some ECU officials hold their breath one last time," reported the *Raleigh News and Observer*. "When the celebration did not deteriorate, ECU's perfect day was complete. Thousands of Pirate fans spilled onto the playing field. The 'E' in the 'P-I-R-A-T-E' lettering on the south end zone was dug up by a dozen or so fans. But stadium security officials reported no fights, no confrontations."

When ECU has the right coach in place, the Pirates can play at a really high level. They went 34–11 from 1975 to 1978 under Dye with six wins over ACC teams. They lost only to three top-10 teams by a combined 13 points during an 8–3 run that earned their first ranked finish in 1983. That comeback win over NC State to finish the 1991 season earned them the No. 9 spot in the final AP rankings—and, to date, meant that they have more all-time top-10 finishes than NC State. And under Skip Holtz, they won back-to-back Conference USA titles in 2008 and 2009.

Their ambition, however, has sometimes led them to aimless places. They left the Southern Conference in the 1970s, both fearing that the SoCon would land in Division I-AA when the top-tier split finally occurred and hoping for an ACC invitation—something that UNC will never allow; hell, UNC fought ECU getting university status and a med school. Two decades of independence worked out well at times but also produced bowl bids in only four of their nine winning seasons. They joined Conference USA in 1997, two years into its existence, and life with conference rivals and genuine peers like Southern Miss treated them pretty well. But administration clearly got antsy during the huge realignment run of the early 2010s. They joined the AAC in 2014, and despite enjoying a level of solid play under ECU grad Ruffin McNeill—they bowled in four of his first five seasons and went 10–3 in 2013—the school panic-fired him after an injury-plagued 5–7 season in 2015.

ECU averaged a power-conference-worthy 46,476 in home attendance over McNeill's six seasons, peaking at 50,011 despite a 5–7 campaign in 2011. But the combination of outrage over McNeill's firing, the ensuing collapse in performance, and a home schedule packed with mostly unfamiliar foes, led to a severe downturn. Even including solid 7–5 and 8–5 campaigns for Mike Houston in 2021 and 2022 (and not including the attendance-limited 2020 COVID season), average attendance has fallen to around 37,000 in the years since McNeill's dismissal. They drew at least 45,000 for 18 straight home games from 2010 to 2012, then did so nine more times between 2013 and 2016. They've done so only twice since: for NC State in 2022 and for Appalachian State in 2024.

"ECU has always had to fight for respect," Andrew Carter said. "They had to fight for a med school, had to fight for funding from the state, had to fight for this and that. It has this underdog, scrappy mentality about it. Most of the people in Greenville probably grew up there. It's not a very transient place like Raleigh is nowadays. Even though from Raleigh proper you can get to Greenville in 45, 50 minutes, it feels like you're a world away from Raleigh, culturally speaking. It's just a different vibe. ECU is not necessarily the party school it once was, but I think it still has that reputation. There's a great barbecue scene—I'll make road trips to Greenville just to have lunch. B's and Parker's are famous barbecue joints. It has its own distinct character and underdog identity, people who want to prove themselves and prove others' perceptions about them wrong. I've always loved my trips out there. ECU embodies the struggle that a lot of schools at that level share."

"My dad went to East Carolina," McGee said. "I write about East Carolina all the time. They made bad moves, but they made the moves they thought they needed to make. When the realignment shifts were happening, East Carolina made the move to the American thinking that's what they needed to do. Because at the time it was like, 'All right, if we align ourselves with this, the ACC is about to expand, and we might finally get the phone call. But we have to be at this level.' And now everyone at East Carolina is pissed because they're not in the Sun Belt," where they would at least get to play rivals like Southern Miss and Appalachian State.

When you've jumped from level to level and conference to conference (and you didn't start playing football until the 1930s), you don't end up with any rivals that you've played 100 times. But ECU has played three FBS programs at least 30 times: Southern Miss, Appalachian State, and NC State. The Pirates are conference mates with none of them. They haven't played Southern Miss since 2013, they've played App State just three times since 2013, and they had played NC State just five times since 2010 before the teams were paired together in the 2024 Military Bowl. (As one would expect, ECU played well and pulled an upset after a late, out-of-nowhere 86-yard touchdown with 1:33 left.) (As one would also expect, there was a brawl at the end, and a pretty good one at that—a ref got bloodied up.)

"They have history with all of these schools going back," McGee said, "and instead of playing them they're playing North Texas and Temple. They show up in droves when they play North Carolina, NC State, App State, or whoever. And then the rest of the year they struggle with attendance because they don't care about that schedule. They have cut themselves off at their feet. Even firing Ruffin McNeill, right? You had a guy in there who, that was the only job he ever wanted in his life. And when you fire him, you're sending a message to the fan base: he was one of your own and had [often] won seven, eight games. You fire him, and then you hand them a schedule they don't want."

Fans watching a team they don't have a connection to playing a schedule they don't care about. If you could distill a doom scenario for college football into one sentence fragment, that might be it. And the last round of realignment seemed to bring this a little closer to reality. "The Big Ten thing is going to be such a fascinating experiment," McGee said. "There's just so many holes in that schedule. Five years from now when everybody has been fed USC-Maryland and still no one cares about it...they're going to have weekends that are just like, ugh, USC-Iowa? Maryland-Washington? Oregon-Rutgers? Who cares, man?

"It's leaving Darlington, simple as that. You've gotta write certain games in Sharpie, and that's just how it is. You make the moves you think are best at the time, but what do fans want? Do the fans want USC and Rutgers? USC fans don't. You take away the games that matter to people, and that's when you're toast. That's when you've lost touch. That's when you're Brian France."

4.

Television—the Cause of, and Solution to, All of College Football's Problems

At this point, it's almost indisputable that *The Simpsons* is America's greatest modern cultural export. More than 35 years and nearly 800 episodes after its debut, it remains on the air. It is perpetually one of the most watched shows on Disney+ in any country, and when anything momentous and/or strange happens in the world, from Donald Trump's election as president to the Siegfried and Roy tiger attack, there's a good chance that *The Simpsons* predicted it. And the Tao of Homer Simpson has been wittily getting nerds through any moment of their day, online and in real life, for decades. "You tried your best and you failed miserably. The lesson is: never try." "Your ideas are intriguing to me, and I wish to subscribe to your newsletter." "If something's hard to do, then it's not worth doing." "Stupidity got us into this mess, and stupidity will get us out." "Kids are great. You can teach them to hate what you hate and, with the Internet and all, they practically raise themselves!" "Television: teacher, mother, secret lover." And, of course, "To alcohol! The cause of, and solution to, all of life's problems."

The Simpsons became a cultural force at the same time that television also began to completely rule and redefine sports, including college football. Rupert Murdoch's Fox, *The Simpsons*' home, shook up the sports world by landing part of the NFL's television package, and stealing famed commentator John Madden, in 1994, just as Murdoch's Sky Sports had done with the English Premier League, sans Madden, two years earlier.

Both rights fees and production value skyrocketed in these sports, as they did for college football, which around this period shifted seamlessly from fears of over-saturation to the glory of nearly *perfect* saturation.

I almost never travel during a given college football season. You could loosely describe my job as "Watch every college football game and write about them," and in 2025, I can watch almost literally any college football game. There are seemingly countless games on air at any moment during one of Saturday's four major windows—early (games generally kicking off at 11:00 AM Central, aka God's Time Zone), afternoon (2:30), evening (between 6:00 and 7:00 PM) and, for the sickos, late (9:00 PM or later)—and this doesn't count the games that have already aired between Tuesday and Friday. Anything that doesn't make one of those networks is probably on ESPN+, Peacock, or maybe FloFootball.com. If you're looking for a particular small-school game, as I usually am at some point on a given Saturday, anything that isn't on ESPN+ or FloFootball is likely getting streamed via a local feed on the home team's website. This comes in particularly handy late in a given season, as the energy shot known as Small-School Playoffs gets rolling.

For a while, in fact, the only thing I *couldn't* watch legally on a given Saturday was whatever was being offered on the Pac-12 Network, which never made it to Columbia, Missouri. I could watch Cortland vs. Susquehanna in Division III, and I could find a choppy feed for Georgetown (Kentucky) vs. Lindsey Wilson at the NAIA level, but I couldn't watch Arizona State vs. Cal.

It's remained true since the first time I caught some random game on ESPN or TBS in the 1980s, and it only grows truer now: the more college football I watch—the actual *game*, not (motions hands at almost literally everything else off the field)—the more I enjoy college football. I am forever indebted, then, for the gains the sport has made on television. TV has drastically increased our shared history, the number of things we have gotten to witness together and remember. It has nationalized a regional game, and while that's come with its own set of drawbacks, the benefits have also been pretty clear. I don't miss having to listen to random Missouri road games on the radio; we always try to romanticize the olden days, but not being able to watch a game you want to watch, even

Arizona State–Cal, sucks. It's a lot more fun being able to watch whatever the hell you want.

Of course, television has also made the pursuit of television revenue the No. 1 driver of decision-making for somewhere between three and six decades now. It's made the sport infinitely richer, but it hasn't always made the sport better. Regardless, it's still pretty incredible to think back to a time when relatively smart people thought the biggest threat to college football was making it too easy to see.

It's generally accepted lore that the first network-televised football game kicked off on September 30, 1939. Glenn Miller's "In the Mood" was just beginning its run of radio dominance, *The Wizard of Oz* had debuted in theaters only a month earlier, and at Triborough Stadium on Randalls Island in New York, Fordham, home of the Seven Blocks of Granite and loser of only two games in the previous three seasons, walloped Waynesburg 34–7 to begin its 1939 campaign. Thanks to an NBC camera on a tripod in the southwest corner of the stadium, some local viewers lucky enough to own a still-rare television—between 500 and 5,000, according to the NCAA—got to watch the blowout from the comfort of their own homes.

World War II obviously slowed television's progress, but by 1945 NBC was aiming even higher. It aired the Army-Navy game, a 32–13 win by an Army team that still has a legitimate claim to "greatest of all time" status, in New York, Philadelphia, and Schenectady. And by the end of the decade, with television sets showing up in American homes from coast to coast, its presence had grown even further. Alarmed by a solid correlation between television's presence and decreased ticket sales, however—according to Keith Dunnavant's *The Fifty-Year Seduction*, an essential tome on the topic of college football's relationship with television, ticket sales dropped by more than 15 percent in the Middle Atlantic region, where TV's presence was strongest—the NCAA voted to prohibit the live broadcasting of college football games. This revealed what would long become a blindspot for the NCAA; as Dunnavant wrote, "What most athletic officials failed to recognize at the start of the game's national television era was the medium's enormous and unprecedented ability to multiply the number of people who cared about the sport. That was the ballgame, and none of the people who crafted the [NCAA's television] plan got it. They were too busy acting out of fear."

There was one primary issue with the NCAA attempting to assert control on this issue, however: it didn't really have any power. In 1951, schools didn't respect or fear the organization, and it had recently attempted to assert enforcement power to no avail. In 1950, following the adoption of the "Sanity Code"—a heavy-handed series of regulations banning the awarding of scholarships for specifically athletic purposes and locking down off-campus recruiting activities—the NCAA recommended expulsion for seven schools that admitted to frequently violating these rules. The recommendation required approval of two-thirds of member schools but failed. The Sinful Seven (Boston College, Maryland, The Citadel, Villanova, Virginia, Virginia Tech, and VMI), foolish as they were to admit to what countless others were undoubtedly also doing, survived, and the NCAA's authority proved toothless.

The University of Pennsylvania, then, was ready to stand up to the NCAA on the grounds of "we can do whatever the hell we want with our home television rights." After all, when a very similar "Broadcasting will kill gate receipts!" debate unfolded around radio broadcasts during the Great Depression in the 1930s, the concept of Home Rule, in which schools or conferences decided their own individual policies, prevailed.

The Penn Quakers enjoyed an all-time run of great form in the postwar years. Under the leadership of head coach George Munger, they went a combined 19–4–1 from 1945 to 1947 (0–2–1 against mighty Army and 19–2 against everyone else), and they spent at least part of every season from 1940 to 1949 in the AP top 10. The northeast was a power center for football talent at the time, and Munger was attracting quite a bit of it. (He was also able to give out more scholarships than rivals like Harvard and Yale, which were not only uninterested in going down that road but were also in the process of deemphasizing athletics in general. This deemphasis easily could have contributed to that northeastern attendance drop referenced above.) The Quakers were a hell of a draw, too: regal Franklin Field, home of long-ago Army-Navy games and, in the 1950s and 1960s, the Philadelphia Eagles—it's where Eagles fans famously booed Santa Claus—regularly brought in more than 60,000 fans for Penn games.

This was a *moment* for Penn football, and thanks in part to ambitious school president Harold Stassen and athletic director Franny Murray, the school wanted to take full advantage. It scheduled football games against nationally relevant programs—Pitt in 1949, Notre Dame from 1952 to 1955, Penn State in 1948 and most of the 1950s, California four times between 1950 and 1955, Duke in 1954—and after selling broadcasting rights for its home games for minor deals throughout the 1940s, it went big, signing a $100,000 deal with ABC for the 1950 season. Notre Dame, which had been broadcasting locally in the Chicago area for years, did the same with the burgeoning DuMont Television Network. The Quakers and Fighting Irish were going to be seen from coast to coast. This rang alarm bells for plenty of ambitious (and suddenly jealous) programs.

Correlation—in this case, between increased television and decreased butts in seats—doesn't necessarily equal causation, but between the falling attendance and the threat of incredible exposure for Notre Dame and Penn, the NCAA acted. And Penn didn't really care. Schools with TV contracts were threatened with sanction, or even expulsion, from the NCAA if they didn't comply and cancel their deals, and while Notre Dame basically took a passive-aggressive, "Fine, but we don't like this" approach, Stassen and Penn correctly felt that this was an antitrust issue and decided to fight. Who needs the NCAA's approval if you can just play your own games, sell your own TV rights, fight a bluffing NCAA, and eventually win?

Unfortunately, there was a problem with the "play your own games" part. The Eastern College Athletic Conference, a loose affiliation of eastern schools that included Penn and most of its closest rivals, told its members they could only play fellow schools that were complying with the NCAA's rules, and most of Penn's scheduled opponents quickly dropped the Quakers. Penn fans wanted to play Harvard, Yale, and Princeton—and Penn's leaders wanted to be associated with Harvard, Yale, and Princeton—more than they wanted a legal fight, and a good TV deal requires good games. Penn suddenly had none. Stassen and Murray, ambitious as they may have been, were forced to acknowledge reality, and Penn begrudgingly canceled its ABC deal. As Dunnavant wrote, "The [NCAA] did not have the legal authority to seize Penn's television rights even with a majority vote of the membership; the body did not have the constitutional power to punish Penn to encourage compliance; and the Ivy boycott looked suspiciously like an antitrust violation. By raising the stakes to a tremendous level—forcing Murray to choose between gambling the future of the program and folding his hand—the NCAA was bluffing with all attitude and no cards." It worked. And it changed everything. With its schools rallying behind it, and behind hard-nosed young president Walter Byers in particular, the NCAA officially controlled television rights for football (even though it didn't care about controlling TV for other sports), eventually releasing its own, limited television deal with NBC in 1951. It was worth $1.2 million, a percentage of which went to funding the NCAA itself. And once they controlled this revenue stream, Byers and company basically controlled the world.

For the next 30 years, Byers negotiated the NCAA's television deal, maintaining the same principles established in the early 1950s. There were strict limitations on both the number of overall games in the package and the number of national television appearances a team could make. These limits were tweaked through the years, and there was occasional in-season awkwardness, like when No. 1 Notre Dame and No. 2 Michigan State had both used up their national appearance allotment before playing a titanic, de facto national title game near the end of 1966. (The solution: air some other game in a couple of remote states so that Irish vs. Spartans qualified as "regional.") Plus, to secure the rights to show big-money games like Ohio State–Michigan or Oklahoma-Texas, a network had to also broadcast a certain number of smaller-school games.

Despite the NCAA's ongoing paranoia about overexposure, however, and despite the self-imposed limitations, ratings were strong, and both the money and stature involved in the deal grew significantly through the years. That became doubly true as ABC used the college football package as a way to experiment and differentiate itself in effort to catch up to mighty NBC and CBS. One of the primary differentiators turned out to be a production man by the name of Roone Arledge. ABC shocked many by stealing the NCAA's college football package from under NBC's nose in 1960, and Edgar Scherick, the first head of ABC Sports, empowered Arledge, then 29 years old and brimming with ideas. From Arledge's

Roone: A Memoir: "'The view a fan gets at home,' baseball commissioner Ford Frick had said, 'should not be any better than that of the fan in the worst seat of the ballpark.' Instinctively, I knew that was wrong. What television ought to be striving for was to give the fan the best seat in the house.... Television could capture it all, and in the 1960s, there was a chance to do it creatively. I wanted to make the game more intimate, and a lot more human."

Scherick told Arledge, the eventual president of ABC Sports and ABC News, to write a memo outlining his vision. And then ABC aimed to fulfill it. "Heretofore, television has done a remarkable job of bringing the game to the viewer—now we are going to take the viewer to the game!" the memo said. "We will utilize every production technique that has been learned in producing variety shows, in covering political conventions, in shooting travel and adventure series to heighten the viewer's feeling of actually sitting in the stands and participating personally in the excitement and color of walking through a college campus to the stadium to watch the big game. All these delightful adornments to the actual contest have been missing from previously televised sports events." Instead of treating viewers like they were lucky to be given a peek into the stadium at all, it was time to treat them like royalty. Arledge outlined concepts that would become required parts of broadcasts for decades to come: pre-shot film from campus; more cameras to catch not only the action, but the faces of coaches, players, fans, and cheerleaders; "video recorders to enable us to replay the decisive plays of the first half at the halftime break." (Instant replay was still a couple of years away.) "In short—WE ARE GOING TO ADD SHOW BUSINESS TO SPORTS!" he continued. "In addition to the natural suspense and excitement of the actual game, we have a supply of human drama that would make the producer of a dramatic show drool." The change in production value was a massive shift, and the "that's not the way we do things" crowd was predictably apoplectic, but this was a slam dunk, an approach that quickly became a requirement for covering virtually any sport.

By the mid-1960s, television had the requisite production value, and ABC had the original voice of the game as well in the sober-voiced Chris Schenkel. The sport also benefited from some absolute epics, even beyond the "regional" 10–10 tie between Notre Dame and Michigan State. In 1967, future Heisman winner O.J. Simpson outdueled future Heisman winner Gary Beban as No. 4 USC beat No. 1 UCLA 21–20. In 1969, with President Richard Nixon in attendance, No. 1 Texas came back to beat No. 2 Arkansas 15–14 in a game that ABC had moved to the end of the season for ratings purposes. In 1971, No. 1 Nebraska toppled No. 2 Oklahoma 35–31 in a genuine Game of the Century, even by typical game-of-the-century standards (1971 Nebraska: another serious G.O.A.T. candidate).

College football as a television franchise was growing rapidly. But it was also still holding itself back. As Dunnavant wrote, the NCAA's and NFL's television packages were worth almost exactly the same amount in 1960, but by 1970 the NFL's package was worth four times more. Television viewers wanted more Oklahoma, more Nebraska, more Texas, more Alabama, more USC, and *way* more Notre Dame, but the NCAA was still terrified of overexposure.

This was becoming increasingly annoying to the sport's bluebloods. Granted, they already lorded resource advantages over their peers, and per-appearance television revenue was only increasing those advantages. In the 12 seasons from 1968 to 1979, nine programs (Alabama, Michigan, Nebraska, Notre Dame, Ohio State, Oklahoma, Penn State, Texas, and USC) hoarded 63 percent of all top-10 finishes, 85 percent of all top-five finishes, and all but one national title. Only Pitt, with its Tony Dorsett–driven run in 1976, broke through the monopoly. Plus, thanks to both an increase in the number of bowl games and the liberalization of bowl bids, these programs were beginning to play each other more, too. Notre Dame accepted a bowl invitation for the first time in 45 years in 1969, and in 1974 both the Big Ten and Pac-8 agreed to break from their longstanding tradition of doling out only one bowl bid each (that is, the Rose Bowl or no bowl). And in 1972, even before the Big Ten and Pac-8 fully joined the party, there were highly rated games among this ruling class in the Cotton Bowl (Texas 17, Alabama 13), Orange Bowl (Nebraska 40, Notre Dame 6), Rose Bowl (USC 42, Ohio State 17), and Sugar Bowl (Oklahoma 14, Penn State 0). In 1973, it was the Cotton (Nebraska 19, Texas 3), Rose (Ohio State 42, USC 21), and title-deciding Sugar (Notre Dame 24, Alabama 23).

Still, they were being forced to leave money on the table, and they knew it. And soon enough, the Supreme Court would agree with them.

Here are 10 of the most relevant and interesting quotes from the decision for *NCAA v. Board of Regents of the University of Oklahoma*, the case that set college football on its current path:

1. "*Beginning in 1979 CFA members began to advocate that colleges with major football programs should have a greater voice in the formulation of football television policy than they had in the NCAA. CFA therefore investigated the possibility of negotiating a television agreement of its own, developed an independent plan, and obtained a contract offer from the National Broadcasting Co. (NBC).*"

   Since the early 1950s, the NCAA had control of the college football television deal because the schools had deferred to Byers in the fight with Penn and, to a lesser extent, Notre Dame. By the mid-1970s, however, deference was harder to come by, at least from member schools particularly interested in football. Members of the ACC, Big 8, Big Ten, Pac-8, SEC, SWC, WAC and major independents (Notre Dame, Penn State, and the like) met in Denver in late 1976 to discuss the formation of a union of sorts. Out of those meetings came the College Football Association (CFA). Big 8 commissioner and former Byers protégé Chuck Neinas was named its leader. The Big Ten and Pac-8 had bailed before the organization's first regular meeting, however—Big Ten commissioner Wayne Duke was one of Byers' closest allies, the Big Ten's lesser lights had voted against joining, and the Pac-8 basically always went along with what its eventual destroyer wanted.

   Led by Neinas, and led in spirit by Notre Dame's Father Edmund P. Joyce, the CFA became an advocacy group of sorts, communicating a mostly unified voice for what the big schools, and their football coaches, desired. And within a couple of years it would explore a TV plan of its own to complement (if you're thinking nicely) or compete with (if you're not) the NCAA's plan. The NCAA seemed a hair more flexible as cable television options were becoming available for schools, after all, and it had no antitrust exemption. As Dunnavant wrote, CFA schools had made 55 percent of the television appearances during the NCAA's 1978–81 TV deal but collected only 49 percent of the revenue. One can question whether six percentage points are worth potentially blowing up the NCAA—I know I am doing so right now—but it was still technically a deficit, and more importantly, the NCAA was still putting strict limits on the size of the pie. In August 1981, the CFA agreed to a four-year, $180 million TV deal with NBC. (The agreement included a boost in revenue if the CFA could convince the Big Ten and Pac-10 to rejoin the party.) After months of making vague threats through media sources—like the *Daily Oklahoman*'s Jerry McConnell, who had reported in May that "NCAA officials say that if members of the College Football Association should negotiate their own television contract and participate in such games on TV, they could be expelled from the NCAA"—the NCAA indeed attempted to lay the hammer down. Byers was a spectacular negotiator and a well-respected administrator, but his control over the football realm was never as strong as he probably would have preferred, and threats (and the peer pressure associated with them) were all he had. And as with Penn 30 years earlier, the threats worked. Enough CFA schools lost their nerve that the deal eventually fell apart.

2. *"The NCAA television plan on its face constitutes a restraint upon the operation of a free market, and the District Court's findings establish that the plan has operated to raise price and reduce output, both of which are unresponsive to consumer preference."*

Perhaps in the spirit of compromise—and with the understanding that the CFA represented a large threat to his power—Byers opened up the NCAA's 1982–85 football television contract to a second network, offering more TV slots in the process. Meanwhile, some within the NCAA suspected that the television issue was actually a secondary concern for the CFA and that general self-governance, as part of a smaller and more like-minded I-A, was the real issue. In December 1981, member schools indeed voted on stricter standards for I-A, and all or most of the Ivy League, Southern Conference, Southland,

MAC, and Missouri Valley were forced to join I-AA. That helped, but it wasn't enough. In September, the universities of Oklahoma and Georgia had filed suit in federal district court challenging the NCAA's ability to prevent the CFA from negotiating its own contract. Andy Coats, former Oklahoma County district attorney and future Oklahoma City mayor, joined the case, which opened in June 1982. The schools accused the NCAA of acting like a cartel, fixing prices and preventing competition. ABC, which had held college football TV rights for most of the last two decades, had encouraged the NCAA to seek an antitrust exemption from Congress; if they tried and failed, however, they feared that might open them up to greater legal challenges. That obviously happened, anyway. The schools won their case in district court, with Judge Juan Guerrero Burciaga calling the NCAA's system that of a "classic cartel," and the NCAA of course appealed. The case moved through the Circuit Court of Appeals, and in March 1984 it was heard by the Supreme Court.

3. *"In some sports, such as baseball, swimming, basketball, wrestling, and track, [the NCAA] has sponsored and conducted national tournaments. It has not done so in the sport of football, however.... With the exception of football, the NCAA has not undertaken any regulation of the televising of athletic events."*

Football was always treated as a different animal by the NCAA, and justifiably so. It was always the organization's bread-winner. Even as evidence slowly emerged that television was in no way a hindrance to game attendance, and even as the blueblood dominance of the 1970s proved that the limitations on appearances and the supposedly competition-friendly insistence on spreading appearances around did nothing to actually help with any sort of parity, the NCAA remained inflexible on these matters. Its 1982–85 television plan said, "The purposes of this Plan shall be to reduce, insofar as possible, the adverse effects of live television upon football game attendance and, in turn, upon the athletic and related educational programs dependent on the proceeds therefrom; to spread football television participation among as many colleges as practicable; to reflect properly the image of universities as educational institutions; to promote college football through the use of television, to advance the overall interests of intercollegiate athletics, and to provide college football television to the public to the extent compatible with these other objectives." The Supreme Court would call into question both some of these purposes and the way the TV deal actually achieved them.

4. *"The [NCAA's television] plan also contains 'appearance requirements' and 'appearance limitations' which pertain to each of the 2-year periods that the plan is in effect. The basic requirement imposed on each of the two networks is that it must schedule appearances for at least 82 different member institutions during each 2-year period. Under the appearance limitations no member institution is eligible to appear on television more than a total of six times and more than four times nationally, with the appearances to be divided equally between the two carrying networks."*

5. *"By participating in an association which prevents member institutions from competing against each other on the basis of price or kind of television rights that can be offered to broadcasters, the NCAA member institutions have created a horizontal restraint—an agreement among competitors on the way in which they will compete with one another."*

The Court agreed that the NCAA was different from a professional sports organization and that the "identification of this 'product' with an academic tradition differentiates college football from and makes it more popular than professional sports to which it might otherwise be comparable, such as, for example, minor league baseball. In order to preserve the character and quality of the 'product,' athletes must not be paid, must be required to attend class, and the like." (We'll revisit that last sentence in another chapter. Basically, the Court was acknowledging the professed realities of college sports rather than declaring them as law, but the NCAA would get a lot of mileage out of that sentence in courtrooms for decades.)

"The integrity of the 'product' cannot be preserved except by mutual agreement," the Court continued, "if an institution adopted such restrictions unilaterally, its effectiveness as a competitor on the playing field might soon be destroyed. Thus, the NCAA plays a vital role in enabling college football to preserve its character, and as a result enables a product to be marketed which might otherwise be unavailable." That acknowledgment was a point in the NCAA's favor. However, "since as a practical matter all member institutions need NCAA approval, members have no real choice but to adhere to the NCAA's television controls. The anticompetitive consequences of this arrangement are apparent.... Price is higher and output lower than they would otherwise be, and both are unresponsive to consumer preference." The demand for televised college football was obvious, and due to the effects of the plan, networks had to pay a higher per-game fee, and consumers got less college football to watch.

6. *"Petitioner argues, however, that its television plan can have no significant anticompetitive effect since the record indicates that it has no market power—no ability to alter the interaction of supply and demand in the market. We must reject this argument."*

I am no lawyer (thankfully), but it has always felt very strange that the NCAA tried to argue that it had no "market power." The Supreme Court thought so, too, striking this argument down with vigor, both on legal terms and as a matter of pure fact. This was a major pillar of the NCAA's overall strategy, and it was doomed from the start.

7. *"It seems unlikely, for example, that there would have been a greater disparity between the football prowess of Ohio State University and that of Northwestern University in recent years without the NCAA's television plan."*

I just enjoy that the Court—most notably, Justice John Paul Stevens, a Northwestern Law grad—managed to pause from its overall point to plant this Northwestern dig in a footnote. (From 1976 to 1981, the Wildcats had gone a combined 3–62–1. Dennis Green justifiably won Big Ten Coach of the Year by dragging them to 3–8 in 1982.)

8. *"The NCAA's argument that its television plan is necessary to protect live attendance is not based on a desire to maintain the integrity of college football as a distinct and attractive product, but rather on a fear that the*

product will not prove sufficiently attractive to draw live attendance when faced with competition from televised games."

This one's my favorite. The Court basically said, "What, your live product is so unattractive that you think people would rather stay home and watch television?" After early data suggested a correlation between increased television viewership and decreased live attendance—not just attendance for the games being televised, but for attendance of *any* games played while games were televised—that correlation had vanished through the years. And, besides, as the Court noted, by that point there was always a game on television while games were being played.

9. *"The television plan is not even arguably tailored to serve such an interest [in equalized competition]. It does not regulate the amount of money that any college may spend on its football program, nor the way in which the colleges may use the revenues that are generated by their football programs, whether derived from the sale of television rights, the sale of tickets, or the sale of concessions or program advertising. The plan simply imposes a restriction on one source of revenue that is more important to some colleges than to others. There is no evidence that this restriction produces any greater measure of equality throughout the NCAA than would a restriction on alumni donations, tuition rates, or any other revenue-producing activity."*

The NCAA's stated intentions were to encourage parity in some way and prevent the biggest schools from deriving too much of a financial advantage. But they were already deriving that advantage in many other ways, and they were already making more television money than their less-televised and less-monied rivals. One of the most positive effects of *NCAA v. Board of Regents* was that those less-televised schools...would end up on television more!

10. *"The collateral consequences of the spreading of regional and national appearances among a number of schools are many: the television plan, like the ban on compensating student-athletes, may well encourage students to choose their schools, at least in part, on the basis of educational quality by reducing the perceived economic element of the choice; it helps ensure the*

economic viability of athletic programs at a wide variety of schools with weaker football teams; and it 'promot[es] competitive football among many and varied amateur teams nationwide.'"

This is from the dissent of Justice Byron "Whizzer" White. White's presence on the Supreme Court was particularly noteworthy, as he was a former college football All-American at Colorado and twice led the NFL in rushing before cutting his career short to attend law school. His Wikipedia page is a delight:

ASSOCIATE JUSTICE
OF THE SUPREME COURT OF THE UNITED STATES
In office
April 16, 1962–June 28, 1993
Civilian awards
Presidential Medal of Freedom (2003)
Career NFL statistics
Rushing yards: 1,321

When the NCAA coined the term "student-athlete" in the 1950s, White was likely the model they had in mind. It probably goes without saying that White was rather old-school in his beliefs in the virtues of amateurism, and as a beneficiary of the collegiate system, he was particularly sympathetic to the NCAA. But his dissent was unconvincing, leaning on perfect-world ideals instead of reality. Star athletes were already likely to choose schools based on levels of dominance or potential NFL preparation instead of "on the basis of educational quality." "Schools with weaker football teams" stood to benefit significantly from a greater number of television opportunities, and again, in terms of "competitive football among many and varied amateur teams nationwide," the 1970s were the least competitive decade in ages. So much of White's arguments seemed to boil down to: *The NCAA is just different, and we should let them be different.* At one point, he wrote, "Limiting the number of television appearances by any college is an essential attribute of a balanced amateur athletic system." It just didn't stand up to reason, which was why he wrote the dissent and not the majority opinion.

So there it was. By a 7–2 vote, the Supreme Court sided against the NCAA, voiding its expanded contract with ABC and CBS and leaving schools to fend for themselves. Oklahoma looked for allies within the CFA to come up with a deal of their own, and Ted Turner's ambitious TBS went hard after Notre Dame. But thanks in part to Father Joyce's advocacy, Neinas ended up negotiating a deal for the entire CFA, primarily with ABC and ESPN, while the Big Ten and Pac-10, still CFA holdouts, pursued their own ABC deal.

What they soon found was that, while Byers' intransigence was a major reason for the NCAA's eventual failure in this realm, it also made him a hell of a negotiator.

Byers, who would retire in 1988 with the organization facing the same level of chaos it was dealing with when he came to power in 1951, had forced the networks to pay handsomely for the exclusivity of the college football package, and without this exclusivity, the price dropped significantly. Ad rates did, too, and thanks to the element of choice, ratings for the biggest games were far lower than they used to be. In the immediate years following the decision, revenue actually decreased on a per-school basis. According to Dunnavant in *The Fifty-Year Seduction*, the Big 8's television revenue fell by 37 percent in the first year of deregulation, and the SEC's fell by 33 percent. Schools would lose well into the hundreds of millions of dollars of TV revenue over the first decade, and with the cost of fielding a major-college football program rising, this created quite a few budget crises in the late 1980s.

From an exposure standpoint, however, the positive effects were obvious for the sport's middle class. As Dunnavant wrote, "Thanks to the massive increase in the number of televised games, lesser programs who rarely appeared on the NCAA series—such as Ole Miss, Iowa State, Washington State, Indiana, and Oklahoma State—could be seen with much greater regularity under the new system." He also noted that Kentucky had as many games televised in the first two years after deregulation than it had in over three decades with the NCAA contract. Conferences were able to find syndication for their games that weren't part of the overall CFA package, too; Notre Dame partnered with WGN, the SEC with TBS, the SWC and ACC with Raycom, and so on. You could easily make a case that both the accelerated emergence of non-historic powers like Florida State and Miami in the back half of the 1980s, plus the improved football stature of a conference like the ACC, which was for all intents and purposes a football mid-major into the late 1970s, were aided dramatically by post–*Board of Regents* deregulation.

▻

The 1982 Independence Bowl between Wisconsin and Kansas State wasn't the most incredible game in college football history. The weather was uncooperative—wind, rain, and atypically cold Shreveport temperatures meant that, despite ticket sales of around 49,000, only 24,684 fans actually showed up—and the teams combined for five turnovers and just 22-for-59 passing. But Wisconsin's Randy Wright threw two touchdown passes, including an 87-yarder on a slant to Tim Stracka, and the Badgers prevailed 14–3. It was at least marginally more interesting than that 1939 battle between Fordham and Waynesburg, and it might have been just as historically significant. It was, after all, ESPN's first live college football telecast. The young network had been airing tape-delayed games for a while, and following *Board of Regents*, ESPN was able to embark on a full schedule of live games in 1984.

And what a slate that 1984 schedule turned out to be:

- On September 1, ESPN showed BYU's 20–14 upset of No. 3 Pitt, a win that allowed the Cougars to surge in the rankings and position themselves to win one of the most unexpected and unlikely national titles of all time.
- On September 15, No. 4 Texas held off Bo Jackson and preseason No. 1 Auburn, 35–27, thanks in part to Jackson suffering a shoulder injury in the third quarter.
- On September 22, Doug Flutie threw for 354 yards and six touchdowns, moving into sixth on the career passing yardage list, as Boston College blew out North Carolina.
- On October 6, No. 14 Miami visited South Bend and thumped No. 16 Notre Dame 31–13, sending the Irish into a tailspin of three

straight losses (the third of which, 36–32 against No. 11 South Carolina, also aired on ESPN).

- On October 13, Vanderbilt nearly erased a 34–6 deficit against No. 12 LSU in Baton Rouge, falling just short, 34–27.
- On October 20 came another near upset: No. 2 Oklahoma, a 28-point favorite, needed a late touchdown from future college football announcer Spencer Tillman to survive Iowa State, 12–10, in Ames, Iowa.
- On October 27, No. 18 West Virginia ended a 25-year losing streak to No. 19 Penn State, scoring 10 fourth-quarter points and picking off a pass in the final minute. Mountaineers fans rushed the field and tore down the goal posts.
- On November 3, at Giants Stadium, Navy nearly ended a 21-year losing streak to Notre Dame, but Fighting Irish kicker John Carney saved the day with a 44-yard field goal with 14 seconds left.
- On November 10, No. 7 Oklahoma State got two touchdowns from Thurman Thomas and finished on a 21–0 run to beat Missouri 31–13, keeping the pace on what would become the Cowboys' first top-10 finish since 1945.
- On November 17, a resurgent No. 18 Auburn got a combined 198 rushing yards from Tommy Agee and an increasingly healthy Bo Jackson, beating No. 15 Georgia 21–12, to briefly get itself back into the SEC race.
- On November 24, No. 11 SMU got three touchdowns from Reggie Dupard and held on for dear life against Arkansas as a 24–3 lead turned into just a 31–28 win.
- On December 1, Texas's Memorial Stadium housed its third-largest crowd ever—attendance levels: strong!—but Texas A&M surged to a shocking 30–0 lead over its hated rival and won 37–12, costing the No. 13 Longhorns a share of the SWC title.
- On December 21, ESPN aired a national title game of sorts when top-ranked BYU beat unranked Michigan 24–17 in the Holiday Bowl. (Rumors flew that top teams like Washington, Auburn, Boston College, and Nebraska had been pursued to play the Cougars, but everyone passed.) After No. 4 Washington took

> down No. 2 Oklahoma in the Orange Bowl on January 1, the Cougars were able to hold off the Huskies in the polls and win the ring.

That's one hell of a season for one network, and it doesn't even include some of the indelible moments that aired elsewhere that fall—Miami's season-opening upset of Auburn; Flutie's miraculous Hail Mary against Miami; Syracuse's shocking upset of No. 1 Nebraska; a trio of second-ranked stunners (Purdue over No. 2 Ohio State, Kansas over No. 2 Oklahoma, Navy over upstart No. 2 South Carolina); a controversial 15–15 tie between Texas and Oklahoma; Maryland's record-setting comeback win over Miami (Miami had an *exhausting* season); an epic Georgia win over No. 2 Clemson, and more. This was just about the perfect season for college football fans to suddenly have a lot more college football at their disposal.

At least in part because of the lower cash flows, of course, the idea of superconferences, which could secure larger portions of the television pie, began to feel like logical, desirable pursuits. So did leaving the CFA. Despite Father Joyce's cheerleading in the 1970s and 1980s, Notre Dame struck an eventually fatal blow to the organization when it reached its own lucrative deal with NBC in 1990. But the organization maintained influence a little bit longer, signing a far more lucrative contract for the 1991–94 seasons, one supercharged by ESPN. Thanks to its ability to draw more and more from cable subscribers (and pull strong rates for advertising on top of that), the self-proclaimed "Worldwide Leader in Sports" was also able to pay more and more for college football (and make more *from* college football), especially with the eventual addition of new networks like ESPN2 and ESPNU.

ESPN is as ingrained within college football as any company has ever been with any American sport. The sheer number of games it airs is staggering (it showed more than 1,200 of them in the 2024 season on ESPN+ alone), but the cultural impact of the *College GameDay* preview show, which began making on-site visits in 1993 and hasn't really stopped since, is also undeniable. Reading the signs that people bring, waiting to see which piece of headgear cohost Lee Corso dons in picking the big game of the day...these things have long been unique to college football and have made it feel both more niche and more universal at the same time. Hell, ESPN has even been involved in EA Sports' college football game (discontinued in 2014 and resurrected in 2024). Rece Davis is talking to you even in your imaginary football universe.

ESPN has many different silos—the digital side, the television side, the programming side, et cetera—and it's noticeable when an ESPN reporter breaks news that ESPN has won a new media rights deal (with a conference or the College Football Playoff), and then other ESPN writers, like me, talk about the impact of it. Even the most honest attempt at neutrality is going to look like state-run propaganda if you squint just right, and such ubiquity has produced nonstop conspiracy theories through the years. ESPN holds influence but doesn't pull strings, and you won't convince an angry fan that there's much of a difference. In Andrew James Miller's and Tom Shales' *Those Guys Have All the Fun: Inside the World of ESPN*, announcer and former *GameDay* host Chris Fowler told the story of his toxic experience during the 1997 Heisman race, one that came down to a battle between Tennessee quarterback Peyton Manning and Michigan cornerback Charles Woodson. "In the weeks leading up to the Heisman announcement, when we talked about it on *GameDay*, I would just point out that if you read the tea leaves, it was not going to be a slam dunk for Peyton Manning," Fowler said. "I wasn't trying to hype Charles Woodson or the show for that matter. The show was going to rate what it rated. I was just doing my job. But there were people at Tennessee who were frustrated and took it very personally. ESPN didn't have the SEC games at that point, didn't have as much of a relationship with the conference as we do now. We were seen as 'the Big Ten Conference' by some people in that part of the world, and we were perceived to have an agenda." That assumed agenda naturally flipped completely when rights changed hands. In the 1990s, SEC fans hated ESPN's "obvious" pro–Big Ten bias; in the 2020s, Big Ten fans hate ESPN's "obvious" pro-SEC bias.

After Woodson indeed pulled an upset, beating Manning by 272 points, Fowler, the host of the Heisman ceremony, was the one interviewing him. "I got a lot of negative feedback," he continued. "The phone was ringing off the hook that night.... It was really, really edgy; very difficult and uncomfortable. And it stayed that way for a while. We didn't go back to Knoxville with *GameDay* for a few years, and when we did, we paid attention to security.

"By the way, I had voted for Peyton Manning to win the Heisman Trophy."

Something similar happened in the home stretch of the 2023 season. The ever-present Kirk Herbstreit, who has cohosted *GameDay* for more than 30 years and who makes countless appearances on other shows as a given season picks up steam, began speculating in mid-November that an unbeaten Florida State could miss out on a spot in the four-team College Football Playoff if one-loss Alabama, with a stronger strength of schedule, were to win out, beating top-ranked Georgia in the process. When FSU quarterback Jordan Travis was lost for the season to injury, things took a pretty toxic turn. His backup looked pretty mediocre before getting hurt, too, and the third-stringer, a true freshman, looked out of his element (as many third-stringers do) as the Seminoles rode defense to an ugly ACC Championship win. With Herbstreit and others constantly repeating their skepticism on ESPN—and with members of the CFP committee inevitably hearing some of this skepticism in the run-up to the final rankings—Nick Saban's 12–1 Alabama team suddenly overtook FSU after upsetting Georgia in the SEC Championship and snagged the No. 4 ranking on the grounds of it being a "better" team than the unbeaten Seminoles. There was no vast, complicated conspiracy to this; Herbstreit and others weren't expressing preferences or rooting for 'Bama over Florida State. They were merely expressing opinions, and anyone who saw a pro-SEC agenda here had to reconcile with the fact that ESPN *also* runs the ACC Network. Again: ubiquity. But things still played out just as the most hardened, conspiracy theory–addled FSU fan on the Internet would have predicted. That person got to pretend to be right about how the world works. Even if there is no agenda, ESPN is big enough that it leaves enough dots lying around for you to connect them however you choose.

It's almost jarring to realize, then, that maybe the most impactful creation of the last 20 years came from somewhere other than ESPN's Bristol, Connecticut, home. On June 21, 2006, Jim Delany's Big Ten announced that, in a joint venture with Fox, it was creating the Big Ten

Network, the first network completely dedicated to covering a single conference. The first game it aired, at the start of the wacky 2007 season, seemed like a dreadful omen: defending FCS champion Appalachian State raced to a 28–14 lead over No. 5 Michigan, held on for dear life, and clinched an all-time upset by blocking a field goal in the final minute. The 34–32 win was the first ever for an FCS program over a ranked FBS team, and it was a humiliation of sorts for the Big Ten. But the conference got the last laugh. BTN was in 60 million homes within a year and was profitable within five years. It quickly turned into a cash cow for Big Ten schools and became a point of envy for everyone else. That set off a predictable chain reaction. The Pac-12 announced it was creating its own network in 2011 and debuted it in 2012; the SEC Network was announced in 2013 and launched in 2014; the ACC Network was announced in 2016 and started in 2019. The latter two were affiliated with ESPN, as was Texas's Longhorn Network, which launched in 2011 and was rendered defunct by UT's move to the SEC in 2024.

Just as television drove conference expansion in the 1990s, conference networks drove a lot of the moves we saw in the 2010s. It certainly didn't hurt that Texas A&M and Missouri both brought the SEC into two new states with large population centers just as the SEC Network was coming to fruition, and the thought of a richly successful conference network drove ambitious Pac-12 commissioner Larry Scott to pursue Texas, Oklahoma, and others in his hopes for a Pac-16. The Big Ten's addition of Maryland and Rutgers in 2013, meanwhile, was nakedly driven by getting BTN access to the Washington, D.C., and New York City markets. (These networks draw a larger chunk of carriage fees in markets in which they have a program.)

These networks have added to conferences' coffers; they've also been fantastic in generating exposure for sports beyond football and men's basketball. Iowa women's basketball player Caitlin Clark, for instance, became a cultural phenomenon of sorts during a four-year career that saw her eventually set the all-time career scoring record. During the final two seasons of her career, more than 25 of her games aired on either BTN or its add-on streaming service, BTN+. If you're a fan of women's hoops, volleyball, softball, wrestling, baseball, or any number of other sports on offer, these are boom times when it comes to your ability to actually watch the sport you love.

Of course, conference networks weren't all slam-dunk successes. After landing Colorado and Utah but not any of the Big 12's heavyweights, Scott's Pac-12 debuted not only a Pac-12 Network but also a series of six regional brands—Pac-12 Arizona (for Arizona and Arizona State), Pac-12 Bay Area (Cal and Stanford), Pac-12 Los Angeles (UCLA and USC), Pac-12 Mountain (Colorado and Utah), Pac-12 Oregon (Oregon and Oregon State), and Pac-12 Washington (Washington and Washington State). The conference also chose to own the network outright instead of pairing with a major entity like ESPN or Fox. Its production value was, by all accounts, outstanding, but I wouldn't know, as I lived in an area it never reached. It never arrived at a deal with DirecTV, a major carrier, and it never got full national buy-in from other carriers. The Pac-12 overestimated itself and its appeal, and the lesser success of the Pac-12 Network damaged its earning potential. That, as much as anything, opened the door for the Big Ten to raid the conference and, eventually, fatally wound it. In a way, the Pac-12's *successes* also ended up damaging the conference's cause. As journalists Armen Keteyian and John Talty wrote in 2024's *The Price: What It Takes to Win in College Football's Era of Chaos*, Scott scored a huge victory in 2011 by scoring a 12-year, $3 billion deal with Fox and ESPN, but it helped to skew the market in such a way that encouraged rival conferences to look for huge moves—like, say, USC and UCLA to the Big Ten—to improve their own rights deals.

As with seemingly every other industry in America, once a big-money hierarchy is established, consolidation probably isn't far away. And consolidation is certainly what we got in the 2020s. The SEC took the Big 12's two biggest brands (Oklahoma and Texas), and by eventually taking not only UCLA and USC but also Oregon and Washington, the Big Ten assured the demise of the Pac-12, its ally and partner for decades, as a major conference. Now, instead of the six power conferences we had in the 2000s (ACC, Big 12, Big East, Big Ten, Pac-10, SEC), we're not only down to four (no Big East, no Pac-12), but we're also looking at a massive gap between the top two and other two.

This gap has left ambitious schools from outside the Big Ten and SEC pretty desperate to close the gap. Florida State, locked into a long-term and, to date, unbreakable-by-lawyers contract in the ACC—and, in 2023, scorned by the CFP committee in favor of an SEC team—has openly flirted with taking on private equity funding. A report by the *Tampa Bay Times* in early 2024 revealed the pursuit of a potential naming sponsor for Doak Campbell Stadium and something terrifyingly called a "super license agreement" with a private equity firm. Nothing good can come from a super license agreement.

The strangest thing about *NCAA v. Board of Regents*, the most impactful case in the history of college athletics, is that no one really expected it—or wanted it—to go as far as it did. In *The Fifty-Year Seduction*, Dunnavant tells the story of Andy Coats, the lawyer who won the case for Oklahoma, Georgia, and the entire CFA, almost pleading with Frank Easterbrook, the NCAA's chosen attorney, during the Court of Appeals process in Denver. "Isn't there some way we can settle this?" Coats asked Easterbrook. He wasn't afraid of losing; he seemed afraid of winning. "Even Coats was torn," Dunnavant wrote. "He kept thinking—hoping—the NCAA would settle, because he understood how his clients benefited from some of the monopolistic tactics he was attacking and how perilous a completely free market might turn out to be. 'I didn't want to go down in history as the man who ruined college football,' he said."

Four decades later, in a 2023 interview with NBC News, Coats said, "I think I screwed up college football across the board." It was, however, the NCAA's own bull-headedness that sent college football down this road. "We tried at every stage to negotiate an agreement of some kind, to limit what would happen," Coats told NBC. "But we learned the 'NCAA' stood for 'Never Compromise Anything at Anytime,' and they wouldn't even talk to us."

It's worth pondering for a moment what might have happened had the NCAA actually agreed to settle the case and allow the CFA schools more leeway in the realm of television rights. The NCAA's 1982–85 television deal was impressive, involving two networks (ABC and CBS), a supplemental package with TBS, and revenue that doubled what the 1977–81 deal brought in. If the CFA had been allowed to keep some of its proposed deal with NBC, it would have multiplied the amount of appearances available, not only for the Oklahomas and Georgias but also for the Oklahoma States and Georgia Techs. In this environment, the Big Ten and Pac-10 might have eventually joined the CFA as well, and with more money flowing in, some of the financial issues that beset schools in the late 1980s would have been eased to some degree. Does this mitigate some of the rationale for the 1990s run of realignment? And would settling have established some sort of permanent detente or just delayed the same inevitable fight?

Regardless, as we've since learned, this wasn't the last time the NCAA's stubbornness made everything a lot more complicated than it needed to be. It chose belligerence over progress, and college football ended up in an awfully strange place because of it.

The lesson is: never try.

5.

Sixty Years of Playoff Debates (and What Do We Owe Bowls?)

On January 1, 1902, Michigan confirmed itself as college football's preeminent program when, following the Tournament of Roses parade in Pasadena, and with Tournament Park charging families $1 to park their horses and buggies, Fielding Yost's incredible Wolverines demolished poor Stanford 49–0, in front of about 8,500 people. The win was so dominant that it convinced the Tournament of Roses Association that maybe a postseason football exhibition wasn't such a good idea. They didn't attempt another one for 14 years.

By the 1920s, however, the Rose Bowl—with its glorious, new Rose Bowl stadium, a venue that genuinely continues to live up to all hype a century later—was bestowing grand status on a number of eventual blueblood programs. USC joined the club with a 14–3 win over Penn State on the first day of 1923. Notre Dame did so after Elmer Layden and the Four Horsemen led Knute Rockne's Fighting Irish to an easy 27–10 humbling of Pop Warner's Stanford in 1925. A year later, a true usurper rose: once it failed to find a properly competitive eastern team to face Washington, the Rose Bowl deigned to invite a dominant southern team for the first time. Alabama rewarded the committee by scoring 20 third-quarter points and holding on for a 20–19 win, eventually called the "Game That Changed the South."

The Sugar Bowl gave TCU greats Sammy Baugh and Davey O'Brien early stages to prove themselves with wins over LSU (in 1936) and

Carnegie Mellon (in 1939), respectively. It granted opportunities to a couple of Bud Wilkinson's first great Oklahoma teams in the late 1940s and gave the South its own championship of sorts—for segregation-related reasons, it must be noted—starting in the 1950s. The Orange Bowl became a regular home for great Oklahoma and Nebraska teams of the 1970s and 1980s, just as the Cotton Bowl did for Texas and other SWC greats. With television becoming an increasingly powerful force, and with the NCAA still afraid to allow major powers on television much during the season, bowls offered fans rare opportunities to watch the teams and players they had mainly read about in the newspapers. Even with Notre Dame refusing all bowl offers for 45 years following that classic 1925 Rose Bowl win, and even with Big Ten and PCC/AAWU/Pac-8 teams continuing to allow only one participant per year into the 1970s, bowls were invaluable to college football's developing national popularity. And both large and small, they have undoubtedly produced some of college football's greatest games:

- Miami's upset of Nebraska in the 1984 Orange Bowl.
- Penn State's upset of Miami in the 1987 Fiesta Bowl.
- Notre Dame's upset of Alabama in the 1973 Sugar Bowl.
- That amazing 2001 GMAC Bowl between East Carolina and Marshall, where the Thundering Herd's Byron Leftwich threw for 576 yards, and Marshall scored twice in the final two minutes to force OT and eventually win 64–61.
- TCU's 31-point comeback against Oregon in the 2016 Alamo Bowl.
- BYU's Hail Mary win over SMU in the 1980 Holiday Bowl.
- Central Michigan's Hail Mary hook-and-ladder against Western Kentucky in the 2014 Bahamas Bowl (which they then wasted by attempting a futile fade route on the game-deciding, two-point conversion; goal-line fades: not even once, friends).
- Notre Dame's 22-point, Joe Montana–led comeback against Houston in the 1979 Cotton Bowl.
- Joe Germaine and Ohio State topping Jake Plummer and Arizona State in the 1997 Rose Bowl.

- The 1964 Cotton Bowl, an easy 28–6 Texas win over Navy but, according to my father, "the first time the nation really got to see Roger Staubach, Heisman winner." A year later, he would go into military service instead of professional football—"an educational experience for a 10-year old at the time."
- Boise State 43, Oklahoma 42 in the 2007 Fiesta Bowl.
- Texas over USC in 2005, of course, and countless other incredible Rose Bowls.

College football's history would be less colorful, and its popularity would have become less widespread, if bowls never existed. But what do we owe them for that in 2025?

On one hand, bowls remain one of the key elements of the sport. Their importance (down) and sheer volume (way up) have obviously changed through the years, but they still litter the television listings throughout December, and I watch at least part of every single one of them. They inevitably give us some of the wildest and most enjoyable moments of a given season—not even including a couple of down-to-the-wire College Football Playoff games, 20 of 35 other bowls capping the 2024 season finished within one score, and three went to overtime. And beyond that, as we've discussed, fielding even a bad college football team is really difficult, and getting rewarded with a trip to a locale of varying degrees of exoticness isn't the worst thing in the world. If we added 20-something more bowls and offered bids to every single FBS program, I would watch all of the new ones too.

On the other hand, a playoff would also have produced plenty of epic moments through the years. And again, the 2024 season's bowls were absolute dynamite despite the presence of the CFP.

From basically the moment that they began helping the sport and its popularity, bowls—more specifically, the executives who ran them—also began doing what they could to hold the sport back and preserve their own power. Long ago, when there weren't very many of them, they may have served the sport well from an exposure standpoint, but they also served as tools for inequality. As Bill Miller wrote for the *NCAA News* more than 50 years ago, "Bowl games and rich television contracts have contributed to the narrowing down of 'attractive teams.'" The teams that typically made major bowls already had the most commitment and resources, and the money and notoriety they earned from playing in these elite games solidified their status for decades to come. That helped to create a ruling class of sorts, a club reluctant to add new members.

Meanwhile, as a playoff slowly became a more logical idea for many in the sport—and as every other level of college football joined both the pros and high school football in finishing a given season with a playoff—bowls used the power of both guilt and guaranteed money to convince higher-ups that a playoff would destroy both bowls and the sport itself. "There seems to me to be no doubt that [a playoff] would work a hardship on our old friends, the bowls," wrote Tennessee athletic director Bob Woodruff to counter Miller in that same 1971 *NCAA News* piece. "A national championship series would undoubtedly take the edge off these traditional games, to the extent that many of them would die from lack of interest. The bowls have done too much for college football to be repaid in that manner." Even when a *post-bowl* playoff was proposed in the 1970s, allowing the bowls themselves to continue to hold influence and help to determine a national champion, Sugar Bowl executive director Mickey Holmes responded with manipulation. "The bowls have been a great friend to college football for a long time," he said, "and how unfair it would be to do something which could destroy us." *Destroy.*

Meanwhile, the hypnotic appeal of the Rose Bowl and its relationship with the Big Ten and Pac-10 prevented a wide array of playoff proposals from gaining traction in the 1980s and 1990s, which meant that by the time the College Football Playoff had finally come into existence in 2014, we had been arguing about a playoff for *more than 50 years*. And even then, the playoff we got added up to a single extra game outside of the bowl structure! It took another 10 years to get anything that resembled a genuine, inclusive tournament.

Though their meaning and importance have certainly changed, bowls have not died in the young playoff era. The Sugar Bowl has not been *destroyed*. But the naked self-interest bowls showed as the playoff debate continued undid a lot of the good they might have done for the sport early on. Bowls are a huge part of the paradox that has always been college football. The sport itself is impossibly unique—huge crowds in strange locales, an ownership-like obsession from fans, all the innate oddity that comes with basing an entire industry around 18- to 22-year-old males and a pointy ball that bounces in unexpected ways—and those things are baked right into the core. But the sport's decision makers and early influencers seemed to spend decades thinking that *any* unique aspect had to be maintained for the sport to remain popular, that major college football had to be different in every possible way. So many otherwise rational people, with steady nudging from well-paid bowl executives, remained eternally convinced that a playoff would ruin the sport. Proclaiming it became a tradition in itself.

The journey to an actual playoff was fraught with speed bumps and guilt trips. Let's look back at the times the arguing grew the loudest. What were the proposals? How did they fail? And how did one finally succeed?

1960: Stu Holcomb's World Series of Football

From an AP report on March 29, 1960: "A college football World Series has been proposed by Stu Holcomb, Northwestern University athletic director. Holcomb said Monday night that he has suggested a football playoff modeled after the NCAA's basketball and baseball tournaments. He wrote Big Ten Commissioner K.L. (Tug) Wilson and NCAA Executive Secretary Walter Byers, he said."

Stu Holcomb was a pretty common product of the day: a former football coach–turned–athletic director. The former Ohio State halfback worked his way up the coaching ladder and landed the Purdue head coaching job in 1947. His 1952 Boilermakers won at Ohio State and claimed a share of the Big Ten title, and he coached future Super Bowl champion Len Dawson there before retiring (career record: 93–75–12) to take the Northwestern AD job in 1956.

Holcomb's most famous act in Evanston was also one of his first: he hired Ara Parseghian of Miami (Ohio) to lead the football program. Northwestern was finding it more difficult to compete in the Big Ten, having gone just 7–27–2 over the previous four seasons after a run of top-10 finishes in the 1930s and 1940s. Parseghian would win just four games in his first two years, but his Wildcats would at least briefly live in the AP top 10 for five of six seasons from 1958 to 1963, reaching No. 1 for two weeks in 1962; they destroyed Notre Dame 35–6 that season, a win that would come back to haunt them a year later when the Fighting Irish, looking for a new head coach, lured Parseghian away.

What *could* have been the most momentous contribution of Holcomb's career quietly fizzled out, but it was a doozy. He envisioned an eight-team playoff that would begin the week after the regular season ended and wrap up by mid-December; it would feature the champions of the AAWU, ACC, Big 8, Big Ten, SEC, and SWC, plus perhaps highly ranked champions of minor conferences or top independents as at-larges. And as an extra carrot, he suggested that some of the massive revenue that came from this event could be directed toward "the American Olympic Fund, educational foundations, medical research, and other authorized organizations operating for the benefit of the public." Walter Byers called the proposal "novel and interesting," but others were less enthusiastic. Asa Bushnell, commissioner of the sprawling ECAC (and a board member on the U.S. Olympic Committee) called it "excessive elaboration of a program which is satisfactory as it is." SEC commissioner Bernie Moore's review: "I could only say I am not enthusiastic about the idea." Big 8 commissioner Reaves Peters expressed concern about December weather. By late April, Holcomb was still selling it—"Think of the possibilities: the best teams in the country squaring off on a Saturday from 12:00 noon until 7:00 o'clock in the evening. What a show that would be!"—and said he was encouraged by the responses he'd gotten. And he seemed to get a pretty big endorsement a few weeks later when Ohio State head coach Woody Hayes, speaking at a coaching clinic, said, "A world series playoff between the top eight teams in the nation will get my support. I think the NCAA will go for it, too. All the other sports have bona fide championships, why not football? It will double the interest in football."

And then...*poof*. Gone. You can hardly find a single additional mention of the Holcomb plan. Just like the proposed Airplane Conference of the day, it was a bold idea that seemed to gain traction in the media and then just got swept under the rug and forgotten. But it would have indeed been a show.

1967: Duffy Daugherty's Eight-Team Bonanza

Michigan State head coach Duffy Daugherty's interest in a playoff seemed to stem from two things: the rise of the AFL and NFL, and his own Spartans' awesomeness. MSU was one of the nation's preeminent programs in the early 1950s under first Biggie Munn, then Daugherty, and after a down period they surged to a combined 19–1–1 record in 1965–66, losing only to UCLA in a classic Rose Bowl to cap the 1965 season and famously tying unbeaten Notre Dame in 1966. There was surely some self-interest in his motivations here, but there's no question that, with two different professional leagues commanding the attention of both the nation and its televisions, college football was going through some existential issues in the mid-1960s. For the first time, a major bowl game and a professional playoff game had been played in the same city, just a day apart, late in the 1966 season: Georgia beat SMU in the Cotton Bowl on December 31, and in the very next day's NFL Championship, the Green Bay Packers knocked off the host Dallas Cowboys to qualify for the first Super Bowl. Far more people paid attention to the latter than the former.

Following MSU's No. 2 finish (and the college/NFL scheduling congestion) in 1966, Daugherty offered his own version of an eight-team playoff, which would start earlier in November and wrap up by mid-December. The year before, according to Ronald A. Smith's *Play-by-Play: Radio, Television, and Big-Time College Sport*, ABC Sports' Roone Arledge had also told the NCAA Television Committee that they would "waste an opportunity if they do not explore nationally the possibility of a bona fide playoff pattern during the three weekends at football season's end to determine a legitimate champion." As the *Houston Post*'s Jack Gallagher wrote for the *NCAA News* in early 1967, "One wonders the impact the pro game might have had at Dallas if it had been competing with, say, Texas A&M vs. Notre Dame in the semifinals of the national championship.... This was for the NFL championship. The winner would go on to the Super Bowl. It was a playoff, an elimination, a meaningful contest rather than an exhibition. Matched against it, the SMU-Georgia contest was a drab affair with scant appeal." In response to Daugherty's push, the NCAA did what the NCAA has always done: appoint a committee to undergo a feasibility study.

The idea seemed to engender quite a bit of support, and Daugherty tried to make it clear to bowl lovers that this playoff could be over before bowl season. (Theoretically, teams could participate in both the playoff and a bowl if they chose to.) But as he also joked at the Football Writers Association of America conference in early August, "This plan is so logical that I know it won't be accepted by the NCAA." Indeed. The Big Ten was forever hesitant on these ideas; SEC commissioner Tonto Coleman, whose conference benefited pretty significantly from its bowl lineup, said no; and Parseghian, now ruling the roost at Notre Dame, rather patronizingly called a playoff "idealistic but not realistic," suggested it would make college football *too much* like the pros, and insinuated that Notre Dame would refuse to take part.

It's hard to have a playoff without the Big Ten, SEC, and Notre Dame. Predictably, things fell apart again. But from this point forward, the debate never really stopped.

1971: Laying Out Both Arguments

In 1971, the *NCAA News* did an interesting job of presenting both sides of the playoff debate, asking North Texas professor and outspoken playoff proponent Bill Miller to lay out the reasons for his point of view while Tennessee's Bob Woodruff explained why he was against such a thing.

"The heart and soul of intercollegiate football is competition," Miller wrote. "Rather than restrict major competitive programs, let us broaden the base for major competition by affording all schools who commit themselves to this program with the opportunity of enjoying the rewards of success." As we are currently living in a time in which we are talking about *shrinking* the base for major competition, this argument feels like a blast of fresh air. That's not the way these things usually work, though.

"Football is the only major intercollegiate sport that does not produce a true national champion," he continued. "There is no way to settle the dilemma of who is champion with our present set up in the NCAA.

A national play-off system, similar to the one utilized in basketball, is needed in order to crown a legitimate champion." Miller proposed going big. Never mind the top six conference champions; he wanted 12 conference champions involved—not only the ACC, Big 8, Big Ten, Pac-8, SEC, and SWC, but also the Ivy League, MAC, Missouri Valley, PCAA, Southern, and WAC, plus four independents to fill out a full 16-team bracket. You could start with regional matchups in the first round, then incorporate existing bowls for later rounds. "The championship game would then take on the same importance as the pros' Super Bowl game," he concluded.

Leaning heavily on conference champions would have produced some strange results: Remember that 1971 Oklahoma-Nebraska Game of the Century? Nebraska's 35–31 win would have eliminated what ended up being the No. 2 team in the country from contention. Meanwhile, we'd have gotten something like this for a bracket in a 16-team, 1971 playoff:

Memphis State (4–6)	at	No. 1 Nebraska (12–0)
No. 15 Houston (9–2)	at	No. 14 Toledo (11–0)
Long Beach State (8–4)	at	No. 8 Arizona State (10–1)
North Carolina (9–2)	at	No. 4 Michigan (11–0)
No. 16 Stanford (8–3)	at	No. 12 Texas (8–2)
Dartmouth (8–1)	at	No. 10 Penn State (10–1)
Boston College (9–2)	at	No. 13 Notre Dame (8–2)
Richmond (5–5)	at	No. 2 Alabama (11–0)

This proposal probably gave too much heft to independents and would have been tweaked after its adoption as the allure of including multiple power programs from the top conferences became too strong. But it was still remarkably inclusive and interesting. The dissent: less so. Including the "bowls have done too much for college football to be repaid in that manner" argument referenced earlier, Woodruff's portion of the essay took on quite a few of the arguments we would continue to see for the next 40 years.

"Here at the University of Tennessee there would be a very serious conflict in the academic area should our team be fortunate enough to qualify," Woodruff wrote. "Because of our fall quarter final examination schedule, it would require special examinations schedules." This was apparently not a concern at the smaller-school level, where they began an NAIA playoff in 1958 and would do the same at the newly created Division II and III levels in 1973. If you want to make academics a priority, then do it. But it's harder to justify that for Tennessee when you aren't doing it for Livingston University (now West Alabama), which won the NAIA title in mid-December 1971.

"With so many good football teams around," he continued, "it would be very difficult for anyone to say just who should qualify for the playoffs and who shouldn't. The severity of regular season schedules would have to be taken into consideration; an 8–2 team playing a strong schedule might be better than a 10–0 team playing a weak schedule, but it would be an impossible thing to prove." Of course, with a larger playoff like the 16-teamer above, most of the teams with the best cases for inclusion would be included. And you know what the best way of determining superiority is? *Having two teams play each other.*

Woodruff went on. "Because of the time involved, the play-off field could not be any larger than eight. We might end up with a national champion that was no more deserving of the title than the so-called mythical champions now selected by wire service polls." Besides the second sentence being a total non sequitur, in 1982, of course, the NCAA expanded the I-AA tournament from eight to 12 teams, then expanded it to 16 in 1986. The Division III field expanded to 16 in 1985, and Division II followed suit three years later. And everyone seemed pretty satisfied with the general deservingness of its champions.

"Finally the biggest unscheduled factor against the playoff is the need for sectionalism," Woodruff concluded, "so that alumni and friends of College Team A will argue and believe with great pride and devotion that their team, which had a great record, was just as good as, if not superior to, another great College Team B in another conference." He legitimately tried to say that fans would prefer arguing to actually watching their team get a shot at a title!

Did anything come of this exchange? Of course not. But it set the talking points for years to come.

1976: A Bowl Workaround

By the mid-1970s, it seemed like a playoff's time had finally come after a *whole decade* of arguing. On January 2, 1976, the Associated Press reported that the NCAA's executive committee had approved of a "college 'Super Bowl' plan" and that it would head to the floor at the NCAA's annual convention. The committee's approval was a big deal, as support for the bowls was typically too overwhelming for a playoff to get votes. But the genius of this proposal was that the entire four-team playoff would take place after the bowls. It would use the bowls to determine the participants. A workaround! As Temple athletic director Ernie Casale, the head of the latest feasibility committee designed to investigate the idea, said in the AP piece, "We realized that we would never get by the convention if we interfered with the present bowl structure." Granted, the major bowls weren't excited about the potential attendance effects of such a playoff—would as many fans travel to Miami for the Orange Bowl or New Orleans for the Sugar Bowl if they thought they might have a semifinal to attend a week later?—but this proposal made it further than most.

A funny thing happened at the convention, however: The discussion about what would eventually become the I-A/I-AA split boiled over. Without knowing how many divisions college football was going to have, it was hard to vote on a playoff and how its money would be distributed. Within a couple of days, the playoff went from having decent odds to "maybe some other time."

1979: Okay, What About Now?

After some fits and starts, the Division I split had finally taken shape, and after another split national title in 1978—Alabama (11–1) won the AP title, USC (12–1) the UPI title—the NCAA's Extra Events Committee recommended the four-team, post-bowl playoff plan to the Division I steering committee. (So, so many committees.) What proponents quickly found, however, was that the workaround they had once found had been eliminated. Bowls were now as virulently against the post-bowl playoff idea as they had been against all other plans. And this time they were organized.

"The bowl people have done a very effective lobbying job," said a College Football Association spokesman after voters overwhelmingly rejected a playoff idea at the summer's board of CFA governors meeting. That would become an increasingly common theme.

(One interesting element of a post-bowl four-teamer, by the way: it was a terrible plan. Picture the end of the 1978 season: No. 1 Alabama takes down No. 2 Penn State 14–7, in a dramatic Sugar Bowl featuring a famous goal-line stand. The Crimson Tide's reward for winning this game in a world with a four-team playoff following the bowls? A semifinal matchup against...No. 4 Penn State.)

The issue itself would come up constantly in the early 1980s, with Joe Paterno and other reliable advocates randomly speaking up about it. And instead of a four-team playoff after the bowls, coaches like Indiana's Lee Corso, future *College GameDay* star, favored a one-game, two-team playoff instead. "Usually at the end of the bowl games, there are two great football teams," he said. "They play." Corso and others even suggested that this title game could be played a week ahead of the Super Bowl in the same stadium. (This would have presented fewer immediate rematches than the four-teamer, but it still would have happened from time to time, as in 1983, when Miami's classic Orange Bowl upset of Nebraska would have been followed by a Miami-Nebraska title game.)

As the major bowl at-large selection process grew more and more political—and as bowls began informally inviting teams earlier and earlier to assure a big name—choosing deserving teams began to matter less than choosing big brands, deserving or not. In the six seasons from 1980 to 1985, there were only six bowl matchups between top-five teams and nine matchups between top-five teams and opponents ranked either in the double digits or not at all. In 1980, Georgia won the national title without beating a team ranked higher than seventh. In 1984, BYU won the title while beating only one ranked team, and that team (No. 3 Pitt in Week 1) ended up going 3–7–1. Regardless, with the ongoing I-A/I-AA debate, the rampant booster-related NCAA violations and *NCAA v. Board of Regents*, all the upheaval of the early 1980s forced this pretty far down the NCAA's priority list, even as the basketball tournament continued to expand and thrive.

The financial issues of the late 1980s, however, would bring a new impetus.

1987–88: Back On (and Off) the Docket

"There will be a national playoff when university presidents discover the money the playoffs would produce is necessary to operate the athletic programs." Alabama's Bear Bryant would deliver a line like that many times in the late 1970s, and it seemed it would be proven true when the effects of *NCAA v. Board of Regents* temporarily limited television revenue and the costs associated with big-time football continued to increase. The 1986 season had also finished with an all-time classic—No. 2 Penn State upsetting No. 1 Miami in the Fiesta Bowl to win the national title—that raked in spectacular television ratings and reminded everyone of what a spectacle particularly big-time games can be. It seemed like the right time to pursue more of those matchups.

In May 1987, the CFA's Long Range Planning Committee presented a series of options to its members—a one-game, "Plus-One"-style playoff following the bowls (Corso's model), a four-team playoff, and an eight-team playoff—and in an August poll conducted by the NCAA, 55 percent of surveyed Division I-A coaches and athletic directors favored a playoff, while 64 percent favored putting it on the next NCAA Convention's agenda. Almost everyone surveyed agreed that the Plus-One format was the best and least bowl-disruptive on the table.

"The NCAA is talking about it now," Louisville head coach Howard Schnellenberger, a title-winning coach at Miami, told the *Louisville Courier-Journal* that summer. "Before, they used foul language to discuss it. The NCAA is generally on the side of the status quo, but I hope to see a playoff system before I die." (He would achieve this goal, but only because he lived into his late eighties.) Meanwhile, CBS commentator Ara Parseghian, a playoff skeptic at best when he was a coach, had flipped all the way to the other side. In the same *Courier-Journal* piece, he endorsed both small (Plus-One) and large (16-team) formats, and in response to bowl executives' seemingly unfounded—and spectacularly hard to believe—claims that a playoff would produce lower ratings and lower ad revenue, Parseghian said, "There's no damn reason why it can't command as much interest. There would be a big pie to cut up, huge money generated by it. It'd be a bonanza like professional football."

As baffling as the "No, playoffs would make *less* money than bowls" logic was, it helped to muddy the waters, as did the continued insistence from the Big Ten and Pac-10 that they were married to the Rose Bowl and would not take part in a playoff. With relevant parties forced to choose between the money in hand that bowls delivered and the unknowns of a playoff, sentiment once again shifted quickly. And at the 1988 NCAA Convention, a resolution to say no to a playoff garnered 88 percent of votes. "The bowls have done a good job of lobbying against it," Texas athletic director DeLoss Dodds said, ever so succinctly. They always did.

1993–94: The "We Need the Funds" 16-Teamer

In early June 1993, Rev. Edmund P. Joyce, the former executive vice president of Notre Dame and one of the founders of the CFA, couldn't take it anymore. He had to take a stand. On the final day of the annual CFA convention, he commanded the podium and took a stand against... militant ladies.

"Frankly, I have been dismayed at the publicity and apparent support the militant women have received by their irrational attack on football as their bugaboo," he said. "They seem to be saying that football is the villain, depriving them of support which they should have, and they will prosper only by football being brought to its knees. As far as I am concerned, this is an Alice in Wonderland scenario. Yet we men have been extraordinarily ineffective in checkmating the campaign of the militant ladies."

It was a trying time for college football, though then again, when isn't it? The NCAA had recently implemented further scholarship limits on FBS programs—they could now max out at only 85 scholarships at any given time—and as the NCAA was attempting to get a handle on gender equity issues, football officials feared there were further spending cuts in store for college athletics' biggest sport. Joyce's stance was, um, assertive enough that even Notre Dame football coach Lou Holtz—who, in his retirement years, would push even more extreme right-wing views on Fox News and Newsmax—wouldn't touch it. "He would have a better understanding of it than I would," Holtz simply said of Joyce. "I'm just a football coach."

In a time in which raising an extra $100 million or so sounded rather appealing, a lot of these officials were giving another thought to the idea of a college football playoff. In 1993, after years of expressing skepticism of a playoff, NCAA director Dick Schultz said "I think, as we look ahead at some challenging times, that we need to put this on our agenda." This was at least the sixth time the NCAA had studied the issue in the last 30 years or so. A settle-it-on-the-field playoff, something long favored by millions of fans and plenty of coaches, which could also serve as a desperately needed cash cow? The appeal was obvious, and the 1990 season had shined a bright light on the bowl system's flaws. With Virginia moving to No. 1 for the first time ever in October, the Sugar Bowl quickly worked to score an early commitment from the Cavaliers. But they collapsed down the stretch and finished the regular season unranked. Conference mate Georgia Tech, meanwhile, surged to No. 2 in the polls, but the Sugar Bowl stuck with Virginia. The Orange Bowl, already hosting top-ranked Big 8 champion Colorado, could have chosen Tech to give us an unexpected No. 1 vs. No. 2 battle, but instead it chose a brand name, No. 5 Notre Dame, as the Buffaloes' opponent. Tech had to settle for a Citrus Bowl battle against No. 18 Nebraska. The Yellow Jackets were impressive enough to snag a split of the national title, but the bowl system had provided only a hindrance to their efforts. And in 1991, unbeaten Washington's commitment to the Rose Bowl prevented a possible matchup against fellow unbeaten Miami. Yet another split title.

In 1992, the Bowl Coalition was created. It was a collaboration between the CFA's collection of power conferences, Notre Dame, and the major bowls not named the Rose Bowl, most of which had taken on corporate sponsorship to increase payouts. This system produced some pluses (No. 1 Alabama vs. No. 2 Miami in the Sugar Bowl in 1992) and some obvious minuses (unbeaten West Virginia getting left out of a No. 1 vs. No. 2 game in favor of one-loss Florida State in 1993, six-win Notre Dame getting into a major bowl in 1994). We also very nearly got another split title in 1994: Unbeaten Penn State, early in its Big Ten tenure and tied to the Rose Bowl, walloped No. 12 Oregon in Pasadena while No. 1 Nebraska used a fourth-quarter surge to get past No. 3 Miami in the Orange Bowl. Nebraska held onto leads in both major polls. No split for the Nittany Lions.

At absolute best, the Bowl Coalition was a minor improvement. It certainly didn't quiet playoff proponents, and it wasn't really drawing eyeballs either. Overall college football attendance dropped for the first time in 35 years in 1993, and cumulative TV ratings for January 1 bowls had plummeted. For six years in a row, the title game of the NCAA men's basketball tournament enjoyed better ratings than the highest-rated January 1 game.

Meanwhile, two decades after the passage of Title IX, the landmark legislation that prohibited sex-based discrimination, the NCAA began to get serious about gender equity at the athletic level. That this push came at a time of increasing budget concerns was certainly inconvenient, and it simultaneously put pressure on football to both a) make as much money as possible to account for increased spending on women's sports, and b) stop hogging the spotlight so much. This became a source of frustration—see: Rev. Joyce and those "militant ladies"—but it also flipped a few more people over to the side of a playoff. One of them was UCLA chancellor Charles Young, who, despite running a Pac-10 school, chaired yet another NCAA committee investigating the merits of a playoff and, more specifically, the money a playoff could produce.

The financial merit of not only a playoff, but a *big* playoff, was becoming pretty obvious, and the roster of proponents included an increasingly influential corporation: Nike came up with some pretty impressive numbers. In a presentation led by both the powerful shoe company and the Creative Artists Agency, the famed talent and sports agency, Young's committee was told that a Plus-One playoff would garner about $30 million, a post-bowl four-team playoff about $60 million, an eight-teamer about $100 million, and a 16-teamer about $200 million. (Bowls promised a total payout of around $70 million.) In January 1994, the NCAA authorized yet another committee, approximately the 4 millionth of the last 30 years, to study the issue. They consulted players like Florida State's Derrick Brooks, and a majority of them said that while extending the season was a bit concerning, they would love the chance to participate in a playoff and prove it on the field. (Brooks also evidently suggested maybe the players should get a cut of the resulting money. I'm going to go out on a limb and guess that probably didn't help the playoff's cause.)

In 2010's seminal *Death to the BCS*, authors Dan Wetzel, Josh Peter and Jeff Passan shared the story of Georgia athletic director Vince Dooley presenting the committee's findings to other SEC ADs in the hopes of garnering support for the idea, only to be coolly shot down by league commissioner Roy Kramer, who said simply, "I think we'll have another option." Sure enough, in June 1994 the latest NCAA playoff committee was quietly disbanded. And within a few weeks, details of a new "Bowl Alliance," championed by Kramer and designed to replace the Bowl Coalition, began to emerge.

The Bowl Alliance was basically the Bowl Coalition in a shinier package. Bowls could bid to host one of the higher-tier bowls, but the alliance still didn't feature the Big Ten and Pac-10 champions, and it of course didn't feature the Rose Bowl. And in 1997, it produced yet another split national title when unbeaten Michigan won the Rose Bowl and unbeaten Nebraska won the Orange Bowl. The bowls continued to convince decision-makers that they could solve all of college football's programs, and they continued doing no such thing.

1998: Hello, BCS

As three years of the Bowl Alliance produced just one No. 1 vs. No. 2 matchup—and perhaps more importantly, after two unbeaten Big Ten teams (1994 Penn State and 1997 Michigan) combined for basically 0.5 national titles thanks to Rose Bowl obligations—some stubborn parties finally came to the table. In the summer of 1997, even before Michigan's half-title campaign, the Big Ten, Pac-10, and Rose Bowl agreed to become part of the Bowl Alliance starting in 1998. And never missing a chance to rebrand, the alliance became the Bowl Championship Series.

As maligned as it would become, the BCS was an unquestionable step forward. We were, at the very least, guaranteed a No. 1 vs. No. 2 finale—hosted by a rotating cast of the Rose, Orange, Sugar, and Fiesta Bowls—to finish the season. Of course, cleanly choosing those teams proved extremely difficult some years, and the formula used to create the BCS rankings (a mix of polls and computer ratings that, at first, included a few other criteria like strength of schedule and a loss penalty) sometimes produced controversial results. Plus, the humans in charge of the formula changed it every time they disagreed with the results, which ruined the point of having an objective portion to the rankings. And in pure college football fashion, there was still enough wiggle room in the major bowl selection process that less historically mighty programs could still get screwed in favor of bigger brands: No. 7 Florida scored an Orange Bowl bid over No. 3 Kansas State (which dropped to the Alamo Bowl) in 1998, and No. 6 Texas went to the Rose Bowl over No. 5 California (Holiday Bowl–bound) in 2004. In 2008, meanwhile, unbeaten and well-proven Boise State was left out of a major bid in favor of a two-loss Ohio State.

Still, the BCS gave the sport one thing it had needed for decades, so it was technically an upgrade. But it still wasn't a playoff. And as the Internet, *College GameDay*, increased television exposure, and plenty of other factors further nationalized the sport, that became less and less acceptable. As Roy Kramer told ESPN's Chris Low in 2023, "I don't think it was so much that people hated the BCS. They just wanted a playoff."

There might have once been a charm to college football's regionality, but it was mostly gone by the late 1990s. "As a New Yorker who loved college football, I was a little bit of an outlier," The Athletic's Ralph Russo said. "I always looked at the sport as a national sport—even when it wasn't, in my mind it was. As a young college football fan in New York City, my most vivid memory was the 1984 Orange Bowl. But it was not just that game, it was that entire day." Nebraska had completely controlled the 1983 season and, with an Orange Bowl win, would have easily laid claim to the national title. But if the Huskers were upset, any number of teams were ready to jockey for position. The national title docket for January 2, 1984, began with unbeaten No. 2 Texas playing No. 7 Georgia in the Cotton Bowl, then No. 4 Illinois heavily favored over a six-win UCLA in the Rose Bowl. In the evening session, the Orange and Sugar Bowls kicked off simultaneously, with the No. 1 Huskers playing No. 5 Miami in Miami and No. 3 Auburn playing No. 8 Michigan in New Orleans.

Nothing went according to plan. Georgia knocked off Texas, 10–9, and UCLA destroyed Illinois by 36 points out west. As Miami was famously winning a classic Orange Bowl, Auburn was surviving Michigan, 9–7. At the end of the day, no one knew if Auburn or Miami—or maybe still Nebraska?—would be voted champion.

"Seeing that all play out almost felt like the NCAA Tournament," Russo said. "There's all these things going on, and they're kind of related to each other. But part of it just didn't make sense to me. As someone who didn't have any of the regional ties, it was like...why can't they just play? Why can't we get No. 1 and 2 here? This is a lot of fun, but...I don't understand. What do you mean, they have to go to the Rose Bowl, and they have to go to the Orange Bowl? There was a charm to that in some ways, and it did make a lot of games important in the postseason, but it also broke my brain. Like in 1994, why can't Nebraska and Penn State just play? What are we doing here?"

2008: Mike Slive's Plus-One

You knew things had grown dire for the BCS from a public relations standpoint when they decided it was a good idea to hire former George W. Bush press secretary Ari Fleischer as an adviser. He didn't waste time coming up with nonsense either. In 2009, he told Politico.com, "Playoff advocates have had an easy ride where they have never been called on to explain exactly how they would create an alternative." Now, the number of different playoff proposals through the years certainly varied. But it was hard to make that case with a straight face when, just the year before, one of the most powerful men in the sport proposed something with pretty easy and specific details.

In 2004, something happened that would be unthinkable today: an unbeaten SEC team was denied a title shot. When the 2004 season produced three unbeaten teams, the BCS could only pick two and went with USC (preseason No. 1) and Oklahoma (preseason No. 2) over Auburn (preseason No. 17). It was honestly justifiable—my historic SP+ ratings graded the Tigers third in the nation behind the Trojans and Sooners—but with three unbeaten teams, someone had to be snubbed. This lit a predictable fire under new SEC commissioner Mike Slive. "I never wanted to see a season again where an unbeaten SEC champion didn't even get a chance to play for a national title," he would later tell ESPN. "I already believed we needed a playoff in college football. I knew after 2004 that we absolutely were going to get there." After years of careful crafting, Slive proposed a simple four-team playoff that incorporated the bowls at first, then added a national title game to the end of the season. But Slive's fellow power-conference commissioners quickly shot his idea down. According to *Death to the BCS*, "The four big conferences that opposed the plan refused to even take it back to their respective presidents for discussion. Their stated fear: the plus-one might prove too popular and too profitable and ultimately expand into an eight-or sixteen-team playoff. 'We felt like there could be...more pressure to add more teams with an ability to get to the national championship game,' Big 12 commissioner Dan Beebe said."

Only college football could decide against something because it might be *too popular*. And not even president-elect Barack Obama could change hardened hearts and minds. In an interview on CBS's *60 Minutes*, Obama lobbied for an eight-team playoff, saying, "I don't know any serious fan of college football who has disagreed with me on this. So, I'm going to throw my weight around a little bit. I think it's the right thing to do." Sorry, sir, no can do. It might work too well.

2011: The Rematch That Broke Down the Last Defenses

"We have playoffs in every sport in the world, I think, except [FBS] college football," former Florida and South Carolina head coach Steve Spurrier was fond of saying. "How can we be right and everybody else be wrong?" Ironically, while power conference commissioners couldn't concern themselves when the SEC was snubbed, they finally ceded ground when the SEC got *both* spots in the BCS Championship.

The defenses against a playoff had already dissipated significantly by this point. The combination of a split title in 2003 and Auburn's snub in 2004 was a big blow, and the success of mid-majors in the 2000s—Utah (13–0 seasons in 2004 and 2008 with BCS bowl blowouts of Pitt and Nick Saban's Alabama); TCU (11 wins per year with three top-10 finishes, a Rose Bowl win and a 12–2 record against power conference teams from 2005 to 2010); and Boise State (four top-10 finishes, two Fiesta Bowl wins, and a 9–2 record against power conference teams from 2006 to 2012)—had furthered a sense that maybe more than two teams were deserving of a shot at the national title. It actually created a slight shift in the way the BCS worked: the powers-that-be added a BCS Championship to the end of the schedule in 2006, opening up two more spots in major bowls and guaranteeing one bid to a team from outside of the power conferences. Once given the opportunity in 2006, Boise State immediately pulled a 43–42 upset of Oklahoma in the Fiesta Bowl in one of the most beloved games in the sport's history.

The money, of course, was still hilariously skewed toward the power conferences, and there were still only two teams getting a shot at the national title, but the little guy was thrown a bone for just about the first time in the sport's history. Plus, the release and popularity of *Death to the BCS* shined a bright light on just how much power the major bowls and major conference commissioners held, how much their decision-making seemed tuned toward maintaining the status quo, and how heavily the money was weighted toward the powers. The anti-playoff foundation was growing awfully rickety. And with one more controversial ranking, the house came falling to the ground.

First things first: Alabama and LSU were the nation's two best teams in 2011. My SP+ ratings had the Crimson Tide and Tigers within a point of each other at the top, with 11–1 Oklahoma State about 5.5 points back. If we had a playoff structure in place, be it a four-teamer or a 16-teamer, odds are solid that we would have ended up with an LSU-'Bama title game. But we didn't have a playoff in 2011, and when Oklahoma State suffered an epic, overtime upset loss at Iowa State late in the season—the Cowboys missed a late, game-winning field goal by what had to be millimeters (if they missed it at all)—it set up an awkward scenario. LSU, with a 13–0 record and a classic 9–6 overtime win over Alabama in early November, was in for sure. But pollsters bumped Alabama ahead of OSU, and even with a disadvantage via the computer ratings of choice, the Crimson Tide got the bid, then dominated LSU in the BCS Championship, 21–0, in a game with the worst title-game TV ratings in five years.

A few months later, the NCAA's presidential oversight committee approved of a four-team College Football Playoff to start in 2014. The hiring of BCS executive director Bill Hancock to hold the same title for the CFP was awfully cynical—Hancock, a genuinely charming man and mostly positive presence, was still quoted in *Death to the BCS* saying things like, "How would band members, cheerleaders, and other students make holiday plans knowing their team might play one, two, or three games on campus during the time they are normally home with their families?" for why a playoff wouldn't work and echoing Fleischer's lame "playoff proponents don't know what they want" line, and now he got to lead the new venture. Still, it was *something*.

Because so many people had grown frustrated with the BCS formula, the CFP's participants would be determined by a committee that proudly rejected computer ratings. (As a formula advocate, I must again note that Alabama got the 2011 bid because of the pollsters, not the computers.) The committee would earn the respect of the college football public with pure *gravitas*. The first CFP committee included former U.S. Secretary of State Condoleezza Rice, all-time great coaches like Nebraska's Tom Osborne and Wisconsin's Barry Alvarez, and nationally respected figures like West Virginia athletic director Oliver Luck and USC athletic director Pat Haden. They would release weekly rankings over the latter half of the season, and no one could *possibly* dispute their opinions, right?

For most of the first 10 years of the CFP era, the committee's decisions were pretty easy. Releasing weekly rankings certainly exposed the committee to (justifiable) claims of inconsistency, but the final results were typically about right. When presented with a tricky choice, however, gravitas didn't produce unassailable logic. In 2014, the CFP's very first year, TCU entered the final week of the regular season ranked third. The 10–1 Horned Frogs beat Iowa State 55–3 in their final game...and fell to sixth, out of a playoff spot. Ohio State (which smoked Wisconsin in the Big Ten Championship), Florida State (which barely beat Georgia Tech in the ACC Championship), and Baylor (which had beaten TCU and therefore claimed the Big 12 title with a win over Kansas State) all jumped TCU.

In 2017, the AAC's University of Central Florida (UCF) romped to a 12–0 record, outscoring opponents by an average of 24 points and beating a pair of ranked opponents late in the season, but the Knights finished only 12th in the final CFP rankings because the committee consistently ain't-played-nobody'd their way into disrespecting mid-majors. They beat Auburn—which had beaten both Alabama and Georgia, the eventual championship game participants—in the Peach Bowl, then went 12–0 *again* the next year and still only peaked at No. 7. Cincinnati pulled the "multiple unbeaten regular seasons" trick in 2020 and 2021, too, and only sneaked into the 2021 CFP because of a particularly weak set of fellow contenders. (The Bearcats trailed Alabama by only 11 in the fourth quarter in the semifinals before losing 27–6 in a result a lot of people used to suggest that mid-majors were indeed unworthy of a title shot. Of course, in the other semifinal, Michigan got annihilated by Georgia from the opening kickoff, and few used that to question the Big Ten's bona fides.)

As mentioned in the last chapter, the worst came in 2023. Long professing that they chose the "best" teams, not the "most deserving"—which completely ruins the point of the exercise, if we're being honest; virtually every other playoff system in the world picks deserving teams—the committee chose 12–1 Alabama, Nick Saban's worst team in 15 years, for the fourth spot in the CFP instead of an unbeaten Florida State team that had just won the ACC despite losing starting quarterback Jordan Travis to injury a few weeks earlier. If there was one thing a four-team playoff was supposed to all but assure, it was that an unbeaten power-conference team would get a shot at the national title. It failed.

2022: Welcome, Bracket Creep

From a purely logistical standpoint, there wasn't much of a difference between the CFP and the system that existed before it. We played the bowls, then had a national title game, just as we did during the end-stage BCS days. The only difference was that two teams would end up playing in a pair of postseason games.

In terms of the way we talk about the sport, however, the playoff seemed to change *everything*. Every outlet, including ESPN (which owned the CFP's TV rights), made the playoff the primary focus of its coverage throughout the season. The CFP offered both a couple of extra shots at the title and a larger sense of disappointment for teams that didn't make it. By the late 2010s, it became common for star players to opt out of what many felt were meaningless bowl games so they could begin preparing for the pros. And it would even eventually happen to New Year's Six bowls, the games that were in the CFP's semifinal rotation—Rose Bowl, Sugar Bowl, Orange Bowl, Fiesta Bowl, Peach Bowl, and Cotton

Bowl—but didn't get to host a playoff game in a given season. This created a sort of "Bowls are dead!!" narrative, even though TV ratings for bowls remained solid.

We also saw teams using early CFP bids to create recruiting advantages and go on dynastic title runs: in 2015, Dabo Swinney's Clemson won just its second ACC title in 24 years, while Oklahoma won its first outright Big 12 title in five years. Both teams would repeat as champions for each of the next five years. Ohio State won its first Big Ten title in five years in 2014, barely missed out in 2015 and 2016 and then won four straight. In the 10 years of the four-team CFP era, six schools—Alabama (eight), Clemson (six), Ohio State (five), Oklahoma (four), Michigan (three), and Georgia (three)—had commandeered 29 of 40 bids, leaving only 11 for FBS's other 120-something schools.

The CFP was a cash cow (for power conferences, anyway), and TV ratings were fine despite the games being played on cable, but there was just enough of a sense of staleness and exclusion that, by 2018, even powerful figures like Big Ten commissioner Jim Delany were expressing openness to the idea of playoff expansion. And in pure college sports fashion, the CFP announced that it was forming a committee. A four-man working group of commissioners Bob Bowlsby (Big 12), Greg Sankey (SEC), and Craig Thompson (Mountain West), and Notre Dame athletic director Jack Swarbrick began meeting to discuss expansion options.

"We met at the very clandestine DFW Grand Hyatt all those times—Jack, Greg, Bob, and I—and we started asking, why should we even be expanding?" Thompson said. "We spent several meetings just saying, why are we at four? Why do we need more? Then we explored literally every number beyond: five, then six, then seven, eight, nine." In June 2021, they arrived at a surprising number. While most in the media had advocated for expansion to eight or 16 teams, they came up with 12, with automatic bids for the top six conference champions, byes for the top four conference champions and first-round home games for the Nos. 5–8 seeds. Quarterfinals and semifinals would take place at the same six bowls already in the CFP rotation.

"The number 12 at the end fell out because it rewarded the top four by not having to play," Thompson said, "and it rewarded the next four by getting them a home game. And then it got to those five autonomous champions"—while most of us use the *power conference* nomenclature, more official administrators have long gone with *autonomy five*—"and it got the Group of Five." This was indeed an intriguing proposal. Offering byes and first-round home games were nice ways of keeping incentives high and assuring that highly ranked teams couldn't sit players and cruise through the end of the regular season. Meanwhile, offering byes to only conference champions was both a fun method for assuring maximum intrigue during Championship Week and quite the benevolent touch from Sankey, whose SEC could have easily gotten multiple top-four seeds in a different system.

The proposal seemed well-received by most, and with no resistance it could have been in place by the 2023 season. But within a few weeks of the proposal, Sankey's SEC shocked everyone by announcing it was adding Oklahoma and Texas from Bowlsby's Big 12. Distrust soared, and three other power conferences (the Big Ten, ACC, and Pac-12) announced they were forming "The Alliance." The goal was...well...I've never really been sure. They briefly blocked playoff expansion (while insisting that they weren't a voting bloc), as if Sankey had secretly planted some SEC-friendly verbiage in invisible ink that would appear once everyone had signed on. They talked about a nonconference scheduling arrangement, but it didn't go anywhere. They talked of wanting to "stabilize a volatile environment," but then the Big Ten mortally wounded the Pac-12 by pilfering USC and UCLA less than a year into The Alliance's (non)existence.

Commissioners against expansion gave vague comments about how it wasn't the right time and how they hadn't had enough discussion and whatnot, but it sure seemed like it was mostly a pushback against Sankey. Regardless, it all proved to simply be a delay. By September 2022, the Big Ten's own realignment moves had destroyed The Alliance, and the CFP's board of managers voted to expand to 12 teams for the final two years of the original 12-season CFP contract (2024 and 2025). It was too late to help 2023 Florida State, but after more than six decades of argument and histrionics, we would finally have a genuine postseason tournament. And sure enough, the 2024 season was a blast. Even as we handed out more mulligans—the first 12-team playoff featured only one unbeaten team, three with one loss, seven with two losses, and one with three—the week-to-week maneuvering was still intriguing, as preseason No. 1 Georgia was up and down all season, Alabama struggled with inconsistency in the first year after Nick Saban's retirement, and both Texas and Oregon spent weeks at No. 1. Plus, early-season upsets like Northern Illinois's toppling of eventual finalist Notre Dame, combined with some wide-open conference title races, gave the season a little bit of a "Has parity reached college football??" buzz.

The journey wasn't perfect: for one thing, we had to get used to an entirely different level of minutiae in conference tiebreakers, as enormous and divisionless conferences don't give you as many head-to-head connections among its members. At one point in early November, it looked like three different Big Ten teams—Oregon, Penn State, and out-of-nowhere upstart Indiana—might get to the finish line at 12–0, which would have been awkward since only two could have made the Big Ten Championship. Plus, it wasn't immediately clear that making the Big Ten Championship would have even been beneficial, as the new playoff seemed to diminish the importance of conference championships in some cases. Both the SEC Championship (Georgia over Texas) and Big Ten Championship (Oregon over Penn State) pitted teams that would each easily reach the CFP field, and in Georgia's victory the Bulldogs lost starting quarterback Carson Beck to injury. They would start backup Gunner Stockton in a quarterfinal loss to Notre Dame. Meanwhile, though the ACC Championship did give us a bid thief (Clemson), a loss in Charlotte barely impacted SMU's CFP status; the Mustangs fell from eighth before the ACCCG to 10th after and still easily reached the field of 12. There were still stakes here, but the decreased impact led to immediate speculation about the future of these games.

Beyond that, the seeding system confused a lot of casual viewers. MWC champion Boise State ranked ninth in the final CFP rankings, while surprising Big 12 champion Arizona State ranked 12th, but they got the No. 3 and No. 4 seeds, respectively, because of the byes for conference champions. It wasn't that different from the NFL system, which hands the top four seeds to division champions—the Los Angeles Rams went 10–7 in 2024 but won the NFC

West and therefore hosted 14–3 Minnesota, the NFC North runner-up, in the wild-card round—but having both a ranking and a seed next to teams' names didn't quite look right. And when the first round produced a series of blowouts and the four conference champions that received byes all lost in the quarterfinals, there was a round of hand-wringing regarding whether the incentive structure worked as envisioned. Still, the system worked pretty well. Michigan's late-season upset of Ohio State knocked the Buckeyes out of the Big Ten race (therefore creating a tougher playoff road for them to follow) and created exactly the existential crisis a fourth straight loss to Michigan is *supposed* to create for Ohio State. That angst just didn't last as long: even with a harder road, the Buckeyes beat Tennessee, Oregon, and Texas by a combined 111–52 to reach the first 12-team final, then fended off Notre Dame with mid-game brilliance to claim their ninth national title.

And then, of course, it was time to expand again. In the spring of 2024, relevant parties had begun to discuss what the playoff would look like starting in 2026, when the initial 12-year contract would expire. A move to either 14 or 16 teams seemed virtually guaranteed, and the Big Ten and SEC pushed for a system of automatic bids, in which both leagues would be guaranteed up to four spots each and the ACC and Big 12 might get multiple bids as well. This is a mockable abuse of power, a way of reminding everyone who's in charge now and making a playoff look more like an invitational. Regardless, since this is college football, the sport that needed 50 years of debate to create a playoff of any kind, nothing is allowed to happen in a timely fashion. Those discussions—along with a debate regarding the seeding process for the 2025 playoff—were still somehow ongoing when this book went to print.

6.

Slippery Slopes and Roster Management

> The NCAA's business model would be flatly illegal in almost any other industry in America. All of the restaurants in a region cannot come together to cut cooks' wages on the theory that "customers prefer" to eat food from low-paid cooks. Law firms cannot conspire to cabin lawyers' salaries in the name of providing legal services out of a "love of the law." Hospitals cannot agree to cap nurses' income in order to create a "purer" form of helping the sick. News organizations cannot join forces to curtail pay to reporters to preserve a "tradition" of public-minded journalism. Movie studios cannot collude to slash benefits to camera crews to kindle a "spirit of amateurism" in Hollywood. Price-fixing labor is price-fixing labor.

Credit where credit is due: while his current job pays better and offers both better perks and spectacular job security, Supreme Court Justice Brett Kavanaugh would have made one hell of a college football blogger. Plenty of us took punches at the NCAA's anti-player-compensation stance through the years, but Kavanaugh's 1,300-word screed at the end of the Supreme Court's 2021 *NCAA v. Alston* decision pretty much topped them all.

Alston was successfully argued by a team led by famed antitrust lawyer Jeffrey Kessler, who had also successfully represented the players associations in both the NFL and NBA and was one of the lawyers most responsible for the establishment of NFL free agency. It severely wounded any hope the NCAA still had about continuing to severely limit the earning potential of its student-athletes. It built on the slow progress created by other court decisions like *O'Bannon v. NCAA* (which allowed athletes to receive limited compensation for their name, image, and likeness) and basically opened the door wide for future lawsuits. *Alston* itself only dealt with payments related to education—computers and other equipment, post-eligibility opportunities—but Kavanaugh rang alarm bells regarding the system as a whole. "The rest of the NCAA's compensation rules are not at issue here and therefore remain on the books," he wrote. "Those remaining compensation rules generally restrict student athletes from receiving compensation or benefits from their colleges for playing sports.... The NCAA's remaining compensation rules also raise serious questions under the antitrust laws." Translation: *File more suits, current and former athletes. You'll probably win.*

This was a 9–0 decision from the Court—those are more common than you might think in this generally divided time, but they still aren't *common* common—and Kavanaugh's quasi-blog post wasn't the majority opinion; that went to Neil Gorsuch. Kavanaugh just really felt like writing about this and tacked on a concurring opinion. He hit all the major notes, like the "lavish new facilities" going up everywhere and athletic directors, coaches, and conference commissioners making millions of dollars while "the student athletes who generate the revenues, many of whom are African American and from lower-income backgrounds, end up with little or nothing." He noted the tough questions that would await a future in which athletes got a cut of the money: What would happen to non-revenue sports? Could you pay some athletes and not others? What would comply with Title IX? Would we need salary caps to assure competitive balance? But just because something produces hard questions doesn't make it the wrong answer. "To be sure," he wrote, "the NCAA and its member colleges maintain important traditions that have become part of the fabric of America—game days in Tuscaloosa and South Bend; the packed gyms in Storrs and Durham; the women's and men's lacrosse championships on Memorial Day weekend; track and field meets in Eugene; the spring softball and baseball World Series in Oklahoma City and Omaha; the list goes on. But those traditions alone cannot justify the NCAA's decision to build a massive money-raising enterprise on the backs of student athletes who are not fairly compensated."

The conclusion: "Under ordinary principles of antitrust law, it is not evident why college sports should be any different. The NCAA is not above the law." By this point, "law" had already become a pretty strong opponent for the NCAA. It had already been about seven years since *O'Bannon* had cracked open the door for future NIL rights and five years since the Supreme Court had struck down the NCAA's *O'Bannon* appeal. It had been a couple of years since the State of California had passed a law prohibiting punishment of athletes for profiting from their name, image, and likeness. It had also already been a couple of years since NCAA head Mark Emmert began making his countless trips to Washington, D.C., in the hopes of corralling congressional support for a national NIL bill that would trump those of the many other states that had followed California's lead.

Following the passage of California's Fair Pay to Play Act, the NCAA's Board of Governors put out an overwrought statement complaining about creating unfair advantages and how allowing athletes to profit off of their NIL would *actually* be unfair to the *athletes*. "If the bill becomes law and California's 58 NCAA schools are compelled to allow an unrestricted name, image, and likeness scheme," the statement said, "it would erase the critical distinction between college and professional athletics and, because it gives those schools an unfair recruiting advantage, would result in them eventually being unable to compete in NCAA competitions.... It isn't possible to resolve the challenges of today's college sports environment in this way—by one state taking unilateral action." The use of *scheme* was catty, and the only reason a state was taking "unilateral action" was because the NCAA, in five years since *O'Bannon*, had taken no progressive action of any kind. When California passed its law in 2019, it came with an effective date of 2023. That theoretically offered plenty of time for the NCAA to establish a dialogue with the state and come up with a compromise. It did no such thing. As with *NCAA v. Board of Regents* 35 years earlier, the NCAA preferred to lose outright than compromise. And lose, it did. Instead of accepting where the winds were blowing, the NCAA fought NIL and player compensation to the bitter end, assuring that when the inevitable happened and the NIL door opened wide, it had almost no control over what followed. And the 2020s have been far more turbulent than they needed to be because of it.

It's impossible to tell the entire story of player rights and compensation in college football a) with anything less than a full-length book, and b) as a completed story with a beginning, middle, and end. The ending hasn't come yet, and the facts are still changing by the week and month. So let's keep things on a pretty macro level. In regard to the player compensation fight, here are seven things I either know or strongly believe about how we got to this point and where we're going:

1. We've Been Arguing about This for a Very Long Time

> One athlete out of every seven engaged in intercollegiate competition is "subsidized" to a point bordering upon professionalism, says a report on "American College Athletics," made public yesterday by the Carnegie Foundation for the Advancement of Teaching after a survey which has consumed more than three and a half years and entailed visits to 130 colleges and secondary schools. The granting of bounties to athletes for no other consideration than athletic ability whether it be in the form of "athletic scholarships," "slush funds," supplied by loyal alumni and local tradesmen, or in the shape of sinecure campus jobs, constitutes "the darkest blot upon American college sport," the report asserts.

That's a quote from the front page of the *New York Times* on October 24, 1929. (If that date looks familiar, that was the day of the Black Thursday stock market crash.)

In the 1920s, when many colleges throughout the nation began to realize that winning at college football was fun and colleges themselves became a bit more working-class, the idea of attracting great athletes via an inducement of one sort or another grew in appeal. As former Notre Dame lineman Michael Oriard put it in 2009's *Bowled Over: Big-Time College Football from the Sixties to the BCS Era*, in the 1920s and '30s, "Football players tended to be those brawny sons of steel-workers and coal miners, many of them recent immigrants to the United States, who were lured to campus by jobs (real or phony) or cash from boosters, as well as by the chance for an education and entry into the great American middle class." He told the story of well-subsidized Pitt players demanding cash payments before agreeing to play in the 1937 Rose Bowl (and Stanford players doing something similar before the 1940 Rose Bowl), Auburn players quitting when their demands for higher pay were refused in 1938, and an LSU player getting cut for trying to organize a union.

With an appalled tone, the Carnegie Report shined a light on "subsidization," exposing and harshly judging "the paid coach, the gate receipts, the special training tables, the costly sweaters and extensive journeys in special Pullman cars, the recruiting from the high school, the demoralizing publicity showered on the players, the devotion of an undue proportion of time to training, the devices for putting a desirable athlete, but a weak scholar, across the hurdles of the examinations." A lot of coaches and higher-ups agreed that the system had been corrupted. But they also took part in said corruption because beating their rivals was both enjoyable and vital to their further employment.

Throughout the first half of the twentieth century, schools consistently found ways to give students more than either the spirit or letters of the rules allowed. And schools were in constant conflict about what *should* be allowed—the Ivy League, the Big Ten, the ascendant and obsessed SEC, and rising programs like Oklahoma and USC all differed in their thoughts on the matter. The NCAA had failed in its pursuit of the "Sanity Code," which was intended to ban off-campus recruiting and all inducements, in the late 1940s, but when Walter Byers both took over the NCAA and discovered that he now had enforcement/intimidation power thanks to the NCAA's TV contract, he and his organization went to work. They created the grant-in-aid, a package to be offered to athletes that included tuition, room, board, and "laundry money." They also, of course, created a term that they would use to rationalize a countless number of rules and punishments in the decades that followed: *student-athlete*.

The term came about when Fort Lewis A&M's Ray Dennison died from an on-field injury and his widow sued for workmen's compensation benefits. In the indelible "The Shame of College Sports," published in the

October 2011 issue of the *Atlantic*, author Taylor Branch wrote, "The Colorado Supreme Court ultimately agreed with the school's contention that he was not eligible for benefits, since the college was 'not in the football business.' The term student-athlete was deliberately ambiguous. College players were not students at play (which might understate their athletic obligations), nor were they just athletes in college (which might imply they were professionals). That they were high-performance athletes meant they could be forgiven for not meeting the academic standards of their peers; that they were students meant they did not have to be compensated, ever, for anything more than the cost of their studies."

"Having subscribed to the fiction," Oriard wrote in *Bowled Over*, "universities then had to live by it. In practical terms, this meant that a football player in the late 1950s and early '60s could quit the team without forfeiting his scholarship, which was not tied in any way to athletic performance or even to participation." Of course, the NCAA would rectify that soon enough, instituting one-year, renewable scholarships in the early 1970s that, according to Oriard, "transformed student-athletes into athlete-students without anyone paying much attention."

2. The NCAA Clung to Amateurism Even When the Olympics and Walter Byers Abandoned It

> Is it wrong for the donor to give the boy the money? No, I'm feeling that it's only the colleges with the rules that say it's wrong. The coaches don't think it's so wrong anymore. The public doesn't think it's so wrong....
>
> I've watched as the Olympics have gradually loosened the rules, and I've heard as the youngsters tell about their income to millions of TV homes. Well, I think there's growing acceptance that they ought to receive those benefits. I didn't sense any shock among the American public or the media about those disclosures.

What anti-establishment firebrand was saying these outlandish things in the mid-1980s, at the height of the NCAA's enforcement era? Walter Byers! The NCAA executive director delivered these quotes in a *Sports Illustrated* interview in 1984, then said similar things to an internal NCAA audience in the years that followed. By this point, even the International Olympic Committee had begun to adjust its views of amateurism and reality. The Soviet Union and other communist nations had long given major support to their Olympic athletes, including stipends and government support (and "jobs" in other sectors that conveniently allowed them to train as much as they possibly needed to), but athletes in the U.S. and elsewhere still had to adhere to strict amateurism rules, which made it difficult for athletes from poorer backgrounds to compete. As television enhanced both the Olympics' popularity and their lucrativeness, the IOC began allowing Olympic athletes to receive compensation from their national Olympic committees for hardship and wages lost during competition. Then, in the mid-1980s, it began to allow outright professionals to compete on a sport-by-sport basis.

As it turned out, viewers didn't mind this shift at all. They wanted to see the best athletes in the world and didn't seem to care much about the spirit of amateurism. But how did others within the NCAA respond to Byers' late-career shift in tone? By basically patting him on the head, saying, "Okay, Grandpa," and sending him out to pasture. "They looked at me as though I had desecrated my sacred vows," he would later say. Byers announced he was stepping down in 1987 at age 65, leaving behind an organization that was growing only fuller with true believers. Byers had created a monster, and he knew it. As Branch wrote in "The Shame of College Sports," after his retirement, "Byers let slip his suppressed fury that the ingrate football conferences, having robbed the NCAA of television revenue, still expected it to enforce amateurism rules and police every leak of funds to college players. A lethal greed was 'gnawing at the innards of college athletics,' he wrote in his memoir." And what a memoir it was. In it, he wrote of a "neo-plantation mentality that exists on the campuses of our country and in the conference offices and in the NCAA that the rewards belong to the overseers and the supervisors. What trickles down after that can go to the athletes."

Even well into the 2000s, the NCAA continued to resist any push for further athlete compensation. As NCAA president from 2003 to 2009, Myles Brand, the first academic to lead the organization, coined an update of sorts for "student-athlete," called the "collegiate model."

According to Joe Nocera in *Indentured: The Inside Story of the Rebellion Against the NCAA*, it was Brand's masterstroke. It emphasized the educational value of athletics, and it "also not only condoned commercialization—it insisted upon it. After all, commercialism had been part of college sports practically since its beginnings. And so it had to remain if college sports was to continue to be financially healthy."

Attend a single NCAA Convention, as I did for the first time in 2025 in the obscene labyrinth known as Nashville's Gaylord Opryland, and you immediately understand why something like the collegiate model might be so seductive. You walk halls lined with pictures of Division II cross-country champions and Division III wrestlers, you see logos for small schools you've never heard of (as with AFCA), and you get constant reminders both that FBS football is merely one of nearly 100 championship sports and that Division I is but one of three divisions. That line that we heard on NCAA commercials for years—that most college athletes "will be going pro in something other than sports"—is indeed true. Nearly every media member there had come to ask about the SEC's latest power grab, or changes to the College Football Playoff and maybe the men's basketball tournament, but everyone at the conference wanted to talk about literally anything *but* that. There were interesting panels on gambling and increasing women's opportunities, and the largest celebration at the conference might have come when the Division I council elected to add women's wrestling to the list of championship sports. In the NCAA's happy place, Division III rowing would matter as much as FBS football. It's honestly admirable. And completely unrealistic.

The collegiate model was indeed seductive, and Brand leaned on it often. "We want to maximize the number of student-athletes competing at a competitive level," he said in his 2006 "State of the Association" speech at the NCAA Convention, "and we do this because athletics participation enhances the educational experience, and enhancing the educational experience of students is the goal of higher education. That is the Collegiate Model of Sports." That sounds great and worthy, but why did this have to include a strict insistence on non-compensation in sports in which money overflowed? Because it just did. From the 2005 convention: "Amateurism is not about how much; it is about why. It is not about the money; it is about the motivation." It would be an *insult* to student-athletes to pay them. It would sully and exploit them.

As Big Ten commissioner for nearly 30 years, Jim Delany did as much as any single person to nuclearize the financial arms race in big-time college football, kickstarting two different rounds of conference realignment and starting the Big Ten Network. That made what he wrote in March 2013, in a comment supporting the NCAA during the *O'Bannon* case, even more breathtaking (and appalling). If the NCAA changed its rules to allow any sort of revenue sharing or "pay for play"—which, by the way, wasn't even the point of *O'Bannon*—he said, "it has been my longstanding belief that The Big Ten's schools would forgo the revenues in those circumstances and instead take steps to downsize the scope, breadth, and activity of their athletic programs. Several alternatives to a 'pay for play' model exist, such as the Division III model, which does not offer any athletics-based grants-in-aid, and, among others, a need-based financial aid model. These alternatives would, in my view, be more consistent with The Big Ten's philosophy that the educational and lifetime economic benefits associated with a university education are the appropriate quid pro quo for its student-athletes." Imagine him telling Urban Meyer, as Meyer was building the Ohio State team that would win the 2014 national title, "Sorry, but if we have to share money with the athletes, we're just going to stop competing at the highest level." And imagine him doing this while pursuing Maryland and Rutgers for pure television revenue purposes.

(Not to be left out of the silliness, Notre Dame president John Jenkins told the *New York Times* in 2014 that, if lawsuits advocating for greater benefits beyond simple scholarships were to succeed, "That's when we leave. We will not tolerate that. Then it really does become a semipro team." Notre Dame rather conspicuously hasn't left a damn thing.)

3. The Courts Turned against the NCAA

Despite the devastating loss in *NCAA v. Board of Regents*, the NCAA's win percentage in court was still pretty good heading toward the 21st century. And even while handing the NCAA a huge loss in *Board of Regents*, a throwaway line in the majority opinion kept NCAA lawyers paid well for years.

Comments made by a judge in an opinion, which are meant as observations and not legal declarations, are known as *dicta*. In discussing what separates college football from professional sports in the *Board of Regents* decision, Justice John Paul Stevens wrote:

> The NCAA seeks to market a particular brand of football—college football. The identification of this "product" with an academic tradition differentiates college football from and makes it more popular than professional sports to which it might otherwise be comparable, such as, for example, minor league baseball. *In order to preserve the character and quality of the "product," athletes must not be paid, must be required to attend class, and the like* [emphasis mine].... The NCAA plays a vital role in enabling college football to preserve its character, and as a result enables a product to be marketed which might otherwise be unavailable.

Justice Stevens was pretty clearly intending to describe what the NCAA saw as the key tenets of this "product." But for years, the NCAA leaned on this quote as if Stevens were declaring that athletes must not be paid and that amateurism rules were valid. In 2021, Justice Kavanaugh officially declared an end to this. "The Court makes clear that the decades-old 'stray comments' about college sports and amateurism made in *NCAA v. Board of Regents* were dicta and have no bearing on whether the NCAA's current compensation rules are lawful," he wrote. Of course, by the time Kavanaugh wrote that, the NCAA was already on quite the losing streak. In 1998's *Law v. NCAA*, the U.S. Court of Appeals for the Tenth Circuit shot down what amounted to a coach salary cap the NCAA attempted to install on antitrust grounds. Meanwhile, *White v. NCAA*, a class-action suit, challenged the NCAA's limitations on the amount of aid a student-athlete could receive, again on antitrust grounds; it worried the organization enough that it did something new in 2008: settle.

Settling didn't stop the coming onslaught. (Strangely, it also didn't make the NCAA more likely to settle in the future.) In 2009, after noticing that EA Sports' *NCAA Basketball 09* was using a player with his exact likeness—with the name of "PF #31"—for a historic 1995 UCLA team, former Bruins All-America power forward Ed O'Bannon, a key cog on that '95 title winner who was still in no way being compensated for use of that likeness, became the face of a game-changing case. His lawyers filed a class-action antitrust suit to challenge the fact that the NCAA could make money off of athletes' names, images, and likenesses and they couldn't, even after they ran out of eligibility. Both Electronic Arts and the Collegiate Licensing Company were co-defendants, but they settled out of court for $40 million. The NCAA insisted on going to trial, and in August 2014 District Judge Claudia Wilken ruled in favor of O'Bannon and company. She didn't immediately declare all NIL rules invalid, but she did dictate that schools should be allowed to cover full cost-of-attendance scholarships to athletes (incredibly, the original grants-in-aid did not do that) and declared that the NCAA had to pay more than $40 million in damages. The NCAA appealed on the grounds that Wilken was not paying proper deference to Justice Stevens' dicta in *Board of Regents*; the appeal was denied, though the appeals panel did strike down an order from Wilken to place $5,000 per year into a trust fund for athletes.

O'Bannon v. NCAA opened the floodgates in terms of class-action suits. A number of those cases were combined into one super-case, *NCAA v. Alston*, that would peel away more layers of the NIL onion. It made its way back to Judge Wilken, who by now had become quite the subject matter expert. She ruled in March 2019 that the NCAA was violating antitrust laws with its restrictions on "non-cash, education-related benefits" like "computers, science equipment, musical instruments, and other tangible items not included in the cost of attendance calculation but nonetheless related to the pursuit of academic studies." She wrote that the NCAA could no longer bar things like tutoring or post-eligibility scholarships and internships. (Why were they doing that in the first place?) The NCAA, of course, appealed this ruling as well, and after the Ninth Circuit upheld Wilken's decision, at one point calling the NCAA "a cartel of buyers acting in concert to artificially depress the price that sellers could otherwise receive for their services," the appeal made its way to the Supreme Court for the 9–0 dunking in 2021. And *that* paved the way for the big one: *House v. NCAA*.

Originally filed in 2020, this class-action suit, led by Kessler and class-action specialist Steve Berman and represented by former Arizona

State swimmer Grant House and TCU/Oregon basketball player Sedona Prince, sought both NIL damages and the white whale of the entire exercise: revenue sharing. In November 2023, Judge Wilken granted certification for damages, and even the NCAA realized it had to settle posthaste. Within months, it agreed to the framework of a settlement of more than $2.8 billion to former Division I athletes and the creation of a model for sharing revenue with athletes moving forward.

From the original filing of *White v. NCAA* in 2006, it took nearly 20 years of legal maneuvering to tear down the NCAA's amateurism apparatus. But down it came.

4. We Never Got the Original Vision of NIL (Or Did We?)

From the moment the NCAA felt the need to settle in *White v. NCAA*, it should have been obvious where things were headed. But instead, we got a series of drawn-out court cases; we also got a series of ridiculous judgments that kept swaying public opinion against the NCAA. Two examples: when a song by Minnesota wrestler Joel Bauman got tens of thousands of hits on YouTube and, more importantly, drew sales on iTunes, the NCAA declared him ineligible in 2013, and when UCF kicker Donald De La Haye refused to de-monetize his popular YouTube channel, UCF was forced to declare him ineligible in 2017. For those of us who were writing about all this a decade ago or more, this was what so much of the NIL fight was about: literally profiting off of your name, image, and likeness—giving lessons, selling autographs at the mall, appearing in local commercials, having your jersey sold in the school bookstore, things like that. But the NCAA was so busy fighting the small stuff that it lost control of the big stuff.

After the *Alston* judgment, the idea of NIL shifted away from local boosters hiring athletes to appear in commercials—though that does also happen, and it's delightful—and toward boosters pooling money together in what became known as NIL "collectives." Florida's "Gator Collective" was up and running by August 2021, mere weeks after *Alston*. Hundreds of other collectives followed suit. Some attempted to secure nonprofit status. It got weird for a while, and it was never what was originally envisioned.

Through collectives, NIL benefits basically became salaries in another name, something schools would offer recruits and potential transfers whether they were supposed to or not. The NCAA still made threats and tried to establish what it relentlessly called "guardrails," allowing athletes to hire agents and profit from the system but still hoping to prevent money from becoming the recruiting inducement it had obviously become. Florida State was fined nearly $2 million, and offensive coordinator Alex Atkins was suspended after allegedly driving a recruit to a meeting in which the Rising Spear collective offered money to attend FSU. And when Tennessee's Spyre Sports collective openly bragged about its efforts in the expensive recruitment of blue-chip quarterback Nico Iamaleava, the NCAA attempted to lay the hammer down. Once again, courts got in the way. The attorneys general of both Tennessee and Virginia filed suit against the NCAA, alleging once again that it was inhibiting athletes' ability to profit off of their names, images, and likenesses. In February 2024 a federal judge granted a preliminary injunction, and the NCAA had no choice but to back down on virtually all NIL investigations for the time being. (The parties reached a settlement in early 2025.)

When Michigan secured a commitment from five-star quarterback Bryce Underwood late in the 2024–25 recruiting cycle, flipping his longstanding LSU commitment, it came with a known, massive offer from Michigan's Champions Circle collective, secured with funding from billionaire software tycoon (and Michigan alum) Larry Ellison, founder of Oracle. The NCAA just had to accept it. So did boosters: booster fatigue, stemming from programs asking the same rich donors for a little more and a little more, over and over, has quickly become an issue for a lot of schools.

In *The Price: What It Takes to Win in College Football's Era of Chaos*, NCAA president Charlie Baker—who took over for Mark Emmert in 2023—told authors Armen Keteyian and John Talty, "I think it was a big mistake for the NCAA not to do a framework around NIL when it had the opportunity. I think there were too many people in college sports who thought no rules would work really well for them. And what everybody discovered is no rules, no accountability, no framework doesn't work well for anybody." Indeed, in the 2020s the NCAA basically doubled down on begging Congress to clean up its mess by granting antitrust immunity and potentially passing a nationwide NIL bill to trump the state bills that were multiplying rapidly. Baker did make waves in December 2023 by proposing a new subdivision in which schools pay at least $30,000 annually to at least half its athletes; it was the first genuinely proactive proposal from the NCAA in ages (or maybe ever?), but the *House* settlement quickly stole the spotlight and became the priority.

There are three main pieces to the *House* settlement. First, $2.8 billion would serve as back pay to recent former athletes who hadn't been able to profit off of their name, image, and likeness. Second, and perhaps most significantly, up to 22 percent of the average power conference program's revenues—around $20.5 million per school to start—could be shared with student-athletes in a given year. Each school could choose its own distribution amounts for each sport. (Early reporting suggested football and men's basketball would command about 90 percent or more of the allocations. In the late days of the Joe Biden administration, the Department of Education sent out a memo suggesting this could be considered a major Title IX violation. Within weeks of Donald Trump taking office, that guidance was rescinded.)

Why 22 percent? It was seemingly drawn from the logic that, when combined with the other aid that students already receive, it approaches the 50 percent or so that most professional players associations arrange for through collective bargaining. It's fair to assume that logic could be subject to legal challenges, though this 10-year arrangement would also include escalators for future years, along with opportunities for reevaluation.

Within the settlement, the NCAA also attempted to assert control over NIL collectives, which could be absorbed by athletic departments with their contributions counting toward the initial $20.5 million cap. Only third-party NIL deals—the originally conceived commercials and business partnerships and whatnot—would be allowed outside of the cap, and any deal over $600 would be reported to a clearinghouse, run by accounting mega-firm Deloitte, that would determine whether it was of fair-market value. Judge Wilken initially expressed skepticism toward the third-party limitations, saying, "I've found that taking things away from people is usually not too popular," in a September 2024 hearing. But after a "clarification" from the NCAA's lawyers in the weeks that followed, the settlement moved forward.

Finally, each sport would be privy to roster limits: schools that opted in,* for instance, would be able to hand out up to 105 football scholarships instead of 85, but even counting walk-ons, rosters would be capped at 105 no matter what. This was an attempt to head off future antitrust lawsuits from athletes—for each sport, the total potential scholarship count went up, though schools weren't obligated to fill them all—but it ended up being a pretty big drag on the proceedings. Even as the scholarship totals were designed to go up, the roster limits themselves were expected to lead to hundreds or thousands of either walk-ons or athletes on partial scholarships losing their spots on rosters. Judge Wilken was initially expected to approve the settlement in April 2025, but she refused to do so until the concerns of these athletes were addressed. And somehow, though it still appears likely that this settlement will be resolved with the loose framework above, official approval dragged on past this book's submission deadline. (Thanks a lot, guys.)

It feels almost quaint looking back at what many of us were advocating for 10–15 years ago and what we actually got. Collectives themselves were far more of a black market than what was intended, and even in the *House* settlement, classifying revenue-sharing payments as "NIL" agreements seems like a stretch in logic, one perhaps designed to minimize potential Title IX issues. But even in these nascent, turbulent stages, NIL in its many forms has still righted a giant wrong (even while creating a few new, smaller wrongs). And antitrust lawyer and athlete advocate Andy Schwarz, a key influence in *White*, *O'Bannon*, plenty of other key lawsuits, and the Fair Pay to Play Act—he was one of the main characters in *Indentured*, too—wants to make it clear: this was absolutely what *he* envisioned. "People are like, 'This is not what NIL was supposed to be,' but it was exactly what I intended," he said with a laugh. "I say this a lot, and people think it's weird, but you can't separate someone's face from their feet. You can only pay them once for their total value. And it doesn't matter whether

---

*Schools outside of the power conferences wouldn't have to opt in to the *House* settlement, and plenty at the lower end of Division I signaled that they wouldn't, believing they could give their athletes better opportunities by simply continuing with their Alston payments and the structure they already had in place.

you call it NIL or athletic performance." There's no telling how this would have unfolded had the NCAA actually attempted a proactive approach, but as Schwarz told Keteyian and Talty in *The Price*, "They kept doing things that put blood in the water instead of getting out of the water and getting some gauze. At core, they're not a business, they're a cult."

5. The Audience Was Never Going to Go Away

In December 2011, Joe Nocera relayed an exchange he had with NCAA president Mark Emmert for the *New York Times Magazine*: "If we move toward a pay-for-play model—if we were to convert our student-athletes to employees of the university—that would be the death of college athletics," Emmert said. "Then they are subcontractors. Why would you even want them to be students? Why would you care about their graduation rates? Why would you care about their behavior?"

"I thought that was such a revealing statement," Schwarz said. "You would make them go to class because you're sincere in your belief that this is *college sports* and them being students is key! He was like, 'Why would we bother at that point if we're paying them?' You should bother because you claim to be an educator. It's this moment where morals and money match up. Those are such easy decisions."

Indeed, the NCAA's slippery-slope arguments always seemed to reveal a complete lack of understanding regarding the draw of their product. Reporting on the O'Bannon trial for the *New York Times* in 2013, Nocera wrote, "The NCAA's legal arguments in the O'Bannon case are almost laughably weak. It argues that if the players were paid, then college sports would lose its appeal. Says who?... It even argues that if O'Bannon wins, schools like Michigan, with its 110,000-seat football stadium, would downgrade its athletic status to that of, say, Amherst. I'm told that there were times on Thursday when people were openly chortling at some of the NCAA's oral arguments."

"The NCAA has done a great job of convincing everybody that 'college' and 'paid' are opposite," Schwarz told Nocera in *Indentured*. "But students get paid all the time." In fact, the draw of college football wasn't that that student-athletes were amateurs, it was that they were *students*. "We love seeing young men who go to our school—for real—representing the school," he said. "We don't really care whether or not they are playing for free." In 2019, as the NIL era was fast approaching, an AP-NORC Center for Public Affairs Research poll showed that 66 percent of adults approved of college athletes earning money from endorsements and sponsorships, and 52 percent thought athletes should receive a cut of the media rights. Public opinion was what allowed state legislatures to know this was a winning policy topic for them. But recent sports history was also loaded with examples of audiences giving zero damns about players making money. The Olympics certainly didn't suffer from their move away from amateurism, and when it comes to a sport moving from a system in which amateurs were consistently paid under the table to an actually professionalized system, there was a very clear example (and success story): tennis.

Late into the 1960s, tour tennis was split between a) amateurs who were eligible for Wimbledon, the U.S. Open, and tennis's other biggest tournaments; and b) pros who barnstormed around the world and actually made good money. But the so-called "amateurs" earned guarantees and under-the-table payments that allowed them to make enough of a living to continue competing as amateurs. In Peter Bodo's *The Courts of Babylon: Dispatches from the Golden Age of Tennis*, he tells the story of two-time Slam champion (and former amateur) Mervyn Rose giving a tour of his house and making references to cash and goods he had received from various tournaments. "Rose's handsome dining room was provided by the French Tennis Federation, and his den by the USTA," Bodo wrote. "Rose invariably ended the tour at the john, bitterly commenting that it represented the stingy contribution made by his native Australian Lawn Tennis Association."

In December 1967, the British Lawn Tennis Association declared that, with amateurism rules unenforceable and "shamateurism" rampant, it was opening Wimbledon and other British tournaments to professionals in 1968. "We should remove sham and hypocrisy from the game," the association's Derek Penman said. "We know that so-called amateur players bargain for payments grossly in excess of what they are entitled to, but without which they cannot live." For years, the International Lawn Tennis Federation had issued an NCAA-like refusal to acknowledge this reality. "For many years now we have tried by peaceful persuasion to get the ILTF to change the rules." Penman said, "but we have met with nothing but a cynical disregard for the present hypocritical situation." Sounds familiar. With Wimbledon playing the role of the California state legislature, the other major tournaments and associations quickly followed suit, and in 1968 tennis's Open Era began. The major tournaments actually featured *all* of the world's best players, the most high-level tennis was suddenly available to a much broader audience, and thanks in part to some spectacular personalities—and the presence of plenty of elite American players—tennis's popularity proceeded to explode in the United States in the 1970s.

6. It's Hard to Be Both Player-Friendly and Coach-Friendly

Just as fans like to predict the demise of college football at all times, coaches like to tell you how broken it already is, especially as it pertains to the current state of roster management and the general football calendar. They're every bit as dramatic and gossipy as fans about it. But that doesn't mean they're wrong.

The transfer portal officially launched in 2018 as, in the NCAA's words, "an NCAA application to manage the transfer process for Division I and II student-athletes." It basically made it easier for players to declare their intention to transfer and be seen by other schools. Over the years, the transfer rules themselves were more liberalized, as well. Historically, players had to sit out a year—and, if transferring within a given conference, potentially forfeit a year of eligibility—if they elected to transfer. Their former programs were also somehow allowed to limit the list of schools to which they were allowed to transfer. But the handcuffs were slowly removed. First, you were allowed to transfer without sitting if you had achieved your degree. Then you were allowed to move once without sitting. Now you can change schools every year if you want, without restriction, though with how tricky transferring credit hours can be sometimes, this might make it a lot more challenging to actually graduate.

When you combine the opening of the transfer floodgates with what was clearly an inducements-based NIL structure (no matter what the NCAA said or intended), you get an absolute free-for-all. In the early 2010s, it was a big deal if you signed even five or six transfers. In 2024, the national FBS average was around 14 transfers per team, a figure the 2025 off-season had topped by the end of the first of two transfer windows.

Between managing the (literal) ins and outs of the transfer portal and an NIL payroll, there's just *so much more* to do now, so many more things a coaching staff can be good or bad at. As an observer, that's honestly pretty fun. For instance, Clemson, Army, and Navy took a combined zero transfers between the 2023 and 2024 seasons—Army and Navy because service academies can't and Clemson because head coach Dabo Swinney just didn't want to. With no help whatsoever from the portal, the three teams went from a combined 20–17 in 2023 to 32–9, with two conference titles and a College Football Playoff appearance, in 2024. Meanwhile, Colorado, Arizona State, and Indiana took in more than 100 transfers between them and improved from a combined 10–26 to 31–9 with a pair of CFP bids. Were there some high- and low-transfer teams that also underachieved dramatically? Of course. But there are more routes than ever to crafting a good team, and that's delightful. Plus, these types of player rights were simply overdue. Ambitious players who were overlooked in high school can move up the ranks and eventually land at their dream school. Others who signed with a big school but didn't stand out can more easily find their level elsewhere and thrive. It obviously doesn't work out for everyone—plenty of players, often responding to poor guidance from under-informed agents (often family members), end up getting lost in the shuffle or landing in a worse situation—but it's a net good. And outside of the very elite levels of the sport, at least, it has resulted in wider distribution of talent, which is typically good from a parity perspective.

Without any order, however, the general roster management process has only become more chaotic. Players have been able to come to their coach, ask for more NIL money (with an implied transfer threat), get it, and then come back and ask for more money a couple months later. This exact situation seemed to play with Nico Iamaleava, who ended up making history in a couple of different ways. Not only did he end up becoming one of the faces of the "NIL as inducement" shift with his openly transactional Tennessee recruitment, but he also became the first major public holdout in April 2025 when he didn't receive what he was asking for after one year of starting for the Volunteers. He missed multiple practices, then entered the transfer portal when UT head coach Josh Heupel elected not to accede to his demands. Within a week, we'd seen another first of sorts:

Tennessee and UCLA basically traded quarterbacks, with the Californian Iamaleava moving back west and new Bruins quarterback Joey Aguilar, having just completed his first spring in town after transferring from Appalachian State, committing to Tennessee. (Meanwhile, Iamaleava's younger brother, Madden, a true freshman at Arkansas, also transferred to UCLA, which left Arkansas attempting to force him to pay an NIL buyout. Be prepared for that term to take on more resonance in the coming years.)

There is hope that the *House* settlement will bring back a little bit of order and standardization in this regard. It could certainly introduce more standardized contract language (with more standardized consequences for breaking said contracts). But the effects aren't yet clear, and even *House* won't de-clutter the calendar. There will still be multiple transfer windows, and teams will still have to sign their freshman recruits in December and/or February with everything else going on. Plus, the length of the freshly expanded College Football Playoff means that the national title might not be decided until the next semester is beginning. So a backup looking for a better opportunity might still feel he needs to enter the portal before his team has even been eliminated from the CFP. This is a lot! And we haven't even mentioned tampering yet—in this case, schools covertly getting in touch with players, perhaps through an intermediary, to convince them to enter the portal. It's rampant, and catching and punishing those who tamper is almost impossible. Coaches complain about tampering constantly while, in all likelihood, doing it themselves.

"The pendulum has swung hard toward player empowerment when it comes to transfer rules," Ralph Russo wrote for The Athletic in April. "It's fair to say we might be in the too-much-ice-cream phase. Bouncing around the country and averaging about a school per season is probably not ideal for players with minimal pro prospects who would benefit from graduating from...somewhere."

Craving order, coaches have also been banging the drum for collective bargaining agreements of late. But collective bargaining typically requires a union or players' association with which to *collectively* bargain. There is no such thing in college sports, and without help from Congressional legislation, even collective bargaining might not slow the stream of lawsuits. There have been legislative attempts at progress in this regard, like Senator

Chris Murphy's College Athlete Right to Organize Act from 2023, but anytime Democrats have been in charge, they've made it clear that this issue isn't much of a priority. (The size of their small recent majorities probably didn't help matters.) Murphy's efforts didn't go anywhere, and they certainly aren't likely to gain traction under Republican rule. Entities like Athletes.org and the College Football Players Association are attempting to make headway in terms of large-scale athlete organization, and there are encouraging signs in this regard, but it's a slow go.

Besides everything else they have to manage, coaches also have to figure out how to build a healthy and sustainable player culture with none of the player continuity. You know you have a good culture when the upperclassmen who have been in the program for four or five years are acting like assistant coaches and holding everyone to high standards when the coaches aren't around. How does that work when you don't have nearly as many guys in the program for that long?

I spoke to Oklahoma State head coach Mike Gundy before the 2024 season. The Cowboys were coming off of a rousing 2023 season in which, after a slow start, they won seven of eight to reach the Big 12 Championship, finished with 10 wins, unearthed an All-America-level star in running back Ollie Gordon II, and better yet, held onto most of their key pieces for what would assuredly be a conference title run in 2024. With the rumored *House* settlement on the horizon, Gundy seemed to think he had found some answers, not that he liked all of them. "The portal and NIL have not only changed the landscape of football, but the amount of hours that I spend, whether I'm at the office or home, has increased considerably over the last three years because of what the portal did with the recruiting calendar," he said. "And now we've added NIL, which has thrown in more of a CEO/business/finance part of it, and now we're going to revenue sharing in the fall of '25. That forces us to hire a front office business manager comparable to the NFL moving forward." Indeed, many schools have created general manager positions, all with slightly different purviews, and Stanford went so far as to hire former star quarterback Andrew Luck as its general manager for football, a position that is actually above the head coach on the organizational chart. That's as "NFL-style" as it gets.

(Actually, no, North Carolina hiring *Bill Belichick* in December 2024 is as NFL-style as it gets. But I digress.)

I wanted to talk to Gundy in part because of his success through the years in the culture-building department. Despite typically fielding rosters with far more three-star recruits than blue-chippers, OSU won double-digit games eight times in 14 seasons from 2010 to 2023, nearly made the BCS Championship in 2011, and nearly made the four-team CFP in 2021. How was he attempting to maintain a solid developmental culture in the new environment? "It's different," he said. "Our culture is the reason we win. We can play better than we're supposed to because of our culture. We brought in outside people to meet with our team weekly, and we continue to talk about building culture and being unselfish and staying committed to each other. You really have to work at it because if you don't have culture, then you have to be just better than everybody else, talent-wise, and that has not happened at Oklahoma State. We have to rely on structure, discipline, and culture. We've worked hard to continue with that, and it's so different than when you had guys in your organization for two, three, four, or five years."

Gundy has seen loads of success. He's Oklahoma State's all-time wins leader, and he thinks about these issues nonstop. And none of that stopped his team from collapsing to 3–9 in 2024. It was the worst season of his head-coaching career. Again: there are so many more things to be good or bad at, and coaches don't have as much control over everything as they once did.

7. Where Is This Heading? Some Guesses

There's nothing scarier than making predictions that will be preserved for posterity in book form, without an edit button to save you. But we're in the middle of so many stories as this book goes to print—ongoing lawsuits, potential legislation, roster management chaos—and I have to spin things forward somehow, for better or worse. So here are some predictions I'm at least 51 percent confident in making (but not much more than that):

The government will eventually bail the NCAA out (with conditions). In 2023, Texas senator Ted Cruz introduced a discussion draft for a potential college athletics bill that aimed to a) prohibit schools from restricting NIL rights (aside from conflicts with codes of conduct), b) create a "standard form contract for NIL agreements," c) formalize agent requirements, hopefully resulting in less poor guidance for athletes, and d) allow for the creation of a "public database used to help student athletes and third parties determine the fair market value of NIL services based on anonymized NIL data from institutions." This was an attempt to bring some order to the NIL process, and in order to help the NCAA—or, in theory, any other future governing body—actually govern, the bill would also e) provide a "safe harbor from legal liability for institutions, conferences, and athletic associations that fully comply with this Act," f) preempt state and local laws with different NIL guidelines, and g) insist that student-athletes are not seen as employees of a school, conference, or association.

With the Senate so narrowly divided and the then-majority Democrats focusing on other priorities, the bill made no progress before the 2024 national election. Following the Republican party's sweep, however, Cruz took over as chairman of the Senate Commerce Committee and told anyone who would listen that an NIL bill would be of the utmost priority.

"I think it is fair and right that athletes receive significant compensation," Cruz said at a press conference in College Station before a Texas A&M football game in 2024. "You have young men and women, 18-, 19-, 20-year-olds, who've developed incredible skills. We're all getting ready to cheer like crazy for a bunch of student-athletes who have developed amazing skills that are also incredibly profitable, that generate millions and millions of dollars for the universities, for the conferences, for the TV stations, for the advertisers. Everyone in the process is making money. I think it's fair that the athletes who've developed that skill, that they be able to enjoy the fruits of their labor." On that, both parties can agree. (They also seem to agree that the NCAA needs to meet certain benchmarks before it gets the antitrust exemption it so desperately craves.)

In 2023 Democratic senators Richard Blumenthal and Cory Booker and Republican senator Jerry Moran also authored the College Athletes Protection & Compensation Act. It aimed to set national NIL standards as well, but its other stated goals included establishing a medical trust fund for athletes and safeguarding health and educational outcomes, things that have only become trickier and more important now that we're asking FBS athletes to play up to 17 games in a season. (Alabama Republican senator Tommy Tuberville, who as Ole Miss's head coach said, "They'll have to carry me out of here in a pine box," in response to rumors that he was taking the Auburn job two days before taking the Auburn job, and who was accused of sneaking out of a Lubbock restaurant while hosting recruits as Texas Tech's head coach so he could take the Cincinnati head-coaching job, also pursued rules that punish players who break NIL contracts.) Blumenthal and Booker (a former Stanford tight end) have been behind many pieces of legislation but couldn't get any of them across the line when Democrats held the majority. With 60 votes required to pass something of this sort—barring some sort of move to cram it into a budget reconciliation package—Cruz acknowledged the need for bipartisan compromise, which likely means concessions on the health care front.

The NCAA backed itself into such a corner that it really is difficult to see it establishing order without help from the government. But there's reason to think the government might step in soon, for better or worse. In April 2025, Yahoo!'s Ross Dellenger reported that Cruz, Booker, Blumenthal, Moran, and Delaware's Chris Coons had already resumed bill negotiations. And in May, after the Trump administration declared that the president was weighing an NIL-related executive order after speaking with both Tuberville and Nick Saban, Dellenger reported on plans of a "presidential commission on college athletics." This is a foreboding and potentially regressive development from a player rights perspective, and God only knows how things might take shape moving forward. Trump's involvement could (but isn't guaranteed to) increase Democrats' resistance, and the *House* settlement likely altered the parameters of the discussion. But I am exactly 51 percent confident, no more and no less, that something will come to pass by 2026. (And yes, I would have predicted that something would pass between 2021 and 2024, too.)

Student-athletes won't become employees anytime soon. If nothing else, the *House* settlement, combined with any sort of government intervention that limits the NCAA's legal exposure a bit, could create a more stable environment, one in which athletes at least know where their money is coming from. That's a welcome change.

In 2024, after leading Holy Cross to the FCS playoffs on three occasions, quarterback Matthew Sluka transferred to UNLV, where he quickly became the starter for a team with CFP aspirations. After a 3–0 start, however, he declared that he was stepping away from the team due to unfulfilled promises. "I committed to UNLV based on certain representations that were made to me, which were not upheld after I enrolled," Sluka wrote on social media. "Despite discussions, it became clear that these commitments would not be fulfilled in the future. I wish my teammates the best of luck this season and hope for the continued success of the program." He would enter the transfer portal again and eventually commit to James Madison and his former Holy Cross head coach, Bob Chesney. (UNLV handed the reins to a *different* FCS transfer, Hajj-Malik Williams, and still reached the Mountain West championship game.)

Sluka's father, Bob, and agent, Marcus Cromartie, claimed that UNLV offensive coordinator Brennan Marion offered them $100,000 as part of his recruitment the previous winter (Inducement! Inducement!), something both Marion and a major UNLV collective, Friends of UNLV, denied. Regardless, the money obviously never arrived, and Sluka was gone. "It sounds like every complaint [Sluka] had between February and August," Dan Murphy said, "was that he would go to the coach and be like, 'Hey, when am I getting my money?' And the coach [be it Marion or another assistant] would just sort of be like, 'Oh, it'll come, just keep working.' I don't think the kid even realized—and I don't know why his agent didn't realize this—that he was asking the wrong guy. He needed to ask the people who actually cut the checks." That would, of course, be the boosters in the collective.

"I think the [*House*] revenue share coming straight from the school will help to make it one-stop shopping," Murphy continued, "where the same guy who's making the offer is the one who actually has to make sure he has the money in the bank to pay it. Schools will know how much they'll be able to spend, and it'll be a bit more professionalized at that point. The main paycheck the players are relying on will be reliable."

Of course, the best way to make sure your payment is reliable is to sign an actual employment contract. It wouldn't change a single thing about the education athletes are receiving, and one of the more dangerous cases still jangling around, at least until the government intervenes, is *Johnson v. NCAA*, a class-action suit in which athletes alleged violations of the Fair Labor Standards Act and argued that they could be considered employees and were entitled to compensation. Previous failed or withdrawn unionization pushes from the Northwestern football team in the mid-2010s and the Dartmouth men's basketball team in the early 2020s used similar logic.

Congressional views on this matter split pretty consistently down party lines—Democrats are open to viewing them as employees, and Republicans like Cruz are not. "Some of the more partisan players in the Senate want students to be treated as employees," the often partisan Cruz said in 2024. "I think that's a serious mistake.... There are an awful lot of college programs that have said it would shut down their athletics if student-athletes were treated as employees." This is a common line, one that schools might actually believe. Between Title IX concerns and ongoing uncertainty about whether *all* athletes would be considered employees (or just those in the more revenue-generating sports), there's a lot we still don't know about how this would work. But an employment model, with an accompanying collective bargaining agreement (CBA), could theoretically work out pretty well for the schools.

"I do not understand the NCAA's adamant disgust with the idea that they could have an employer-employee relationship with their athletes," Andy Schwarz said. "That would allow them to get into a union bargaining situation, which, if done wrong—and that's the most likely outcome: done wrong for the athlete's point of view—would result in this incredibly supine union that they could push around." Student-athletes are never in the talent pool for very long, any union would struggle to hold onto any sustained wisdom or leadership, and the strongest unions are the ones with lots of that. "There's the current world, and there's this CBA world, which is so much better than the current world if you're trying to keep costs down. But it is just anathema to the ethos of the NCAA. They would rather harm themselves economically."

Of course, none of that matters. With Cruz and Republicans now in charge, any successful legislation will come with anti-employment mandates. Barring a successful executive order, Cruz would still need help from Democrats to reach 60 votes in the Senate, but that could probably be achieved through compromises on health benefits. Now, a lack of employment status doesn't negate the possibility of the NCAA or conferences negotiating a CBA-like arrangement with something resembling a players' association. But it remains to be seen whether such an organization can wrangle enough signatures from athletes to control part of these negotiations.

There will be no sports-based government entity and no breakaway from the NCAA (at least, not a useful one). In many countries across the world, there is some sort of government department that oversees sports, be it China's General Administration of Sport; Ghana's Ministry of Youth and Sports; Ireland's Minister for Tourism, Culture, Arts, Gaeltacht, Sport, and Media; the UK's Parliamentary Under-Secretary of State for Sport, Media, Civil Society and Youth; or the plain old Ministries of Sport found in lots of countries. As things have grown messier within college sports, and as the NCAA has further proven its own limitations in addressing the messiness, the idea of a government entity overseeing college sports has begun to resonate a bit.

Granted, Cruz's own Commerce Committee fulfills this role to a degree, but Cruz has long been adamant that a ministry of sport is a no-go. "There are some pieces of legislation that have been filed that have either the government or a quasi-governmental entity making the rules," he said in 2024. "I think that's a bad idea. I promise you, if you have politicians deciding what constitutes pass interference, that ain't good." That's obviously a politically loaded talking point, but the idea of adding another layer of bureaucracy to an already bureaucracy-heavy structure could have obvious drawbacks, and it's not hard to see a political position succumbing to posturing and lobbyist influence and not even slightly improving matters. The best-case scenario is an NCAA-like organization competently running college sports. And since the NCAA has failed to do that for decades, at least for college football, another idea has begun to resonate: a *new* NCAA of sorts, perhaps one only overseeing college football.

There's one thing to always remember, though: the NCAA is run by and reflects the interests of its schools, the same ones that would be represented by and influencing some new entity. A new organization might be able to act more nimbly at first, but it's not worth anyone's time to build new offices and design new letterhead for what would quickly just become NCAA 2.0. There is an avenue for an entity like the College Football Playoff to take on governing responsibilities, and if nothing else that might provide a better opportunity to organize athletes—it could be established in the bylaws that playing for a designated CFP school could require membership to an Athletes.org type of association—but never forget that the same schools would be in charge and causing most of the same issues from which the NCAA has suffered.

We will see future fights over the percentage of revenue being shared. Maybe it will be over that 22 percent figure from *House*. Maybe it will be in regard to how much money football has to share with other sports. Maybe the reaction to a Trump order or commission will fill law firms' coffers for years. But history tells us how things usually go. "When you give players more, they don't suddenly say, 'Okay, great, thanks,'" Murphy said. "When you give them a bigger stack to stand on, they can see more clearly how much they're worth. Football players are gonna realize, 'Wait a minute, we're generating all this money. Why is it being shared among all of our other sports? We deserve a way bigger piece of this.' And that's where the next lawsuit or the next movement to organize players is headed, I think."

Inequality within college football will only grow in the coming years. And either those in charge will do something about it or they won't.

7.

Tall Poppies and Sports Socialism

"Every school is somebody's favorite school." That's what EA Sports senior VP Daryl Holt said to ESPN in May 2024 as buzz built for the return of one of the most beloved sports video games in existence: *EA Sports College Football.*

First called *Bill Walsh College Football* upon its release in 1993, it had no official licensing agreements with the NCAA or its schools, so teams had names like South Bend (instead of Notre Dame) and S.C. (instead of USC). It was fun from the start, but it picked up real team names a couple of years later, then an actual NCAA license—and a new name: *NCAA Football*—starting in 1997, my freshman year in college.

The game was a rite of passage for college football fans of a certain age. Three friends and I stayed up all night multiple times to bring Missouri a long-awaited national championship—after a couple of extremely Mizzou-esque failures—in Hatch Hall in the fall of 1997. My obsession with it during a particularly deep bout with senioritis definitely damaged a couple of grades a few years later, too. I'm too old for it now; the level of detail it provides, the game's increased adaptability (when you find something that works, it doesn't keep working forever), and my own decreasing video game dexterity all meant this game was not for me. But I still bought a PlayStation 5 with the sole purpose of playing the game for about eight total hours before accepting that. Those eight hours were still an absolute rush of nostalgia. And blowout wins on the lowest difficulty level.

Each year from 1993 to 2013, the game's rosters would feature nameless players who *looked* like college football's stars but were called things like "QB #16" instead of, say, "Denard Robinson." In the later years, you could download and install fully named roster files that users had painstakingly crafted, but EA itself couldn't include them because the NCAA's quest to maintain the pretense of "amateurism" took us to very silly places. The game's popularity was unwavering, but because of the eventual legal issues surrounding college athletes and their names, images, and likenesses, EA stepped out of the realm of college sports for 11 years.

Once NIL rights became a thing, EA slowly shifted back into action. The NCAA had elected not to renew its naming rights, but EA announced in February 2021 that it would be bringing the game back anyway. It would now be known as EA Sports College Football, and this time EA would be paying athletes to appear. Athletes had to opt in to inclusion, and anyone who did would get a $600 check and a copy of the game; certain stars would be part of an ambassador program and make more. "We went through all this process not really knowing how many players we're gonna have," principal game designer Ben Haumiller said, "and are the players that sign up gonna be the ones that you're expecting to see? It is great that you get all these players, but if you don't have Luther Burden III, do you really have Missouri? That was a big concern with the opt-in process—how do you wrangle all of these college-aged kids to do anything?"

Turns out, it's pretty easy when The Video Game is involved. Barely a week after the opt-in process started, more than 10,000 athletes had signed up. They added a few thousand more in the months that followed. The per-athlete fee rose to $1,500 for 2025's game, and we'll see what happens with future iterations of the game—it wouldn't be a surprise if athletes became both more demanding and more organized regarding how they're compensated. But for the first go-round, things went spectacularly well. And when the game was released in July, it quickly blew any sales expectations out of the water. "We didn't really know what the forecast was going to be because we've been gone for so long," Haumiller said. "We knew there was pent-up demand. We knew previous sales numbers, so we did a pretty conservative forecast for what [the] year would be, and we beat [that] forecast in a week and a half." There were 5 million unique players registered in the first week after launch. In terms of dollar figures, it was the most successful sports video game in U.S. history.

"We hit a record even before the game was launched!" Haumiller said. "We were in that pre-release window where you had to buy the special edition to be able to access it, and those first four days were like the four biggest days of simultaneous users in our studio history. 'Are we gonna get to a million users tonight? Holy shit!' It was just beyond wildest expectations from our side, but also we hit the expectations of users from all this time away. I think that was the biggest challenge."

From the game play to the stadium likenesses, the game was rebuilt from scratch. It had plenty of different modes—you could just fire it up and play Team A against Team B, of course, and there was an online mode if you wanted to test yourself against others. There was a "Road to Glory" mode, where you could create a prospect and try to become a star, from high school into college. But most of the people I know and/or follow on social media immediately tried to do the same thing I did in 1997, and 2002, and many years in between and after: win a national championship with Louisiana-Monroe. Or Kent State. Hawaii, maybe. Akron. There are many ridiculously hard jobs in FBS, and there was nothing more enjoyable than taking one of those schools to pretend glory.

I'm not saying the video game's absence caused us to stop caring about underdogs. But even if correlation doesn't equal causation, it's interesting to look back at the world that existed in 2013, its last year before hiatus.

In 2013, we were a mere decade removed from a time when the MAC briefly ruled the world. In the same 2003 season in which Miami (Ohio) finished 10th in the AP poll—thanks in part to future NFL star quarterback Ben Roethlisberger—three MAC teams beat ranked teams on the same day: Marshall over No. 6 Kansas State, Toledo over No. 9 Pitt, and Northern Illinois over No. 21 Alabama. (Three weeks earlier, NIU had beaten No. 15 Maryland, too. Did the video game's return cause NIU's 2024 upset of Notre Dame? Who's to say?) Meanwhile, we were barely six years removed from Boise State's epic 43–42 upset of Oklahoma in the 2007 Fiesta Bowl, a game that featured a game-tying, 50-yard, hook-and-ladder touchdown with seven seconds left in regulation, a game-winning two-point conversion on a Statue of Liberty play, and, for good measure, a postgame marriage proposal from Ian Johnson, the Bronco who scored the game-winner.

That win kicked off a genuine rise to prominence for BSU. The Broncos finished that season ranked fifth in the AP poll, and with quarterback Kellen Moore taking over behind center and throwing for nearly 15,000 yards, they would proceed to go 50–3 from 2008 to 2011, beating six power conference teams—including ranked squads Virginia Tech, Georgia, and Oregon (twice)—and losing only to TCU (twice) and, in another of the century's greatest games, a Nevada team quarterbacked by future NFL star Colin Kaepernick. If we add up the final AP poll rankings from 2006 to 2011 and give out 25 points for finishing No. 1, 24 for finishing No. 2, et cetera, Boise State ranked third in this six-year span, ahead of mighty USC and behind only Ohio State and LSU. TCU was also in the top 10, just ahead of mighty Texas.

Cumulative AP Poll Rankings, 2006–11

1. Ohio State
2. LSU
3. **Boise State**
4. USC
5. Alabama
6. Florida
7. Oklahoma
8. Oregon
9. **TCU**
10. Texas

Mountain West rivals BYU (22nd) and Utah (24th) were in the top 25, as well.

Boise State wasn't just good for a mid-major or good for a former junior college—the Broncos were genuinely one of the best programs in college football. My SP+ ratings adjust heavily for conference quality and strength of schedule, and in this time period BSU still rose as high as sixth in SP+. They would have had a puncher's chance at winning the title had a 12-team playoff existed in 2010 or 2011. TCU would have been a major contender in 2009 and 2010, too.

In 2013, we were also only about six years removed from maybe the most beloved season of all-time.

Like any sport without capped revenue or spending, college football has a pretty well-defined balance of power, with the same blueblood programs having taken turns dominating the sport for basically the last century. When things go awry, however, it can be spectacular. Blip years have saved us from monotony throughout the sport's history. Coaching changes or retirements, tactical innovations, ill-timed injuries, and plain old funky bounces have caused random seasons to go completely off-script. The universe always rights itself, but the blips are life-givers.

In 1956, for instance, Notre Dame, Alabama, and Texas went a combined 5–24–1, while Iowa finished third in the AP poll, and Oregon State and a pre-glory Miami both finished in the top 10. In 1959, three different SEC teams fielded their best teams in ages (Ole Miss, LSU, and Georgia); 24 teams made appearances in the top 10; Michigan and Ohio State went a combined 7–10–1; and Oklahoma lost as many games (three) as it had in the six previous seasons combined.

In 1967, an unranked Oregon State beat three different top-two teams in four weeks (Purdue, UCLA, and USC); Michigan and Ohio State went a combined 10–9; Wyoming finished sixth in the AP poll; and Indiana made its only Rose Bowl.

We got a trio of blip years just as cable television was discovering the sport, too. In 1983, four different teams finished in the top 10 despite starting the season unranked (Florida, BYU, Illinois, and national champion Miami), while five preseason top-10 teams *finished* unranked. In 1984, six different teams ranked No. 1 (the most ever), 25 different teams spent time in the top 10 (also the most), BYU won the national title, preseason No. 3 Pitt went 3–7–1, and defending national champ Miami lost via both a Doug Flutie Hail Mary and a 31-point second-half comeback by Maryland. Whew. And after all that, five different teams reached No. 1 in the AP poll in 1985, too, including Iowa (for the first time in 24 years) and a banned-from-the-postseason Florida; a top-five team lost to an unranked opponent for four straight weeks; and Air Force finished in the top 10.

In 1990, the national title was split between a Colorado team with zero previous titles, whose two most famous plays that year were a fifth down (against Missouri) and a clipping penalty (against Notre Dame), and a Georgia Tech team that began the season unranked and got relegated to the Citrus Bowl. Oh, yeah, and a record 18 different teams made appearances in the top five.

In 2000, 16 different teams appeared in the top five, three top-five teams lost to unranked opponents in the opening month, and Oklahoma stormed to an out-of-nowhere national title after averaging five wins over the previous six seasons.

Only 1984 and 1990 can even come close to the glory of 2007, though.

In just the second season after the last ride of Vince Young, Reggie Bush, and Co., college football ceased making any sense. USC's offense wobbled under the weight of QB injuries and slightly diminished talent; Texas's next generation of stars was still figuring things out; and Nick Saban's first Alabama team was not ready for prime time, losing to Louisiana-Monroe late in the season. The spread offense was taking over, and some of its earlier progenitors—Oregon, West Virginia, Missouri, Kansas—derived competitive advantages from it and made huge runs. FCS powerhouse Appalachian State, with its own delightful, run-centric offense, beat No. 5 Michigan in Week 1, and then Oregon, spurred by new coordinator Chip Kelly's incredibly fast-paced spread, ran circles around the Wolverines the next week.

The balance of power looked rickety early in the season, then completely fell apart. In Week 5, No. 3 Oklahoma (Colorado) and No. 4 Florida (Auburn) fell to unranked foes, while No. 5 West Virginia lost to No. 18 South Florida, an upstart. The next week, No. 2 USC fell as a *41-point favorite* to Jim Harbaugh's first Stanford team, and we were *really* off and running. In Week 7, top-ranked LSU fell in overtime to Kentucky, while No. 2 Cal (!) fell to Oregon State. South Florida, in just its eighth FBS season, charged to No. 2 the next week and immediately lost to Rutgers (which had at one point risen into the top 10 itself). Boston College rose to No. 2 for the first time in 65 years and lost to one of Bobby Bowden's worst Florida State teams. Then the only seemingly infallible team to date, top-ranked Ohio State, allowed 260 rushing yards, threw three interceptions, and lost at home to Illinois.

By mid-November, it looked like the nation's three best teams were LSU, Oregon, and Oklahoma. But Oregon quarterback—and, for a moment, Heisman front-runner—Dennis Dixon suffered a season-ending knee injury, and the Ducks got blown out by unranked Arizona. Oklahoma quarterback Sam Bradford suffered a concussion against Texas Tech, and Mike Leach's Red Raiders won 34–27. Over Thanksgiving weekend, LSU suffered an amazing 50–48 overtime loss to Arkansas, and in the most watched game of the regular season, No. 3 Missouri knocked off No. 2 Kansas at Kansas City's Arrowhead Stadium. Heading into championship weekend, we were looking at a potential BCS Championship game between No. 1 Missouri (!) and No. 2 West Virginia (!). Except the Tigers collapsed in the second half of the Big 12 Championship and fell to Oklahoma, and thanks in part to an injury to star quarterback Pat White, WVU suffered a forever-traumatic 13–9 loss to Backyard Brawl rival Pitt.

By the end of the season, 17 different schools had appeared in the AP top five, more than any season except 1990. Twenty-four different teams appeared in the top 10, too, second to only 1984. An unranked team upset a top-five opponent 13 times, five more than in any previous season. LSU lost two different overtime games as the No. 1 team. The No. 2 team lost seven times in nine weeks. Oklahoma lost three times as the No. 3 team. There was so much chaos that it circled back around to order: we ended up getting a seemingly normal Ohio State–LSU matchup in the BCS Championship. Thanks to a second-quarter surge, the Tigers became the first two-loss team to claim a title in the "final polls taken after the bowls" era. The only thing that would have made this season better would have been an equally chaotic 12-team playoff at the end of it.

The late 2000s and early 2010s almost made EA's video game feel realistic. You could turn a former junior college in Boise into a powerhouse. You could take historic also-rans like Utah, Cincinnati, TCU, Kansas, or Oklahoma State nearly to the top of the polls. Hell, you could win a

Heisman with a Baylor quarterback (Robert Griffin III in 2011). Almost literally anyone could beat anyone on the right Saturday. When the authors of 2010's *Death to the BCS* proposed not only a college football playoff, but a 16-team playoff that actually included every conference champion, from the SEC to the Sun Belt, it didn't seem particularly outlandish.

No matter how fans were reacting to this chaos, however, this was for many a bug to be fixed, not a feature to be celebrated. In a December 2010 panel of conference commissioners in New York, Big Ten commissioner Jim Delany tried to bully a supposed peer. With the recent success of mid-major programs and an ever-so-slight increase in the opportunities they received after political pressure, there was a growing sentiment that, since mid-majors could clearly hold their own, they should get even more opportunities to do just that. As Sun Belt commissioner Karl Benson was talking about his schools proving themselves on the big stage, Delany cut him off. "The problem is, your big stage takes away opportunities for my teams to play on the stage they created in 1902." (That was when Michigan won the first Rose Bowl. Never mind that only one other Big Ten team would play in the Rose Bowl in the next 45 years.) "The notion that over time by putting political pressure on, it's just going to get greater access, more financial reward, and more access to the Rose Bowl, I think you're really testing," he continued.

Big 12 commissioner Dan Beebe, whose conference would be nearly cannibalized a few months later when Delany's conference decided to expand, got even chestier. "Don't push it past this because if you push it past this, the Big 12's position is we'll just go back to the old [bowl] system," he said. "You're getting the ability to get to places you've never gotten before. We've Jerry-rigged the free market system to the benefit of those institutions and a lot are institutions that don't even fill their stadiums." Nice opportunities you've got here. I'd hate for the free market to take them all away.

For starters, it is openly silly to pretend as if every power conference program fills its stadium. During the 2010 season that was wrapping up as Beebe made those remarks, seven power conference teams averaged under 40,000 in home attendance, and another five averaged under 45,000. At the same time, the Mountain West's BYU and Utah were averaging 61,381 and 45,459, respectively, and good old East Carolina was averaging 49,665. But leaving that aside, both Delany and Beebe knew how the other half lived and still said what they said. They had each served stints as commissioner of the Ohio Valley Conference in the 1980s and 1990s. (For that matter, current SEC commissioner Greg Sankey once ran the Southland Conference.) But they still believed that the only way to do their jobs effectively was to never give an inch and never think about the greater good. If someone else was getting an opportunity, that was an opportunity they weren't getting instead. Zero-sum, all the way.

Both of these men, by the way, also got into the commissioner business after serving time as NCAA attack dogs. In 2016's *Indentured*, Joe Nocera tells the story of Delany charging Mississippi State and lineman Larry Gillard with NCAA violations because Gillard had received a $12 discount—one he didn't know about, and one also often received by students who didn't play sports—from a clothing store in the 1970s. Gillard was suspended for three seasons for this evidently grievous violation, and when Mississippi State got a court restraining order that allowed Gillard to continue playing ball, the NCAA eventually forced the school to vacate all of its wins in the seasons Gillard played. Because of $12. Beebe, meanwhile, was the NCAA's director of enforcement when the NCAA was ramping up both its investigations of and sanctions against SMU and other schools in the 1980s.

Delany and Beebe both ended up as symbols for both of the NCAA's failed priorities. Whenever the organization had a chance, it declared its actions were built around two main principles: amateurism—namely, minimizing the exploitation and commercialization of its athletes (as the NCAA defined it, anyway)—and competitive balance. Indeed, one of the NCAA's primary arguments in *NCAA v. Board of Regents* was that, in addition to protecting attendance, limiting television exposure was intended to protect the ideal of competitive balance. If teams were on TV all the time, the logic went, they could develop significant advantages in both revenue and recruiting. Predictably, the Supreme Court ripped these claims apart. If competitive balance had actually mattered to the NCAA, they'd have long been seeking ways to cap or re-distribute other revenue streams. Instead, they were simply seeking to limit the one stream that happened to also give them all their control over the sport.

Twenty-five years after *Board of Regents*, and against significant odds, it appeared we were actually drifting toward something resembling competitive balance. Maybe it was just a blip that would right itself over time—that's usually how these things go—but it was awfully fun watching college football turn into its video game universe. And the words and actions of commissioners like Delany and Beebe showed just how badly the sport's powers wanted to snuff that out.

Again: correlation isn't causation. But The Video Game returned in 2024 to a very different universe. We had still seen plenty of mid-major charges in the first 10 years of the CFP era, like UCF in 2017 and 2018 and Cincinnati in 2020 and 2021. And in 10 years of New Year's Six games, in which the best team from the Group of Five conferences played against one of the nation's top 12 teams, the mid-major team went a serviceable 4–6. The sport's powers, however, had again circled the wagons. They absorbed certain programs—Utah (Pac-12) and TCU (Big 12) were called up to power conferences in 2012, while Cincinnati, UCF, BYU, and Houston were brought in by the Big 12 in 2023—which served to shut up some of the loudest critical voices of the time. Utah senator Orrin Hatch, for instance, sure didn't seem to care as much about potential antitrust issues once his home-state Utes landed in the Pac-12. And when the opportunity presented itself, the power conferences (two in particular) figured out how to hoard even more of the money.

In 2024, when negotiations took place for how revenue would be distributed for the expanded CFP when the new contract began in 2026, the freshly expanded SEC and Big Ten, now on far friendlier terms than during the Alliance days, began to throw their collective weight around in an unprecedented way. While pushing to expand the playoff further—and, allegedly, to secure as many as four automatic bids each in what would turn a playoff into more of an invitational (and allow them to potentially create lucrative "play-in games" on championship weekend)—they also arranged to increase their takes from 16 percent of playoff revenue each to about 29 percent starting in 2026. (Here's your reminder that schools in these conferences are already looking at making nearly $50 million more per year in media rights than schools in other power conferences.) The ACC and Big 12 increased their percentages from 16 percent to only about 17 percent, and the more than 60 remaining Group of Five schools and independents went from sharing 20 percent of the revenue to sharing only about 9 percent. Leveraging their power to the fullest, the Power Two went even further, securing a memorandum of understanding from the other FBS conferences that gave them the final say for any future CFP changes.

They arranged a rather different distribution, however, when it came to paying the nearly $3 billion settlement with former players deprived of NIL benefits in the *House v. NCAA* case. While the four remaining power conferences would stockpile over 90 percent of future CFP money, they only had to cover about 40 percent of the *House* expenses paid by conferences, while the Group of Five and conferences with either no football teams or teams below the FBS level covered 60 percent. And many people called this a good thing because it might prevent the top schools from breaking off into a super league for a little while longer. How benevolent of them!

Psychologist Robert Zajonc once espoused what he called the "mere-exposure effect," in which mere exposure with something builds familiarity, and familiarity creates a more positive assessment of it. You could make a pretty good case that the reverse is also true. Less exposure to the greatness of mid-majors—through the limiting of their opportunities, through the depletion of their ranks via promotion of certain schools to power conferences and most importantly through further financial separation (and, perhaps, through the lack of "I'm going to win the national title with Akron!" video game dynasties)—has made us less accepting of their potential, or at least of a world in which their potential will be recognized. This is the world in which the video game returned.

Now, college football will never be completely orderly. Underdogs will always rise, at least briefly, and upsets, occasionally spectacular ones, will always be part of the sport. In 2023, James Madison, in its second year since moving up from FCS, won 11 games and finished 20th in SP+ despite enjoying barely one-third the revenue stream as teams like Kentucky (22nd in SP+) or Clemson (23rd). Troy won 11 games and finished 26th despite making less than one-quarter what Wisconsin (29th) pulled in. And in 2024, perhaps in another nice homage to the previous EA Sports era, Boise State fielded maybe the best player in the country in running back Ashton Jeanty and went 11–2, losing only to two top-five teams (Oregon and Penn State). Oregon, in fact, needed two return scores to survive, 37–34. And despite all the limitations that come with being a service academy team, Army finished 12–2, losing only to Notre Dame and rival Navy. (Navy went 10–3 itself, recovering from a midseason funk to beat not only Army but also Oklahoma in the Armed Forces Bowl.)

But even with the transfer portal and early-stage NIL decisions distributing talent a bit more evenly, financial heft still reigned. Of the top seven teams in 2023's year-end SP+ rankings, six were among the nine most high-revenue schools according to the most recent data in the *USA Today*'s revenue database. The top two teams on that revenue list? Ohio State and Texas, who reached the semifinals of the first 12-team CFP in 2024 alongside two other old-money programs, Notre Dame and Penn State. The 2024 season gave us some mammoth early upsets, and the expanded playoff gave us so much more to track; this provided a delightful feeling of parity during the regular season. But when it was time to actually decide the title, favorites rolled. The first-round games were decided by an average score of 36–17 (each winner led by at least 21 points at some point), and the only upset came in the semifinals, when Notre Dame narrowly beat Penn State as just a 1.5-point underdog. The Boise State and Army stories were incredible to follow, but look at the moving goal posts: I just celebrated mid-majors that finished the season ranked 29th and 37th, respectively, in SP+. In an earlier era, BSU ranked in the single digits.

Given enough opportunities, a mid-major could obviously pull a playoff upset. If, or when, it happens, it will be spectacular. And if the portions of the *House* settlement related to third-party NIL deals actually survives legal challenges, it's possible that the richest programs in college sports might not actually be able to outspend everyone else so drastically moving forward. But the current $20.5 million spending cap is still far higher than almost any Group of Five program will be able to reach, and college football's haves have thrown their weight around remarkably well in recent years that it's almost impossible to imagine them ever accepting a slightly more even playing field. The balance of power has become so demonstrably one-sided that some of the same people who were once shouting for a 16-team, all-conference-champions playoff—something like what we have at virtually every other level of the sport—have begun to reluctantly advocate for a Group of Five–only subdivision and playoff. "Power conferences don't see the massive gaps between themselves and everybody else as a problem to be erased, but an advantage they will build upon," Rodger Sherman wrote in a newsletter advocating for exactly that in May 2024. Sherman, a former colleague of mine at SB Nation, has long championed mid-majors and virtually every minor sport, but "the power leagues will never give, and only take. This is not a symbiotic relationship, but a predatory one."

It's a perfectly valid point, one based in obvious reality. And I'll be honest: I would gleefully write a 5,000-word preview for a hypothetical Army vs. Boise State national title game at the end of a hypothetical G5 playoff. Few things are more in my wheelhouse. But I have an allergy to anything that basically amounts to "Screw these powerful folks, we'll just [give them exactly what they want]." A G5 playoff would represent an enormous defeat, one that would allow the most selfish and predatory rulers of this sport to win. It would confirm that no more Boise State–style sudden rises would be allowed to happen.

Hell, it might even prevent us from winning a title with Boise State in a video game.

▻

I'm going to try to sell you on the idea of sports socialism. And to do so, I'm going to take you to Australia.

If you're of a certain age (read: mine), your lasting memory of Australian Rules Football might be when a nascent ESPN showed it in the 1980s and you first saw an official give what can only be described as a double-finger-guns signal, signifying a six-point goal. (There is also a single finger gun for a one-pointer called a "behind.") That's honestly pretty great as far as first impressions go, but further impressions will probably be positive too. It is an awesome game, one an American football fan would warm up to quickly. The games are long, and the field—sorry, *pitch*—is huge and oval-shaped. There are fast food ads everywhere you look (KFC: huge in Australia, apparently), and success requires contributions from players of all sorts of shapes, sizes, heights, and speeds. When the game is over, the winning team's cheesy anthem plays overhead. It's probably a familiar tune, too: when the Sydney Swans win, for instance, you'll hear a song with the tune of "Cheer, cheer for Old Notre Dame..."

The AFL is the NFL of Aussie Rules; it sprang from Australia's most successful regional league, the Victorian Football League—Victoria is the state that houses the greater Melbourne metropolitan area and about one-quarter of Australia's population—in 1990. The VFL began ramping up its commercialization and merchandising efforts in the 1980s, shifting from a board of (self-interested) directors to an independent commission, moving its clubs from aging, local venues to larger and newer (and less personal) ones and expanding to cities like Sydney, Perth, and Brisbane in the 1980s, then Adelaide and Fremantle in the 1990s, and to the Gold Coast in the 2010s. It has plans to field a team in Tasmania (named, of course, the Devils) in the late 2020s.

The sport itself shifted from regional to national in a process not entirely unlike college football, right down to an often unwelcome level of corporatization. Now, if you squint just right, you could say this seems like a closed-gate super league of sorts forming from a successful regional league that expands to incorporate other areas. Considering what many think college football is moving toward, that's not the type of example I would prefer to share right now. But Australia has truly committed to nationalizing its sport in a *representative* way. And it is absolutely obsessed with parity.

"Australians will tell you we love an underdog more than anyone else," said Max Laughton, an editor and commentator for Fox Sports Australia. "I'm sure other countries do, too, but we have this individual Australian concept of Tall Poppy Syndrome, cutting down the biggest poppy at any point. There is always an idea of, 'We don't want anyone getting too big for their britches.'"

Laughton and I began interacting on social media as I was getting more and more into the AFL and he was getting further immersed in American football. “I’ve followed probably 20 years now, starting with the NFL stuff but then getting into college,” he said. “I think the first [college] game I watched was the USC-Texas Rose Bowl. So, good start.” I asked Laughton what the most confusing part of the college football universe was as he was getting to know the sport. “Probably the complete acceptance of what recruiting was,” he said. “‘Oh, yeah, it’s totally above board, no one’s paying anyone,’ and yet everyone is paying players. And the fact that the NCAA wants to think it has power and doesn’t... there just needs to be some sort of governing body [for college football] when there absolutely isn’t.” Tell me about it.

Like plenty of other leagues, the AFL has more or less used the NFL as its model for financial success. “There are always people wanting to make AFL like American sports ’cause we look up to them like big brothers,” Laughton said. “But we can’t be completely the NFL. There’s just not enough money in the game. Salary caps are still like $14 million (U.S.). There’s no acceptance of contracts being publicly available—we don’t know what players make except for reports. And you can’t freely trade players, you can only trade players with their acceptance.” But a lot of the parity measures that the NFL worked to implement have come pretty naturally Down Under. “There is just no concept of concentrated capital in our sports,” he continued. “We have no private ownership for teams, and every sport is run by a league which, to a broad extent, also runs the sport itself. So the AFL has these dual duties of, ‘We’re running the professional league, but we’re also running local leagues. We’re running the rules of the sport for all leagues.’ They can’t just purely focus on the pro level.” (He refreshingly presented this as a good thing. In college sports, the NCAA represents both Texas and D-3’s Texas Lutheran, but we often reference that as a bad thing because Texas doesn’t get whatever it wants. It only gets *most* of what it wants.)

The AFL has its historic powers. Going back to the start of the VFL, Collingwood, Essendon, and Carlton have combined for 48 titles—sorry, *premierships*—since 1897, while smaller Melbourne-area clubs like St Kilda, North Melbourne, and the Western Bulldogs have combined for just six. But in the 35 seasons since the AFL officially formed, 14 of the current 18 clubs have won at least one premiership, and only one team, the Hawthorn Hawks, has won as many as five. Collingwood, Essendon, and Carlton have combined for just two titles, both from Collingwood, since 2000. "The AFL is probably right now more equal than it's ever been," Laughton said. "And that's been the stated intention of the league for some time. So that's been a success."

Like American pro sports, the AFL distributes talent via a draft, with the worst teams picking first. The league has been liberal in its allotting of extra draft picks and priority picks based on free agent losses and sustained on-field problems—*too* liberal, perhaps, which has caused some issues with tanking at times. But with the sheer volume of good players required to win (and no single position as important as the quarterback in American football), rebuilds take a while. And the salary cap assures that just about everyone has to rebuild at some point. "You can never have rebounds as quick as you've got with, like, the Texans getting C.J. Stroud," Laughton said. "But you can still get some level of balance."

The latest mini-dynasty run came from the Richmond Tigers, another former VFL club, which won three premierships in four years from 2017 to 2020. They went from winning 74 percent of their regular-season games in that run, to 50 percent from 2021 to 2023 to just 9 percent, two wins from 23 games, in 2024. Thanks to losses both on the field and in free agency, they entered the off-season with eight of the top 24 picks in the late 2024 draft. (They ended up using six of them.) "It's been an accelerated version of the normal cycle," Laughton said. "It is very normal to see a team be good, get to the top, and then rebuild. It is just a natural accepted way of things. Teams like Geelong [15 finals appearances in 16 years, with four premierships] and Sydney [13 finals appearances in 15 years, with one premiership and three Grand Finals losses] have rebuffed that, but that is what is supposed to happen."

Instituting extreme parity measures basically means doing favors for less-supported, less-historically successful clubs at the expense of a league's royalty. That feels risky. But average attendance was at 37,455 per game in 2024, up more than 60 percent from 1990, the AFL's first season, and TV ratings for the Grand Final—which is required to remain free to air by Australia's "anti-siphoning" laws that regulate media companies' access to major sporting events—have been relatively steady throughout the 2000s.

The AFL has attempted to prove that parity measures can benefit the sport as a whole. And Australia has gone even further in other leagues and sports. In both the National Rugby League and regional, lower-level football leagues like AFL Victoria, they use what is called a "player points system" (PPS), in which you literally get so many points to put together a roster (and certain players are worth more or less than others). As writer Alina Schwermer put it (translated from German) in *Futopia: Ideen für Eine Bessere Fussballwelt (Ideas for a Better Football World)*, "[National Rugby League] franchises are allowed to pay what they want, but no one is allowed to put together a dream team. If you gather too many good players, you have to give some away.... Salary expenses can hardly be controlled, but players in the squad can. And while the salary cap is primarily about giving the players less of the cake, the PPS looks very directly at the competition itself."

"[PPS] is an idea where you don't have a salary cap, but players are assigned points based on their perceived talent and past reputation," Laughton said. "So a retired AFL player who goes back to play for his local team will count for a lot of points for that team. Players who've been at high-level leagues who go back down will count for more."

"Values can be developed further," Schwermer wrote. "In Australian football, the Victoria region introduced a similar system in 2016, with additional elements. Weaker clubs or clubs from sparsely populated regions can purchase more points than the competition, while champions can purchase less. There is even an attempt to compensate for locational disadvantages." Schwermer even envisioned how to go further with the idea. "A final instrument would be possible: if players develop particularly positively at a club, the club receives points. This creates an incentive not to just leave young people languishing on the bench, but to invest in youth work themselves, even though the particularly talented ones may soon be gone. The PPS is an approach that has the chance to bring systemic change."

▻

Let's revisit a quote from *NCAA v. Board of Regents*. In response to the NCAA's ludicrous insistence that limiting television exposure protected competitive balance, the Supreme Court said, "The television plan is not even arguably tailored to serve such an interest. It does not regulate the amount of money that any college may spend on its football program, nor the way in which the colleges may use the revenues that are generated by their football programs, whether derived from the sale of television rights, the sale of tickets, or the sale of concessions or program advertising. The plan simply imposes a restriction on one source of revenue that is more important to some colleges than to others. There is no evidence that this restriction produces any greater measure of equality throughout the NCAA than would a restriction on alumni donations, tuition rates, or any other revenue-producing activity."

The NCAA indeed failed spectacularly at both justifying amateurism as a core concept and maintaining competitive balance. The only thing it could ever actually stop was athletes getting (legally) paid. And even when it instituted some sort of competitive balance measure, it came from different motives. Dropping the scholarship limits for football to 95 in the 1970s and then 85 in the 1990s prevented the most powerful schools of the day from hoarding athletes that could be of use to other schools and allowed for some level of talent redistribution; both moves came about, however, because of widespread budget issues, not a thirst for parity. Meanwhile, when someone actually proposed a more even spread of revenue and balance, the bluebloods threw a hissy fit. In the 1970s, Long Beach State president Stephen Horn proposed a more even distribution of television revenues, and the most powerful schools called Horn a communist and threatened to leave the NCAA altogether.

(It's funny how your viewpoint shifts when you do and don't hold power, by the way. In *The Fifty-Year Seduction*, Keith Dunnavant quotes Florida State's Bobby Bowden about the changes of the 1970s, saying, "The scholarship limits gave everybody a fighting chance," as Bowden was building his FSU program from scratch. But when further scholarship limits were instituted in the 1990s, Bowden, then in charge of a football dynasty, hated them, telling *Sports Illustrated*, "They're just going to water it down until it can't compete with the pros for the attention and dollars. They're just going to produce an inferior product.")

(It's also funny how these cost-saving measures didn't actually save costs. When the scholarship limits went down, coach salaries and facilities investments went up.)

If you ask a college sports writer where he or she thinks things are headed in terms of revenue distribution, they will probably paint a pretty specific picture: now that the SEC and Big Ten have secured so much of the college sports pie, they'll say, at some point the Ohio States and Alabamas, the financial heavyweights within these conferences, will start to wonder why they have to split media rights revenue evenly with the Marylands and Mississippi States within their conferences. They get bigger TV ratings, after all, and with the smaller schools in these conferences knowing how lucky they are to have a lifeboat to the big-time, the Ohio States have all the leverage. And isn't that what college sports are all about—financial leverage?

The ACC agreed to such a model in early 2025, crafting a distribution system based largely on television viewership that would have allowed Florida State to make far more than its peers, even while going 2–10 in 2024. It was a victory in that it made programs like FSU and Clemson less likely to leave in the short-term, but a) other conferences that conjured up such models to satisfy their bigger names, like the Mountain West (Boise State) and West Coast Conference (Gonzaga), eventually lost those programs anyway, and b) Alabama and Ohio State don't have anywhere to go. And why the hell does Ohio State need more money anyway? According to publicly available estimates, its athletic department brought in more revenue in 2023 than all but about five NHL teams. Even as we face a future that involves sharing revenue with athletes themselves, why does Ohio State need more when it already makes more than the *Boston Bruins*? How does the tallest poppy growing even larger help college sports? Why does *everything* have to end up a zero-sum exercise?

The answer, of course, is, "Because that's how it works with seemingly every other industry in America." But that's never going to be an acceptable answer. Athletic departments, and college football programs in particular, are community institutions. They prop up hundreds of college towns and economies throughout America. They should be supported and, when necessary, subsidized, almost as public goods. We've been taught to reflexively gag at the word "socialism" in his country, but the idea of *sports socialism*—which I'll basically define as any system through which income/revenue is redistributed in a way that props up programs or schools that have fewer natural resource advantages (and/or didn't get a head start by investing heavily in football in, say, the 1920s)—has powered the NFL for decades. The playing field in the most lucrative league in the world is also the most equal. The Dallas Cowboys might be the single biggest brand in world sports, and they haven't won a Super Bowl since 1996. Attempts at parity haven't hurt either the Cowboys' or their league's popularity or general lucrativeness.

Obviously parity measures are tricky when it comes to college sports. You can't institute a draft, as fascinating as it would be to force the next Trevor Lawrence or Bryce Young to ply his trade at Kennesaw State. And while we already have a player rating system for incoming college football players—they're called recruiting rankings—a PPS for college football, limiting the number of recruiting stars you can have on your roster, probably isn't going to get very far. (That does sound pretty damn fun, though. I'll call the SEC offices about it, just in case.) We're finally getting somewhere in terms of both player freedom and player compensation, but those freedoms will forever lead to players choosing schools with the best history of success and professional development, and those schools will always have the most money at hand. Hell, that still tends to be the way it works in Australia, too: the better AFL free agents pick Collingwood over St Kilda far more often than not.

Still, the goal doesn't have to be perfect parity, a world in which Michigan and Central Michigan have equal opportunity for success. The goal is to assure that blip years can happen every so often, that the haves and have-nots are just close enough to each other that the Davids can occasionally flip the table over and make things really messy for the Goliaths, even if order is always eventually restored. Every school is somebody's favorite school, after all, and that should be respected.

▻

In the last chapter, I mentioned that it's hard to be both player-friendly and coach-friendly. Well, it feels even harder to be both player-friendly and *parity*-friendly. For starters, the increased scholarship limits associated with the *House* settlement—moving the limit from 85 back up to 105—could bring talent hoarding back into vogue, even though free player movement should still assure that talented players won't be stuck on Georgia's fourth string unless they want to be. Beyond that, when pure bidding power drives recruitment, it creates a pretty clear food chain. The authors of *The Price: What It Takes to Win in College Football's Era of Chaos*, talked to Maryland head coach Mike Locksley and athletic director Damon Evans about schools like Maryland becoming a Macy's of sorts, losing its best players to "the Saks Fifth Avenues of college football" but also losing its backups to schools further down the food chain. The question, they wrote, was "whether it was willing to pump in the resources to elevate to the Saks Fifth Avenue level. If not, it risked slipping down to Target." Granted, they could also acquire stars from further down the food chain; this is the way it works in club soccer, and clubs that are particularly adept at talent identification and development can consistently shine in this environment. But soccer clubs pay what are called transfer fees for the right to sign players. When Borussia Dortmund acquired a young Jude Bellingham from Birmingham City in 2020, they paid a €30.2 million fee, and when he became a massive star and moved to Real Madrid three years later, the European giants paid Borussia Dortmund €103 million. If you're good at developing young talent, you're probably pretty well-compensated for it. But there's a certain buy-and-sell aspect here that won't exist in any likely college football structure.

When star quarterback Vernon Adams moved from Portland State to Oregon as a graduate transfer in 2015—he would throw for 2,643 yards and 26 touchdowns in 10 games for a nine-win Ducks team—Rob Ash, then Montana State's head coach, was appalled. "We're Division I like the other level," he told ESPN at the time. "Our guys need to start and finish at the same school. We cannot be perceived as a farm system or

Triple-A ballclub or anything like that.... It's going to be potentially a very difficult, bad situation for FCS with really good players that we recruit, we develop, being tempted to move on for that fifth and final year."

"That's my famous quote," he said more recently. "But that's what it's become. Every team's a farm system now for everybody else. We built our programs on player development. We would take ranch kids from Montana that played a bunch of different sports and also worked on the ranch all their lives that hadn't really focused on football. We built 'em up and put weight on 'em and got 'em in the weight room and taught 'em fine points of the game, and when they were juniors and seniors, they were outstanding. We had two straight Buck Buchanan Award winners for best [FCS] defensive player in the country—one was a walk-on from Billings [defensive end Caleb Schreibeis], and another one was a scholarship recruit, but he was not a five-star guy by any means [defensive end Brad Daly]. They're just Montana kids who were fantastic workers. And neither one would've played their junior or senior season for us."

Schools like Montana State have managed to establish a high level of play at the FCS level—in 2024, in fact, the Bobcats went 15–1 and reached their second FCS title game in four years. But they did so despite losing three linemen (two on offense, one on defense) to starting roles at the FBS power-conference level. Idaho, meanwhile, enjoyed a breakout 2023 and proceeded to lose seven starters to FBS. Four became power-conference starters. There were no transfer fees involved.

To some degree, the cost of doing business in this new era might simply be that you have to do *more business.* You lose a few guys up the ladder, you pull in some guys from elsewhere, and on you go. The transfer portal era has opened up wonderful opportunities for players and genuinely seems to have redistributed talent in an interesting way. But there are trade-offs. First, your fans might not be able to connect with their transient roster quite as deeply if the names are changing more constantly—that's not a problem if you're winning, but it could cause them to check out a bit faster when you're not. Second, all programs become more transactional and less developmental. And when your playing field is tilted in general, we know which teams and conferences are more likely to take advantage of anything new that the sport has to offer.

How might we go about leveling the playing field a smidge? Well, in the short-term, we won't. The SEC and Big Ten run college sports, and there's no one around to tell them no. But things change. You never know when there might be a future opportunity to steer the conversation in a more positive direction. So let's talk for a moment about caps, floors, and sharing money.

The *House v. NCAA* settlement included a projected spending cap of $20.5 million in revenue to share with athletes for any school that opted in for the 2025–26 academic year. The NCAA wasn't able to implement nearly as many restrictions on NIL collectives as it wanted—it's only *sort of* a cap—but it's still an attempted cap. That's good for parity, right? Not in a way that doesn't punish athletes. A cap is clean(ish) and easy(ish), and it certainly attempts to limit how much the richest schools can pull away from the field, but a) the richest schools will always figure out ways to outspend the field, and b) caps also cap the total amount of money that can go to athletes.

Andy Schwarz, long a champion of athlete compensation, suggests raising floors instead of capping ceilings. "A salary minimum is great, especially a salary minimum with enough revenue sharing to make sure that Wake Forest can afford it," he said. "You don't need any caps other than that, and you end up forcing Wake to spend more money than they want to. It's not economically rational for Jacksonville in the NFL to spend as much as they do on talent, but they have to, and the NFL has these structures in place to fund it. Players would be better if there was no ceiling, just a floor and [revenue] sharing." A lot of schools that have opted in to play the *House* game won't be willing or able to give anything close to the maximum $20.5 million to its athletes, but if revenue were distributed such that lots of schools could pay a *minimum* amount—say, $12 million, $15 million?—the overall dollar figure going to athletes (and the quantity of athletes benefiting from the system) would increase overall. And perhaps Wake Forest, or even Montana State, could afford to hold onto a few more of its players.

"Great athletes want as many schools in the top [payment] tier as possible," Schwarz continued, "it's as many jobs as possible. And the smaller schools want it—'Sure, subsidize it so we spend more than is rational and we have more fans than is rational.' It's big schools that don't want that." In fact, there's nothing big schools seem to want *less* than subsidizing the competition.

Dr. Steve Horn didn't mind making people angry. As a five-term U.S. representative from 1993 to 2003, he broke from his Republican party to vote against oil drilling in the Arctic and supported abortion rights and gun control. That could get you ostracized pretty quickly. But nothing he could do in Congress was going to light a room on fire the way his pursuit of NCAA changes in the 1970s did. Horn became president of Long Beach State in 1970, as the LBSU athletic department was dealing with an epic list of alleged NCAA violations. As he worked with the NCAA to clean up the program—something that included allowing ultra-successful (and, shall we say, rules-defiant) basketball head coach Jerry Tarkanian to leave for UNLV in 1973—he began to realize just how tilted the playing field really was in college sports. So he brought what he called "modest" changes to the 1976 NCAA Convention. "I got interested in discovering the cause of a lot of these problems," he later said. "I felt the cause was simply money and greed. And the fact is, the rich were getting richer and the rest of the institutions were sort of just there to vote occasionally and serve as cannon fodder for the major institutions." He proposed drastically limiting football scholarships, far beyond the eventual cut to 95, and creating far more even revenue distribution from the NCAA's television deal—he wanted 50 percent of the revenue to go to Division I schools and 50 percent to be split among Divisions II and III. "As far as I'm concerned, Notre Dame and Ohio State can be on TV every weekend," he told the media during the 1976 convention, suggesting that might earn even more money for the NCAA's TV deal. "But I want what they do to help all members of this association." He earned the nickname of Robin Hood, and as soon as major conferences like the Big 8 fell to their fainting couches and threatened to leave the association, the NCAA's executive council shot down the proposal.

There has never been an appetite for a genuine, college football–wide, revenue-sharing mechanism among schools. In fact, since *Board of Regents*, there has really only been the opposite. So we have to consider this one *particularly* theoretical. But let's attempt a useful thought exercise: acknowledging that revenue data is murky and can be manipulated to tell certain stories, the *USA Today* revenue database, which features data for public schools only, shares that in fiscal year 2023, five FBS schools (Alabama, Georgia, Michigan, Ohio State, and Texas) were credited with over $200 million in revenue while nine reported under $30 million (Ball State, Bowling Green, Jacksonville State, Kent State, Louisiana-Monroe, Louisiana Tech, Northern Illinois, Ohio, and Southern Miss). If you were to create a pool of money in which every FBS school pitched in just 3 percent of its revenue* and it was divvied out equally to all 130-something schools, you would end up in a situation where those $200 million schools make about 1.8 percent less (losing about $4 million each) but the sub-$20 million schools would make 7.9 percent more (gaining about $2 million each). If we were to raise this to 10 percent each—QUICK, TO THE FAINTING COUCHES—the top schools would still end up with over $190 million each (Ohio State would still be over $230 million!), but Louisiana-Monroe's revenue would go from barely over $19 million to over $26 million.

The gains would boost FBS's smaller schools more than the losses would limit the big boys. And considering how much damage smaller schools are already able to do when they have their act together, it wouldn't take much to make a big difference. In 2024 alone, among those sub–$30 million teams listed above, Northern Illinois famously upset Notre Dame, Bowling Green lost to both Penn State and Texas A&M by one score, Jacksonville State won Conference USA and ranked second nationally in rushing yards per game, and Ohio won the MAC despite getting wrecked by transfer portal losses and a poor NIL situation. Imagine if these schools had a few extra million to potentially develop talent even better or keep their better players a little longer?

---

*In this case, we're talking about all revenue, not just media rights. Media rights money made up only about a quarter of Ohio State's overall $251.6 million haul in 2023, after all, and as Alina Schwermer pointed out in *Futopia*, "If just media revenues are distributed more equally, the top teams that earn well through exclusive sponsorship gain an even greater advantage because the upper middle is weakened."

We're obviously nowhere close to real, comprehensive, inter-conference revenue sharing. Hell, it feels like we're closer to the opposite, as evidenced by both the "Ohio State lords its leverage over Minnesota" idea above and the fact that, when the CFP was officially expanded, we added nearly $1 billion in revenue with some handshakes and the stroke of a proverbial pen, and elected to give most of the new money to the SEC and Big Ten instead of funding the future of the sport. Still, you wouldn't have to trim the tall poppies much to create a healthier football environment for a lot of schools, and we shouldn't stop yelling that from whatever rooftops we can find.

Actually, there's one more option if we want to bring actual merit to college football: promotion and relegation. But let's stick a pin in that one and return to it in a bit. First, we have to talk about who actually makes decisions.

8.

Who's Actually in Charge of College Football

In 1920, professional baseball was in crisis. The Black Sox scandal, in which eight members of the Chicago White Sox—star outfielder "Shoeless Joe" Jackson; co-aces Eddie Cicotte and Lefty Williams; four other starters (first baseman Chick Gandil, shortstop Swede Risberg, third baseman Buck Weaver, and outfielder Happy Felsch); and a key backup infielder (Fred McMullin)—were indicted and accused of throwing the 1919 World Series, had, along with allegations of other fixed games, shaken the sport to its core. Baseball had been governed by a National Commission consisting of three parties with extreme self-interest: National League president John Heydler, American League president Ban Johnson, and Garry Herrmann, president of the Cincinnati Reds team that had beaten the White Sox in the World Series. Its leadership proved lacking in this moment, and its questionable independence severely damaged perceptions. Herrmann resigned from the commission in 1920, and the commissioners couldn't agree on a new third member.

In early October 1920, days before the start of that season's World Series between the Brooklyn Robins and Cleveland Indians, leaders of the Chicago Cubs, Chicago White Sox, New York Giants, and Pittsburgh Pirates proposed a tribunal of, in the words of the *New York Times*, "three of America's biggest men, with absolute power over both major and minor leagues." A letter sent to every major and minor baseball club said, "If baseball is to continue to exist as our national game (and it will) it must be with the recognition on the part of club owners and players that the game itself belongs to the American people, and not to either owners or players."

The letter stated that "the present deplorable condition in baseball has been brought about by the lack of complete supervisory control of professional baseball," that "the only cure for such condition is by having at the head of baseball men in no wise connected with baseball who are so prominent and representative among the American people that not a breath of suspicion could be ever reflected." It concluded, "The practical operation of this agreement would be the selection of three men of such unquestionable reputation and standing in fields other than baseball that the mere knowledge of their control of baseball, in itself, would insure that the public interests would first be served, and that, therefore, as a natural sequence, all existing evils would disappear." This tribunal would have the power to punish players, strip owners of their franchises, "establish a proper relationship between minor leagues and major leagues," you name it.

This proposal, first discussed by Cubs shareholder A.D. Lasker, became known as the Lasker Plan. Perhaps unsurprisingly, a number of clubs—particularly, those in the American League still loyal to the strong-willed Johnson—initially balked at the idea, to the point where the National League considered beginning an entirely new league with a few insurrectionist AL clubs, including the New York Yankees and Boston Red Sox. But all necessary parties eventually came to the table, and figures as grand as former president William Howard Taft, General John J. Pershing and former treasury secretary William G. McAdoo were under discussion for the tribunal.

The search pretty quickly began to revolve around a single figure: Judge Kenesaw Mountain Landis. A known baseball fan and an occasional showman on the bench, the 54-year-old Landis was known primarily for his antitrust judgment against Standard Oil, issuing the corporation a $29.2 million fine in 1907, equivalent to almost $1 billion today. (The U.S. Court of Appeals would eventually strike down the verdict.) He was regarded as tough but thoughtful, a grand figure but a supporter of the everyman. He would go on to serve as the sport's first commissioner, a one-man tribunal, until his death in 1944.

Landis proved ruthless and uncompromising when he felt he needed to be. Despite all of the indicted "Black Sox" being acquitted in a criminal trial, Landis still banned them from baseball for life, stating, "Regardless of the verdict of juries, no player that throws a ball game; no player that undertakes or promises to throw a ball game; no player that sits in a conference with a bunch of crooked players and gamblers where the ways and means of throwing ball games are planned and discussed and does not promptly tell his club about it, will ever play professional baseball." For better or worse, he stuck to that decision through the years despite both legal and emotional appeals. Early in his tenure he even suspended star Babe Ruth for participating in a postseason barnstorming tour without permission, even though he didn't really know how the public would respond to such a decision. (Ruth was evidently booed in his return to the field, giving Landis affirmation and confirming his absolute power.)

Landis wasn't a ruthless traditionalist, however. The All-Star Game was created under his watch in the early 1930s and proved to be a big hit, and while he didn't seem to approve of the development of farm systems, in which minor league clubs developed affiliations with major league clubs to develop and promote their talent through the ranks, he also didn't stop it, choosing only to step in on a case-by-case basis. He was far from infallible—you can certainly find inconsistency in some of his decisions, and Lord knows baseball didn't exactly speed toward integration under his watch. (Jackie Robinson's major league debut came two and a half years after Landis' death. He might not have stopped that from happening had he still been in charge, but he certainly wasn't pushing owners to become more progressive in this regard.) But he provided as steady a hand as possible, and both the trust in and popularity of baseball grew under his watch.

Absolute power? A dictatorial hand over the sport you've loved since childhood? Man, sign me up. That sounds amazing. Sure, I've never issued a billion-dollar fine to anyone, and my strongest bona fides regarding my general incorruptibility probably stem from the time I went on *The Paul Finebaum Show* and proclaimed that Cincinnati should have ranked higher than the SEC's Texas A&M in the 2020 College Football Playoff rankings. But that qualifies as speaking truth to power, right?

In 2017, while at SB Nation, I indeed decided to run for college football commissioner. Granted, there was no such election and no such position, but it felt like a good use of time all the same. "College football needs someone to make long-term decisions," I wrote. "College football needs someone who can reflect the interest of programs at every level: Alabama, Alabama-Birmingham, North Alabama, and all."

There was an explosion of commish talk in 2016, thanks to a number of issues like College Football Playoff selections, conference schedules (mainly that some conferences play eight conference games and others play nine), and high school satellite camps, an issue that was all the rage for a few months and then vanished from consciousness altogether, to the point where I don't even feel the need to define it here. "There needs to be somebody that looks out for what's best for the game," Alabama's Nick Saban said at the time, "not what's best for the Big Ten or what's best for the SEC or what's best for Jim Harbaugh, but what's best for the game of college football—the integrity of the game, the coaches, the players, and the people that play it. That's bigger than all of this." (Harbaugh was at the center of the satellite camp issue that I'm still not going to explain further.) But even with Saban's high-visibility comments, nothing came of it. Nothing ever comes of it.

Through the decades the only thing everyone has seemingly agreed on in this sport is the need for a commissioner figure.

> Charley Trippi, one of the all-time greats in college and professional football...said college football today needs a national commissioner to direct the game on a national basis. Trippi...charged that the National Collegiate Athletic Association is "controlled by the Big Ten." He said he felt no conference in the nation should have any kind of monopoly in the game. —*Macon News*, 1958

> You don't think we need a commissioner and a set of rules to make things even? We're the only sport in America that doesn't have the same set of rules for everybody that plays.... Everybody goes to their own neighborhood and makes their own little rules.
>
> —Florida State head coach Jimbo Fisher, 2016

I think there's a perception with the public that perhaps college football doesn't have its act together because there are so many different entities pulling in different directions.

—former Baylor head coach Grant Teaff, 1994

We need somebody running college football. We need somebody that is not biased based on a conference and that is out of the financial impacts of it as well, because if you're just making the decisions which are in the best interests of the student-athletes and college football, then I think you can do it. But if you're biased by a specific conference or if you're impacted by making all your decisions based on revenue and earnings, then we're never going to get to a good place.

—Penn State head coach James Franklin, 2024

What this business needs is a commissioner who has the best interest of the game in mind. There needs to be somebody who creates a structure in which people just don't cannibalize each other.... The NCAA president doesn't have any legal authority to do much, in his defense, because they've given away that authority over the course of the last 60 years.

—West Virginia athletic director Oliver Luck, 2011

Somebody could finally say, "Well, I listened to everybody, but here's what we need." When you have one voice, it just helps you. Instead of, "The Big 12 says they want this, and then the SEC, nah, we hate that. And the Pac-12 says this." We don't make ourselves look too intelligent, to be honest with you, because we don't have one common message coming out.

—TCU head coach Gary Patterson, 2016

I think we need to have a...commissioner. I think football should be separate from the other sports. Just because our school is leaving to go to the Big Ten in football...our softball team should be playing Arizona in softball. Our basketball team should be playing

> Arizona in basketball.... And they'll say, well, how do you do that? Well, Notre Dame's independent in football, and they're in a conference in everything else. I think we should *all* be independent in football. You can have a 64-team conference that's in the Power Five, and you can have a 64-team conference that's in the Group of Five, and we separate, and we play each other. You can have the West Coast teams, and every year we play seven games against the West Coast teams and then we play the East—we play Syracuse, Boston College, Pitt, West Virginia, Virginia—and then the next year you play against the South while you still play your seven teams. You play a seven-game schedule, you play four against another conference opponent, division opponent, and you can always play against one Mountain West team every year so we can still keep those rivalries going. Not that I've really thought about this, not that I've spent a lot of time on this. [Sure, Coach.] But I think if you went together collectively, as a group, and said there's 132 teams and we all share the same TV contract, so that the Mountain West doesn't have one and the Sun Belt doesn't have another and the SEC another, that we all go together, that's a lot of games, and there's a lot of people in the TV world that would go through it. You can sponsor each one—instead of calling it Group of Five and Power Five, you can call it Amazon, Nike...you can have a lot of different things. But I think if we still do the same and take all that money...that money now needs to be shared with the student-athletes, and there needs to be revenue sharing, and the players should get paid, and you get rid of [NIL], and the schools should be paying the players because the players are what the product is. And the fact that they don't get paid is really the biggest travesty. Not that I've thought about it.
>
> —UCLA head coach Chip Kelly, 2023

Kelly's spiel, spoken at a pace faster than his fastest old Oregon offense at a press conference before UCLA's LA Bowl appearance, made waves. In a way, he was basically calling for a *College Football Association* of sorts, an all-of-FBS league that could negotiate a huge television contract to be divvied out in a fair manner. In a perfect world, maybe that's what would exist. But as with any other "In a perfect world..." construct, the real world prevailed instead.

The waves continued after Kelly's comments. In January 2024, Nick Saban retired in part because he was frustrated with all the different demands of the NIL era. In February, Saban told ESPN's Chris Low, "If my voice can bring about some meaningful change, I want to help any way I can, because I love the players, and I love college football. What we have now is not college football—not college football as we know it. You hear somebody use the word 'student-athlete.' That doesn't exist." A company man until the end, Saban suggested that either SEC commissioner Greg Sankey or Alabama athletic director Greg Byrne might make a good commissioner for the sport. ("They would be more qualified than I am. They're in it every day and know all the issues.") In December 2024, Penn State head coach James Franklin expressed frustration with the state of the college football calendar and the fact that his backup quarterback, Beau Pribula, felt he needed to hop into the transfer portal before the Nittany Lions' College Football Playoff journey began to make sure he had a solid home for the winter semester. His solution? "Let's get a commissioner of college football that is waking up every single morning and going to bed every single night making decisions that's in the best interest of college football. I think Nick Saban would be the obvious choice if we made that decision."

Did anything come of that? Of course not. But that just means I'm still a candidate, right?

Back in 2017, my campaign platform consisted of nine pillars intended to maximize both the athlete's experience and the fan's enjoyment of the sport:

1. A student-athlete bill of rights to ensure proper health care options, guaranteed undergraduate scholarships, and freer transfer rules.
2. A modernized definition of amateurism that allowed players to profit off of their name, image, and likeness.
3. The return of the EA Sports video game. (Hey, you have to throw some red meat to the base, right?)

4. A fairer recruiting landscape that allowed players easier releases from their letters of intent if a coach left and explored changes to signing periods and regulations surrounding official visits and other recruiting rules.
5. A system of promotion and relegation that incorporates actual merit into the sport's power structure. (This one's always on my mind.)
6. An expanded playoff.
7. Ditching unequal conference divisions in favor of a system of permanent rivalries and a larger rotation of opponents.
8. Increasing creativity and flexibility in nonconference scheduling. (One idea: a "BracketBuster Saturday" in November in which everyone in FBS gets paired off based on in-season results.)
9. Changes in clock rules that stemmed the recent increases in average game times, which had reached nearly three and a half hours per game.

It's been about eight years since I put that list together, and damned if I haven't gotten a lot of what I wanted: we've seen either partial or complete success for items No. 1, 2, 3, 4, 6, 7, and 9. That's a hell of a success rate, especially considering how hard it is to actually institute change in this sport at times. But it feels like a lot of the forces I was responding to at the time—mainly, massive disorganization within the sport and an ever-increasing imbalance between haves and have-nots—have only gotten worse since 2017. Why? BECAUSE WE STILL HAVE NO COMMISSIONER! Any change that could have produced progressive outcomes only made the imbalance worse because when no one's in charge, that really means that the most powerful and self-interested figures in the sport are in charge. And their only goal is to reinforce the power structure.

"I can't tell you how many times I heard [former Big Ten commissioner] Jim Delany say two things," former Mountain West commissioner Craig Thompson said. "One: 'You didn't bring the Rose Bowl, or the Orange Bowl, or the Sugar Bowl, or the Fiesta Bowl, so [you get] whatever we decide you are worthy of.' He also used to say, 'The world cares more about 6–6 Michigan than 12–0 Utah, and until you realize and understand that and accept that...' and I got it. But we always seemed to find a way to work together for the good of the cause, the good of the overall enterprise. Great, you started the Rose Bowl, but was it all bad that TCU beat Wisconsin in the Rose Bowl [in 2011]? That Utah beat Alabama in the Sugar Bowl [in 2009]? Did the enterprise come crumbling down? No. We're trying to look at the good of the cause and what's best for the second most popular sport out there, and what I always had in the back of my mind trying to protect was how we could make sure that people give a damn about college football."

For somewhere between 10 and 30 years, Delany was the sport's most powerful figure. He kickstarted multiple runs of conference realignment, and the Big Ten's creation of the Big Ten Network turned out to be a game-changer. But college football's most powerful figure was also doing everything he could to keep other conferences' ambitions in check, to almost limit the sport's potential growth in other areas of the country.

"When people talk about wanting a commissioner, what they're really asking for is someone whose job it is to look out for the betterment of the sport as a whole," said NBC Sports' Nicole Auerbach. "I know it sounds really pollyannaish and idealistic, but you don't have someone whose job it is to look out for the greater good. So you have competing interests. You have an NCAA president who has certain motivations and goals—and major college football is not even under their purview. And then you have all these different commissioners, and it makes a lot of sense that we ended up in a position where conferences started hiring outside of college sports. They hired businesspeople, they hired media executives, and then those people believe that their goal is to advance the interest only of their conference because that's how those jobs work."

"Lately, it seems like we've morphed into, 'I've gotta feed the beast,'" said Thompson. "'I've got 18 schools, 16 schools...' In 2023, there were five autonomous conferences with an average membership of 13 schools each. Now we've got four autonomous conferences with an average membership of 17. We've gone to that consolidation, and a commissioner is paid to protect his 14, 16, 18 school interests. But, man, it just doesn't seem like we care as much about how we just keep this thing going, how we keep 80,000 people, 50,000 people, hell, even 30,000 people coming to games."

Now, professional sports have proven rather definitively that you can be disorganized and inequality-friendly with a commissioner atop the organizational chart. Just look at the last 35 years for most of Europe's biggest soccer leagues or large swaths of Major League Baseball's history—baseball had all the inequality a fan of capitalism could possibly crave, especially in the 1990s. And, hey, having an occasional tyrant like David Stern in charge didn't stop the NBA from basically being ruled by three teams for decades—from 1980 to 2002, the Los Angeles Lakers, Boston Celtics, and Chicago Bulls won 17 of 23 titles. Even in the NFL, all the parity measures in the world couldn't stop the teams that employed either Tom Brady (New England, then Tampa Bay) or Patrick Mahomes (Kansas City) from winning 10 of 24 Super Bowls from 2001 to 2024.

It's also not hard to see how a dictatorial figure like the Landis-style commissioner I dream of becoming could get corrupted. (*I* wouldn't, of course—you can trust *me*—but others might.) Just look at FIFA. Soccer's world governing body has become downright cartoonish in its catering to the richest and most dictatorial powers in the world, a trend that has only grown since Gianni Infantino took over as president in 2016. (His Wikipedia page doesn't beat around the bush, featuring pictures of Infantino with Russia's Vladimir Putin, Saudi Arabia's Mohammad bin Salman, and Donald Trump.)

You can obviously manage things quite poorly with a commissioner in charge. But the only thing worse might be *not* having one. Professional organizations have commissioners, and at its highest level college football is now a professional organization of sorts. But a quote from Notre Dame president Father John J. Cavanaugh from the late 1940s still rings impressively true: "The type of reformers I refer to are those who play with the question for public consumption, who seem to say that an indefinable something has to be done in a way nobody knows how, at a time nobody knows when, in places nobody knows where, to accomplish nobody knows what. I wonder if there are not grounds to suspect that the reformers...protest too much, that their zeal may be an excuse for their own negligence in reforming themselves."

Before Landis, baseball's National Commission was basically the equivalent of college football being run by Sankey, Big Ten commissioner Tony Petitti, and Alabama athletic director Greg Byrne. Eventually, the public lost trust in this self-interested group, but more than 100 years after the Black Sox scandal, college football still rides with this type of arrangement. In fact, you could make the case that it has shifted even *more* toward self-interest.

For most of 140 years, college football has had a de facto ruler of sorts. The identity of that figure says quite a bit:

1888–1906: Walter Camp. One of the sport's first great players, he also established most of its defining characteristics—downs, 11 players on the field, the line of scrimmage, lines on the field, the safety, slush funds (that one never made it into the official rule book)—and dominated the game as it was defined before the legalization of the forward pass. He also continued to name All-America teams well after he stopped coaching. He felt an ownership of the sport that no one else has matched since.

1906: Teddy Roosevelt. According to Taylor Branch's "The Shame of College Football" in the *Atlantic*, when football's brutal tactics resulted in more and more collegiate deaths—there were a reported 25 of them in 1905—Roosevelt, a big fan of the sport serving his second term as president of the United States, "summoned leaders from Harvard, Princeton, and Yale to the White House, where Camp parried mounting criticism and conceded nothing irresponsible in the college football rules he'd established. At Roosevelt's behest, the three schools issued a public statement that college sports must reform to survive, and representatives from 68 colleges founded a new organization that would soon be called the National Collegiate

Athletic Association." In 1906, the forward pass was legalized, and the game slowly began to open up a bit.

1906–16: The presidents of Harvard, Yale, and Princeton. In the days of baseball's National Commission, college football had its own unofficial commission. And in the years following Roosevelt's summit, the country's three preeminent football schools continued to both play it as well as anyone (they went a combined 199–29–25 from 1906 to 1914) and serve as the relative faces of the sport.

The list of school presidents from this time includes an anti-football force in Charles Eliot, who served as Harvard president from 1869 to 1909 and once said, "Football cultivates strength and skill kept in play by all the combative instincts, whereas the strength most serviceable to civilized society is the strength which is associated with gentleness and courtesy." (He was also anti-baseball because of curveballs. No, really: "I understand that a curve ball is thrown with a deliberate attempt to deceive," he said. "Surely this is not an ability we should want to foster at Harvard.") He was succeeded by A. Lawrence Lowell, however, who learned the exposure benefits of the sport when he agreed to let the Crimson play in the 1920 Rose Bowl (a 7–6 win over Oregon). Among these presidents were also Yale's Arthur Twining Hadley, a major football supporter about whom Roosevelt once said, "It is a great comfort to have among the two or three leading college presidents one who can always be relied upon to say what is wise and sane as well as fearless," and Princeton's Woodrow Wilson, a future U.S. president.

1916–24: The Rose Bowl. Following Michigan's 49–0 walloping of Stanford in 1902, organizers of Pasadena's Rose Parade decided maybe a football game wasn't the best way to raise funds for the parade. But after attempting a number of other events, including ostrich races, they realized that nothing beats football. Washington State and Brown were invited to play at Tournament Park in 1916, the Rose Bowl stadium took the game over a few years later, and this East-West invitational became a national title game of sorts. It provided a breakout stage for emerging powers like USC (with a 14–3 win over Penn State in 1923), Notre Dame (27–10 over Stanford in 1925), and Alabama (20–19 over Washington in 1926). An invitation was the ultimate sign of legitimacy in a time when schools were discovering how intoxicating being good at football could be.

1924–36: Knute Rockne and Grantland Rice. "Outlined against a blue-gray October sky, the Four Horsemen rode again. In dramatic lore they are known as Famine, Pestilence, Destruction, and Death. These are only aliases. Their real names are Stuhldreher, Miller, Crowley, and Layden. They formed the crest of the South Bend cyclone before which another fighting Army football team was swept over the precipice at the Polo Grounds yesterday afternoon as 55,000 spectators peered down on the bewildering panorama spread on the green plain below." Grantland Rice wrote with a flourish and spent a lot of words sharing college football's glory with the nation as a columnist for the *New York Tribune*. And no one benefited more from Rice's mythmaking than Rockne and his Notre Dame teams. (That game that Rice was describing in his famous passage above? A 13–7 Irish win over Army. You'd have thought they'd won 102–0.) Rockne died in a plane crash in 1931, but Rice's mythmaking continued for a while longer as he named All-America teams. No one's opinions held greater sway.

1936–51: Nobody? The Associated Press began polling its writers to create official college football rankings in 1936, and along with the creation of the Heisman Trophy in 1935 it prompted the slow nationalization of the sport. With no conference proving consistently stronger than any other and the rules of amateurism and college sports getting interpreted rather differently from region to region, you could say this was an incredibly decentralized time.

1951–84: Walter Byers. For three-quarters of a century, whoever has controlled television has controlled the sport. Once Penn and Notre Dame backed down and Byers realized he and the NCAA had real power thanks to their control over the national TV contract, he was college football's official ruler. Powerful coaches like Bear Bryant and Bud Wilkinson became particularly huge figures in this time, and we know that bowl officials had outsized control, but Byers held the purse strings and at least 51 percent of the power.

1984–93: Chuck Neinas and Edmund P. Joyce. Following *NCAA v. Board of Regents*, you could say that the CFA, presided over officially by Neinas and in spirit by Joyce, Notre Dame's executive vice president, held the greatest control over college football. If there was ever an opportunity for the creation of a genuine power structure and commissioner position, this was likely it. And out of desperation, the sport actually tried to take a step in this direction until the FTC threatened to get in the way.

As Keith Dunnavant noted in *The Fifty-Year Seduction*, during the budget crises of the late 1980s, the National Association of Collegiate Directors of Athletics (NACDA) began working to move both the CFA's television contract with CBS and the Big Ten's and Pac-10's deal with ABC back under one umbrella. "College athletics was hemorrhaging, and the leaders of the effort believed a single, noncompetitive package could pump an additional $20 million per year into the system—and turn back the clock."

In January 1989, Gannett reported that, in pursuit of a unified deal, ADs were "awaiting word from the Department of Justice and the Federal Trade Commission on what structure can be used for such an agreement. The request was made in the attempt to find a way to limit the televising of games without violating federal antitrust laws. [Tennessee athletic director Doug] Dickey said there will be no progress until groups hear from the federal government." By April, it was clear that they weren't going to hear from the FTC for quite a while. "If the FTC matter runs its full course, it'll take five years," Neinas told the *USA Today* in a piece that also featured an incredibly revealing quote from Arkansas athletic director Frank Broyles: "The FTC has indicated that the two packages are too large to meet the federal courts rulings. They want it to be more like college basketball: one conference per network. So you're likely to see a reorganization or reshaping of conferences. The bigger the conference, the larger its TV market share and potential TV income." In August 1990, the FTC declared that the provisions of the CFA's contract with ABC violated federal antitrust law; in August 1991 one of its own administrative judges ruled that the agency didn't have jurisdiction over the CFA and withdrew its antitrust complaint. But it was too late. "The bigger the conference, the better" had already driven a *lot* of decisions by that point, and college football had already decided to travel down the superconference highway.

School presidents also began to get more involved around this time. In 1984, the NCAA formed the Presidents Commission with presidents from Divisions I, II, and III, and charged it with setting the agenda for the organization. In theory, this seems high-minded and logical, a variation of the "biggest men" that baseball sought in 1920; it assures that officials with loads of academic experience are keeping an eye on college athletics, which, since this is *college* athletics, establishes solid priorities. In practice, however, it means that fewer people with genuine, institutional knowledge are casting votes on important matters. In an interview in 1990, Texas women's athletic director Donna Lopiano said, "Presidents drive me up the wall. They come in two days, three or four times a year, and they think they understand what's happening in this world called athletics. They do not." This turned out to be an idea like term limits in politics: you think it will produce less embedded, self-preservational power, but instead it just gives more influence to the lobbyists and unelected officials—or, in this case, athletic directors and conference commissioners (and, initially, bowl executives)—who know how to work the system.

"I think part of the governance challenge here that really needs to be reexamined is the role of the university president," said Matt Brown, founder of the Extra Points newsletter and another former SB Nation coworker. "Right now, the university president—and for ideologically good reasons—has a lot of on-paper power for negotiating the College Football Playoff. They're the ones that decide conference realignment, and they're the ones that make some structural recommendations. But they don't have the subject matter expertise. Most of them are out of their depth. And, if we're being honest, a couple of the guys who have really made athletics a priority and have wanted to swim in those waters have screwed it up."

1993–2002: Roy Kramer. "I think we'll have another option." That's the quote from chapter 5, when Kramer, the SEC commissioner, quietly put to death Vince Dooley's ideas for a playoff in the early 1990s because he already knew what was coming down the pike. Kramer had already taken a huge risk in expanding the SEC, splitting it into divisions, and crafting an SEC championship game in the early 1990s. When it worked out, and the SEC became an absolute cash cow, Kramer became king until his retirement in 2002. Without Kramer, we don't get the Bowl Alliance or the BCS—for better or worse—as he was a primary architect for both. And without Kramer, the conference arms race doesn't ramp up quite the same, either.

2002–19: Jim Delany. You could maybe say that NCAA president Myles Brand, he of the "collegiate model" and a reinvigorated enforcement department, was a co-commish of sorts for part of this period, and the SEC's Mike Slive, who succeeded Kramer in 2002, was a co-commish for another part. But in this era, Delany became the sport's senior leadership figure. (The fact that Slive wanted a Plus-One playoff in the mid-2000s and Delaney didn't—and we didn't get one—certainly hints at who held the most sway, too.) And if it wasn't true before the establishment of the Big Ten Network and the early 2010s round of realignment, it was definitely true afterward.

As the sport's pseudo-commissioner, Delany pushed the arms race forward while holding back progress on the playoff and NIL fronts as long as possible (as evidenced by his ridiculous Division III reference in the previous chapter). "At times, Jim Delany presented himself as caring about the greater good," ESPN's Adam Rittenberg said, "but the actions haven't necessarily backed that up all the time. I remember Delany standing outside the Big Ten office in Rosemont [Illinois], by the O'Hare airport, and saying, if players want to get paid, that's what minor leagues are for. He was so anti–where we're at right now. But he was anti-playoff until he wasn't. He was a guy that tried to look around the corner, but he was a pretty staunch traditionalist in many ways as well."

2019–present: Greg Sankey. Delany retired in 2019 after three decades in charge of the Big Ten and was replaced for three and a half years by relative college sports newbie Kevin Warren. Sankey, who had taken over the SEC upon Slive's retirement in 2015, therefore became the new ruler. By 2021, he was expanding the league and serving as the face of the committee that ended up recommending expansion to a 12-team playoff. And when CFP expansion found resistance, he embraced a more mercenary approach.

Regardless of how it came about, conferences have acted on solely their own behalf for decades, and the only way that will ever change is if there's a nationwide crisis of some sort—be it of the budgetary variety or something else—and/or if the Big Ten and SEC willingly decide they have too much power and elect to cede some. That's not something that tends to happen in this or any other industry. "If things are gonna get done, it's really up to the Greg Sankeys and Tony Petittis of the world to fix some of these problems at this point," ESPN's Dan Murphy said. "You need somebody who's genuinely incentivized to act in the greater good of the whole overall sport. And college football has never had that."

As Rittenberg put it, "Tony Petitti told me this straight up when I interviewed him: his job is to do what's in the Big Ten's best interest. He works for Big Ten presidents." And considering his television background—more than a decade as a senior vice president with CBS, more than a decade in charge of the MLB Network—it's pretty easy to suss out what those presidents might be looking for from him.

De facto leaders aside, this decade has seen a pair of instances that positively begged for leadership that didn't exist:

The disastrous COVID season. As with seemingly every other industry in America, college football emerged from the 2020 COVID-19 pandemic less prepared than ever for the next disaster. The attempts to get a season off the ground in the summer months, with every single conference doing something slightly different than everyone else and the NCAA able to only establish loose guidelines thanks to the U.S. government's dismal handling of the issue, proved beyond a shadow of a doubt how having a singular voice would help in a time of crisis.

Throughout June and July, despite testing and isolation protocols, schools took turns battling COVID outbreaks as they brought athletes back to train. (LSU and Clemson were among those hit particularly hard.) At the same time, a lot of athletes found their voices and grew empowered during the protests following George Floyd's death at the hands of a Minnesota police officer that summer. Florida State's Marvin Wilson called out head coach Mike Norvell when he made some awkward comments about having reached out to each player individually to discuss the tragedy, and in early August a group of Pac-12 athletes penned a letter that was posted at The Players' Tribune, threatening to opt out of the entire season if demands for improved COVID safety protocols, a greater focus on social justice, and revenue sharing from the league were not met. Syracuse players would sit out the first two days of fall camp with similar demands.

With studies emerging in regard to COVID's longer-term health effects, the Ivy and Patriot Leagues canceled their fall sports in July, and eight of 13 FCS conferences decided to push their football season to Spring 2021. But with so much money on the line in major college football—Wisconsin athletic director Barry Alvarez stated that the school could lose more than $100 million if the football season was canceled—FBS conferences plodded onward with their plans. Most major conferences decided to move forward with conference-only schedules, leaving independents and Group of Five conferences in a tricky spot, but each conference was producing its own tentative plans and protocols (and committing different levels of money to them), which is just dreadfully inefficient.

Things came to a head in early August. On August 9, Clemson's Trevor Lawrence and Ohio State's Justin Fields became the leaders of the #WeWantToPlay movement. "We all want to play football this season," a statement by Lawrence and others read on social media, but they wanted certain needs addressed: "Establish universal mandated health & safety procedures and protocols to protect college-athletes against COVID-19 among all conferences throughout the NCAA.... Give players the opportunity to opt out and respect their decision.... Guarantee eligibility whether a player chooses to play the season or not.... [and] Ultimately create a college football players association." Meanwhile, with the pandemic's numbers skyrocketing in the summer months, the MAC and Mountain West announced they were postponing their seasons. (Conference USA, meanwhile, announced it would play an eight-game season.) After an emergency meeting of power conference commissioners on August 9, the Big Ten and Pac-12 both announced that they would be pushing their seasons to the spring, citing concerns about long-term heart damage from COVID and the need for rapid-response tests to properly protect their athletes. It sure seemed at the time like these conferences thought the other power conferences would follow their lead, but instead, the Big 12 announced it would be moving forward in the fall. The ACC and SEC elected to play in the fall, too, and in mid-September, after the scattershot season had begun, the Big Ten announced it would begin an abbreviated campaign (in empty stadiums) on October 24. The Pac-12, MWC, and MAC followed suit in the following days.

On August 10, at ESPN, I wrote, "Recent months have proven that while a lack of uniformity can be charming in many ways, there are times when more proper and concrete leadership is needed. Even if it had to create different protocols for sets of schools based on the money available for testing, a body with real governing power could have ensured that health standards (and the enforcement for violating those standards) were as stringent as they could be for guiding schools through this pandemic. It could have made sure athletes across the sport were all receiving the same information. It also could have taken charge in the scheduling process to ensure we didn't waste a month waiting for each individual power conference to come up with its own plan for playing this fall. Some schools and conferences have done quite well given the circumstances, but they shouldn't have had to take this on without firmer guidance." The next day, I wrote, "There is not even enough leadership in the country's most popular college sport to get five leagues to work together during the most wicked problem in 75 years. Why exactly does an NCAA-type governing body exist if it cannot help guide schools through extraordinary circumstances such as these?" It was maddening. In the *Atlantic*, Amanda Mull wrote a line I wished I had come up with myself: "Given months to prepare for competition, college football has buckled under the weight of its own nonsense."

By the end of the "season," over 125 games had been either postponed or canceled due to outbreaks, including Michigan–Ohio State and many bowl games. Miami (Ohio) and Ohio were able to each play only three games, and seven teams (Arizona State, California, Colorado State, Kent State, UMass, Washington, and Washington State) were able to play only four. Washington went 3–1 and earned a spot in the Pac-12 Championship but had to forfeit its opportunity; Oregon, just 3–2, stepped in and won the conference title. Eventual national champion Alabama played 13 games that fall while fielding what honestly might have been Nick Saban's best team (and the best team of the 2020s); runner-up Ohio State played only eight games.

There's nothing saying we will have another pandemic to deal with anytime soon—there's a nonzero chance, of course—but with the increasing impact of climate change and what it might do with future large-scale cancellations or plain old travel costs, it's fair to assume there will be more disasters to collectively deal with in the future. And from start to finish, the saga of 2020 exposed exactly how and why college football's leadership void needed to be rectified. Absolutely nothing happened to rectify it.

The Alliance (and its repercussions). You had to feel for Bob Bowlsby in January 2022. The previous summer, he'd been stabbed in the back by a frequent collaboration partner when the SEC's Greg

Sankey took Oklahoma and Texas from Bowlsby's Big 12 and left the conference scrambling to survive. And now he was being stabbed in the front, with distrust of Sankey a clear driving force for other commissioners—namely, those of the other three power conferences (the ACC, Big Ten, and Pac-12, aka The Alliance)—voting down the proposed playoff expansion that Bowlsby, Sankey, and others had worked on for months. Asked why others were against expansion following a fiery meeting in Indianapolis before 2022's national title game between Georgia and Alabama, Bowlsby simply said, "You'll have to ask them."

"This is my 35th year as a Division I commissioner," the MWC's Craig Thompson told media that day. "I've been on the [Division I] Council twice, the men's basketball committee twice. I've been in a lot of meeting rooms with a lot of peers. I have never seen the hardened positions and, 'We're not going to budge, not going to give, don't want to talk about compromise.' I've never seen that in intercollegiate athletics."

"It's been a frustrating process," Bowlsby continued. "Everybody is more concerned about their own silo than everybody else's. The first time around Jim Delany and Mike Slive got past their individual concerns to do what is best for college football. That's why we got to a playoff. That hasn't happened this time."

Sankey, meanwhile, simply called the proposed expansion an "enormous give" on the part of his conference, which was doing just fine with the four-team playoff. For the second time in five seasons, after all, SEC teams were dueling in the national title game. "In December 2018, conference leaders from those not in the SEC were loudly and publicly calling for expansion," he said. "We were not. I don't know if anybody has noticed, but [the SEC is] doing very well in the current system. I'm more than willing to continue forward [with four teams]." A month later in an interview with ESPN's Heather Dinich, he was even more precise: "We were willing to adapt to modern expectations to create opportunities," he said. "Others weren't willing to adapt to create those opportunities. So we'll have to rethink our views as at some point this process reengages." Translated from commissioner-speak: *Fine, you want me to be the bad guy? I'll be the bad guy.*

"That Indianapolis meeting before the championship game, Bowlsby is just livid, comes out and flames everybody," said Ralph Russo, who was in attendance in Indy. "And afterward, Sankey's tone at that point was very much like, 'Hey, we're done compromising.' In the moment you think, well, he's just playing hardball, but I do wonder if he just stayed pissed and if he just determined it at that point." It sure seems to have driven a lot of Sankey's decisions since. "You have this [*House*] settlement," Russo continued, "and you have all this pressure with these laws that wasn't happening at that time, so there is a practicality to hoarding the money. But in retrospect you go, okay, yeah, they were done playing nice."

"I really feel Greg was sincere and legitimate saying, 'I'm giving up something here,'" said Craig Thompson. And when the playoff expansion plan was revealed in June 2021, it quickly proved popular. But the SEC's announced acquisition of Oklahoma and Texas weeks later set off a massive domino effect in terms of both conference realignment and epic distrust. Now, you can make the case that *Sankey* didn't make that move, *Oklahoma and Texas* did. "He did not call Oklahoma and Texas, they called him," said ESPN's Ryan McGee, "and if you don't take those phone calls, you should be fired. So I understand why he did it." One could say that he should have looked out for the good of the sport and told them to stay where they were, but for all we know, they would have then immediately called the Big Ten and knocked down a lot of the same dominoes. Regardless, no one was in charge to tell either Sankey or OU and Texas no. In response, the silly-from-the-start Alliance formed to basically fulfill the same function. And in less than a year, it had both set in motion Sankey's heel turn and devoured itself (when the Big Ten took USC and UCLA from the Pac-12).

"The playoff ended up a good idea used for bad," Russo said. "You have this great power, and you will use it to crush everybody. Greg is a true believer. I do hope that his essence and his background allows him, after they're done gathering as much of a war chest as they can to pay the players—because clearly that's what they're doing, just gathering as much as they can because they know this new system is coming—that there's going to be some kind of epiphany here where they realize, 'We need to keep these other schools viable.'"

Because Sankey is now the sport's de facto commissioner, it's up to him—and his presidents—to realize that. There's no one to do that for him, and the Big Ten's Petitti is clearly happy allowing Sankey to sit at the front of the table. This was all clear years ago, but once again, nothing happened to change it.

Of course, nothing *can* happen—there's no *place* for a commissioner in college football's structure. There's no National College Football Office for him or her to occupy. England has spent the last few years working toward an "independent football regulator" (IFR) to oversee soccer as a whole in the country—in a lot of the same ways we're talking about here—and it might create an intriguing model to follow. Or it might prove to totally lack independence from either partisan government or financial influence. We'll see. Regardless, as long as Ted Cruz and Republicans are in charge in Washington, D.C., there will be no move toward a government position or department. (And if Democrats take charge again at some point, they've already made it clear that this isn't a high priority of theirs.)

The creation of the College Football Playoff as an entity might have produced an opportunity for a leadership structure of sorts—imagine a situation in which schools must opt in to CFP membership (which features a set of rules and protocols you must follow) to compete for the CFP title—but it doesn't appear we're anywhere close to that at the moment. Among other things, expanding the CFP's governance potential would again require a vote from Sankey and Petitti to strip themselves of power. "It could come through the CFP," Nicole Auerbach said. "They already have a governance structure. In theory, they could build that out and add all of the bureaucratic pieces they would need to truly govern the sport. But you would need the people who are powerful now to be willing to give up some of that power for the collective good of the sport—you would need to have a willingness from the SEC and Big Ten commissioners, or those schools in their

> leagues, to give up power to have a collective, centralized, powerful figure. They would have to feed authority to that figure or board or whatever it is to allow them to make decisions that they would then have to agree with. It's just hard to imagine that that would happen.
>
> "I think it would have to come through the CFP," Auerbach continued. "I think you could hire someone who is really forward-thinking and creative, have a built-out structure around it and truly lead from that. That's where all the money is, and that's what ties these leagues together: the postseason. But you do have to have full buy-in from all the people who currently wield the power in the current model."

▻

"I think any governance system probably has to shift power away from the presidents," said Matt Brown, "and either more toward on-campus, subject-matter experts, which are athletic directors, or toward agents—not sports agents, but people that presidents and ADs give that power to. That could be a centralized commissioner. That could be a different board." Right now, however, it's nothing. And without anyone atop the pyramid, any change that could be good for the sport just exacerbates the haves-versus-have-nots divide that already exists.

Writing about the possibility of interleague play in Major League Baseball in the early 1970s, Roger Angell wrote, "The plan is startling and perhaps imperfect, but it is surely worth hopeful scrutiny at the top levels of baseball. I am convinced, however, that traditionalists need have no fear that it will be adopted. Any amalgamation would require all the owners to subdue their differences, to delegate real authority, to accept change, and to admit that they share an equal responsibility for everything that happens to their game. And that, to judge by their past record and by their performance in the strike, is exactly what they will never do." He was right and wrong: it did come into existence, but it took 25 years to do so. We've been talking about a college football commissioner for far longer than that, and there doesn't yet appear to be much of an appetite for subduing differences or delegating real authority. And it's hard to imagine that changing without some sort of Black Sox–level emergency.

Then again, we can only envision what we know to envision. "Our imagination is bound by our experiences," Russo said. "And that's making it hard to see where all this could possibly go. I feel like there's a conclusion here that nothing in our collective experience could have brought us to. There's just something, some other event, that is going to influence college football, probably an outside event. I say that because the history of college football is riddled with outside events totally influencing the power structure. It's demographic movement—where the population goes within the United States. It's wars. It's segregation and desegregation. All of these things. So is the next thing something that completely disrupts the university system? Is it something that disrupts the U.S. government?" Lord knows the early months of the second Trump administration have upended plenty of status quos in plenty of ways that could infiltrate the universe of college athletics, from funding of the Department of Education to the heavy thumb Trump has put on how the economy works in general. "I think that's the hardest part about thinking about where this could go. It's just not in our collective mindset."

At best, a commissioner figure could for the first time give the sport a vision to follow and a steadying hand for guidance. At worst, he or she would reinforce the divides and inequality that have already been established, furrowing his or her brow and talking about how great and deep college football is and how hard it is to satisfy everyone before simply giving the SEC and Big Ten whatever they want.

Regardless, I'm keeping my hat in the ring. **CONNELLY 2025** (or 2036, or 2048, whatever it ends up being).

9.

Soccer Fans Rejected a Super League

In the late 1980s and early 1990s, football's power brokers pushed for a new, more lucrative championship format and a more television-friendly set of matchups.

I know, I know. We've already told that story. But in this case, I'm talking about *European* football. Just as television was completely redefining both college football and every major professional sport in the states, things were following almost the exact same path with the biggest sport in the world, soccer. And it started, more or less, with a bad draw.

On September 16, 1987, in the first round of the 1987–88 European Cup—a tournament pitting each of Europe's league champions against each other—Spain's Real Madrid took down Diego Maradona and Italy's Napoli 2–0 in Madrid, with a penalty goal from midfielder Michel and an own goal from Napoli midfielder Fernando de Napoli. (Fernando de Napoli! Amazing! Imagine a Florida wide receiver named John O'Florida.) At the time, the game was mostly noteworthy because it was played behind closed doors, with a listed attendance of just 499, as punishment for Real Madrid fans throwing objects onto the field (sorry, *pitch*) and interrupting a match in the previous year's European Cup. But a very important person was annoyed that these teams were playing at all.

For each round of the European Cup, the pairings were decided by a random draw. (Whereas we're used to painstakingly seeded tournaments in the U.S., there's always been more of a whims-of-fate feel to tournaments in sports like soccer and, to a lesser degree, tennis.) Other first-round matchups in 1987-88, like Cyprus's Omonia Nicosia vs. Ireland's Shamrock Rovers or Finland's Kuusysi vs. Switzerland's Neuchatel Xamax, didn't exactly jump off the marquee. Italian cable impresario (and future prime minister) Silvio Berlusconi, owner of Napoli rival AC Milan, was baffled as to why UEFA, European football's organizing body, was okay with allowing no-name clubs to advance in the competition while either Real Madrid or Napoli was guaranteed to go out in the first round.

There was a wonderfully romantic aspect to this, as with just the right draw and a couple of great performances, it seemed anyone could go all the way—Romania's Steaua Bucharest did so in 1985–86, followed by Portugal's Porto in 1986–87, the Netherlands' PSV Eindhoven in 1987–88, and Yugoslavia's Red Star Belgrade in 1990–91. But to Berlusconi, there was serious television revenue potential going to waste. He wasn't wrong. He and others thought that European's grandest clubs should be playing each other far more often and for far higher stakes. He envisioned a super league of sorts, as either a replacement for or complement to the European Cup. UEFA, which also liked money and wasn't interested in a challenge, changed its competition's format in the following years. It introduced a group stage to what it would now call the Champions League, assuring that big names would get a healthy number of matches (with the major gate and television revenue associated with that), and it soon expanded its field to give the most successful leagues multiple bids.

The new Champions League was an absolute money firehose, and it didn't take long for its effects to become noticeable. And, as with college football, a player-friendly court decision helped: the Bosman ruling of 1995 banned restrictions on player movement. (Incredibly, a player's club had been able to block his move to another club even after his contract had expired.) This dramatically increased freedom of player movement, and the allure of playing in the Champions League became a major draw for signing the world's best players. It also assured that only teams that were frequently playing in the Champions League could pay the salaries required to land those players. Success bred success, which bred more success, and if a usurper attempted to spend big and join the club, it was virtually guaranteed to run into serious financial problems. Within many countries, clubs that were successful early in the 1990s ripped off long, dynastic title runs with these new advantages; meanwhile, after teams from nine different countries reached the finals in the last 10 years of the European Cup, only teams from the five richest soccer countries (England, Spain, Germany, Italy, and France) have reached the Champions League finals since 2005.

During this same period, English football was experiencing its own power consolidation. Throughout much of the 1980s, the heads of England's more ambitious clubs—in particular, Arsenal, Everton, Liverpool, Manchester United, and Tottenham Hotspur—grew frustrated at other clubs' lack of ambition and their satisfaction with settling for lower television revenues. England's top league sat atop a four-division pyramid called the Football League (now the English Football League, or EFL) with a promotion-and-relegation structure (the same type found in almost every soccer country) sending teams up and down within the pyramid each year. Television revenue was split evenly between the more than 90 clubs in the pyramid, and Liverpool and Manchester United began to wonder why they had to share money with minnows like Tranmere Rovers and Scunthorpe United.

The Premier League formed in 1992–93, the same year as the first Champions League and right around the time that Notre Dame and the SEC were leaving the College Football Association. It would serve as England's top division, and it would still promote teams from and relegate teams into the second division, but it would negotiate its own, far more lucrative television contract (won, initially, by Rupert Murdoch's BSkyB). With enhanced production value and an explosion of money, it would become an NFL for England and the most lucrative league in the soccer universe.

For the last two decades, English clubs, plus soccer royalty like Real Madrid, FC Barcelona, and Bayern Munich, have dominated the highest level of the sport. But this wasn't enough. The richest and most powerful clubs desperately wanted to become even richer and more powerful. Throughout the Champions League era, rumors constantly flew regarding the formation of a Berlusconi-esque Super League. Longtime Real Madrid president Florentino Perez seemed forever obsessed with the idea, and when financial losses associated with the COVID-19 pandemic—which forced cancellations and led to months of games without fans (and the money fans paid)—crippled a good portion of European soccer, Perez and others struck.

On April 18, 2021, 12 clubs—three from Spain (Atlético Madrid, Barcelona, and Real Madrid); three from Italy (AC Milan, Inter Milan and Juventus); and six from England (Arsenal, Chelsea, Liverpool, Manchester City, Manchester United, and Tottenham Hotspur)—announced the formation of a breakaway Super League, with around $4 billion of backing from American investment bank JP Morgan. (Why no German clubs? We'll get to that in a bit.) An initial statement declared that the clubs were doing this for the good of the game: "The formation of the Super League comes at a time when the global pandemic has accelerated the instability in the existing European football economic model," it said. "Further, for a number of years, the Founding Clubs have had the objective of improving the quality and intensity of existing European competitions throughout each season, and of creating a format for top clubs and players to compete on a regular basis." They were clearly believers in good, old-fashioned, trickle-down economics, in which the rich are allowed to make as much money as they possibly can, and it magically benefits everyone. "It's a format to prevent football, which is losing interest, from dying," Real Madrid's Perez would say of the Super League, despite a lack of convincing evidence that soccer was even slightly losing interest.

Three days later, every English club withdrew itself from the Super League after *spectacular* fan backlash.

The day after the initial announcement, irate Chelsea fans blocked the team's bus on its way into the stadium for a match against Brighton. Both inside and outside the stadium, they chanted things like, "You greedy bastards, you're ruining our club!" and, "Fuck Perez!" (Perez, naturally, responded by saying there was almost no one there, and besides, they were all plants.) Nearly every major supporter group for the English clubs released furious statements; UEFA threatened major sanctions; and eventually everyone but Real Madrid, Barcelona, and Juventus—maybe the three clubs most jealous of and threatened by the Premier League's money-printing machine—backed out. The Super League isn't *officially* dead because Perez won't ever let the idea go. But with England's

Football Association announcing that any English clubs participating would be banned from playing domestically, and fans making their voices pretty clear on the matter, it's unlikely that English teams will ever be involved. Without them, you don't have a full, genuinely *super* league.

The histories of European soccer and college football rhyme in many ways, from local teams serving as cultural touchstones to the rampant inequality that both sports have proven capable of generating through the years. We certainly saw success beget more success in the beginning of the CFP era, just as we did with the Champions League, and vague "super-league breakaway" rumors have floated around college football since even before Berlusconi bought AC Milan.

In 1974, the *Texas Monthly*'s Paul Burka wrote a piece called "The Decline and Fall of the Southwest Conference," which included the following passage. "One Longhorn athletic official puts it bluntly: 'We're subsidizing the conference,' he says.... The search for more money, not a desire to play stronger opposition, is behind the occasional talk of a Super Conference that would see Texas pulling out of the SWC to join an elite organization of the nation's traditional football powers." That same year, Arkansas head coach Frank Broyles, always one for a memorable quote, made the media rounds proposing the same super-conference idea. "An irreversible gap is developing between the schools making money off athletics and the schools that aren't," he told the *Atlanta Constitution* that January. "The way our budgets are now it's so much more difficult for a school on the way down athletically to fight its way back. We're going to see a lot of schools drop football and that will be a tragedy. We've got to get them back on sound programs and realistic schedules." Apparently the only way to help smaller schools was to force them to stop competing with richer schools and not to, you know, *create a more even playing field*. Some were even talking about moving back to one-platoon football, aka iron-man football, where everyone plays both offense and defense, to increase competitiveness instead of simply sharing money. It's amazing how creative you can get when you take by far the most obvious solution off the board.

USC's John McKay supported the super league idea, too, but both Arkansas (SWC) and USC (Pac-8) were playing in conferences with a significant amount of dead weight at the time. Alabama's Bear Bryant had no interest in it, saying at a February 1974 coaches clinic, "That Super League, that's a little fast for me. Independents haven't had it that good. You build crowds by rivalries—we can just open the gates now and 70,000 will drop in. Yes, sir, you think long and hard before you leave your neighbors. The Super League—it might be all right up there in the Ozarks." (There is no wrong time to poke fun at the Ozarks.)

The tenor grew a bit more toxic, of course, when Long Beach State's Stephen Horn brought his television revenue sharing plan to the table and football's bluebloods—who, by the way, were (and still are) rewarded for "subsidizing" the sport by getting to win most of its titles—reacted as if, "How about we give more television dollars to Long Beach State and Grambling since the big boys already have all the other revenue advantages?" was akin to lighting the Constitution on fire and attempting to install communist rule in the White House. But, eventually, instead of limiting things to 40 or so teams as often rumored, the breakaway idea evolved into what would become the I-A and I-AA split.

The idea of a super league has rarely been far from the surface since. When *NCAA v. Board of Regents* came down, columnists everywhere began speculating that it would lead to the same 40-team (or so) breakaway. The same happened during the budget crises of the late 1980s. We got distracted by the idea of superconferences during the rounds of realignment in the 1990s and 2010s, but even as power conferences have accumulated more money and independence, they still like to complain that they are being held back by smaller schools. When the four-team CFP came into existence in 2014, the NCAA actually voted to award schools in the power conferences "the right to make their own rules on several issues affecting athletes and competition," according to a *New York Times* article that also called the move "the first step toward an aristocracy in college sports." But they still demand more autonomy. They are still doing so even though they acquired far more money and independence.

If there's a difference in the 2020s, it's that while revenues are ridiculously high for the richest schools, many desperately fear missing out on whatever comes next. Some relevant quotes for you [emphasis mine]:

> It was never our intention to cause such distress, however, when the invitation to join the Super League came...we did not want to be **left behind** to ensure we protected Arsenal and its future.
>
> —the Arsenal board, April 2021

> The possible participation of Chelsea and City has been described by sources as more out of a desire not to be **left behind**, than a fervent desire to lead the charge.
>
> —The Athletic, April 2021

> I just want us to be prepared...I don't want Florida State to be **left behind**. I consider us part of the ACC, but...we've got to be prepared no matter what the options are.
>
> —Florida State president John Thrasher to the *Tallahassee Democrat*, July 2021

If you ask anyone who works in or around college football where they think things are headed in the coming years, they're pretty much all going to predict the same thing. Some details differ, but the idea is always similar: a separation of the sport's biggest brands into a stand-alone league of 20, 30, 32, or 40 teams. Some hedge and guess something larger, like 48 or 64 or 80. You can't find many people who say they *want* it to happen, but coaches think it will, many media members think it will, and FOMO could assure it: when everyone acts out of the fear of missing out and getting left behind, the thing everyone says is terrible becomes a self-fulfilling prophecy. And American sports fans don't take to the streets to express their anger about terrible things all that often.

As with seemingly every other industry in this country, private equity seems poised to drive us further and faster down the least appealing road. It has spent the last few years expanding its reach within the soccer universe. Sometimes that has taken the shape of club ownership: RedBird Capital's vast investment portfolio includes ownership of Italy's AC Milan, France's Toulouse FC, and a minority stake in Liverpool FC. Sometimes it has basically resulted in clubs or leagues selling future revenue for immediate cash injections: CVC Capital Partners, for instance, gave Spanish LaLiga clubs cash in exchange for about 8 percent of the league's audiovisual rights for the next 50 years. (Call this the business equivalent of those credit cards I signed up for in college, with the bad interest rates and free T-shirts.) And sometimes it has simply produced epic disasters. Take 777 Partners: its founders were, according to a $600 million fraud lawsuit against them, "operating a giant shell game at best, and an outright Ponzi scheme at worst," but were still able to grab either shares or outright control of clubs in Spain (Sevilla), Italy (Genoa), Germany (Hertha Berlin), Belgium (Standard Liege), France (Red Star FC), Brazil (Vasco da Gama), and Australia (Melbourne Victory) from 2018 to 2023. They also nearly came to an agreement to purchase England's Everton. The Everton purchase fell through, however, and as everything was falling apart around it, 777 had to sell off all of its shares in 2024, leaving virtually every club it touched in worse shape than it found them.

It's a little trickier for private equity to find a stake within college football since you can't really purchase a university or its athletic department. You can't then sell its parts to some other entity a few years later either. But the Pac-12 attempted to recruit investors from this world in the late 2010s, and in 2024 word emerged via CBS and others that the Big 12—which has also explored selling its own naming rights (picture the "Allstate 12")—was in conversation with CVC Capital Partners for one of those "future money for immediate money" deals, trading up to a 20 percent ownership stake in the league for a cash injection of up to $1 billion. That same year, former Florida State quarterback Drew Weatherford made the media rounds talking about a new private capital partnership between RedBird and his Weatherford Capital, called Collegiate Athletics Solutions. Yahoo! reported that "Weatherford and [RedBird's Gerry] Cardinale are seeking five to 10 programs to invest in as little as $50 million and as much as $200 million. They are in 'deep conversations' with a 'handful' of programs." Now, private capital and private equity (PE) aren't the same things; *equity* suggests a level of ownership that Weatherford went out of his way to insist wasn't involved here. But you do have to figure a group investing $200 million in an athletic program might have some pretty clear ideas about how that athletic program should streamline its spending in the name of efficiency—how many employees to lay off, how many sports to cut, et cetera. As former CFP executive director Bill Hancock put it in a 2025 article for *D CEO Magazine*, "Would a PE owner care about women's soccer, cross country, or wrestling? I think we know the answer." Regardless, one way or another, someone's going to invite the PE vampire into the house. After a presentation from RedBird before the national title game in January 2025, an industry source told ESPN's Heather Dinich that "there's not a chance in hell another year's going to go by with someone not tapping into some kind of third-party money." That will work out fine for some and catastrophically for others.

The largest PE-related headlines in 2024 came from stabs at a super league. In April, a group called College Sports Tomorrow (CST), a collection of college administrators and professional sports team owners—people with experience dealing with PE, if not PE investors themselves—pitched a super league of 80 teams (70 permanent programs, plus 10 promoted from and relegated to the mid-major ranks) divided geographically, and with almost no nod to history, into divisions like "Plains" (Iowa, Iowa State, Kansas, Kansas State, Minnesota, Nebraska, and Wisconsin, plus the decidedly non-"Plains" BYU, Colorado, and Utah) and "Midwest" (Cincinnati, Illinois, Indiana, Louisville, Michigan, Michigan State, Northwestern, Ohio State, and Purdue, plus a Missouri program that has never been conference mates with any of these schools). The regular season would consist of teams playing 14 games across 15 weeks, followed by a 16-team playoff.

That fall, CST also proposed a different idea: a tiered, 136-team, FBS-wide outfit with promotion and relegation and potential collective bargaining with athletes. At least in this one Missouri was paired with some of its former Big 8 mates.

In October 2024 came a much more PE-forward proposal, a pitch called "Project Rudy." (The name was inspired by famous former Notre Dame walk-on, Rudy Ruettiger, who also inspired a 1993 film and, in 2011, was charged with securities fraud and fined hundreds of thousands of dollars.) Private equity firm Smash Capital proposed a 70-team super league basically consisting of the four current power conferences. The media rights for these leagues would be consolidated under one giant deal and tiered so that the best programs earn far more than the rest. All games against Group of Five and FCS opponents would be eliminated, and schools would see an immediate cash injection of more than $5 billion (taken, of course, out of future earnings). It seemed like a pretty straightforward way for PE to insert itself into what was otherwise the haves-and-have-nots status quo.

If there's any major, super-league realignment on the horizon, it's easy to look toward the early 2030s. The media rights deals for the Big Ten (2030), Big 12 (2031), SEC (2034), and ACC (2036) all expire within a reasonably short range, and even the CFP's updated arrangement will likely expire in 2031. Groups like College Football Tomorrow have been reminding school presidents that pooling media rights like the NFL and improving schedules to increase marketable games is the way to pull in more money, and this would be by far the most logical time to attempt that. And in spring 2025, Senator Ted Cruz even broached the topic of an antitrust exemption for college sports to pool rights in exactly this way.

The problem with virtually any super league-style proposal, however, is that there's simply no reason for the SEC or Big Ten to agree to any of them. They already have all the advantages they want. On Fox's *Triple Option* podcast in October 2024, in response to the Project Rudy proposal, Greg Sankey said, "I've studied it a little bit and I come back to, I don't want to dumb down the Southeastern Conference to be a part of some super league notion with 70 teams that some people speculate would happen. They want to be us, and that's on them to figure it out, not on me to bring myself back to earth." And at a media gathering after a summit meeting with Sankey in Nashville that same month, the Big Ten's Tony Petitti said, "I have yet to see a single thing in any plan that I've learned details about that contains things that we couldn't do ourselves and do with other colleagues." Maybe we'll find that giant and unwieldy conferences, unbalanced conference schedules, packed (and often strangely-timed) television windows, and a silly playoff structure that looks somewhat rigged all create so much dissatisfaction and pushback that, combined with a heaping dose of economic instability, the two behemoths are willing to discuss something new. But again, history doesn't suggest that pushback for *anything* will be particularly strong.

Petitti, appointed to replace Kevin Warren in 2023, and Sankey spent most of 2024 getting to know each other and throwing their collective weight around. Their recent summits have served as a nice reinforcement of the old line from economist Milton Friedman: "The key insight of Adam Smith's *Wealth of Nations* is misleadingly simple: if an exchange between two parties is voluntary, it will not take place unless both believe they will benefit from it." They used brute force to both maximize their own shares of future revenue from the freshly expanded CFP—making it clear that if the Group of Five schools who were barely seeing any increased revenue whatsoever were unhappy about it, they could choose not to participate at all—and to spread liability from the *House* settlement among a wide group.

These two conferences have almost all the brands required for a true college football super league to come into existence, and they're pretty happy with life at the moment. "Maybe what we're going to find out is, we are in the Super League," The Athletic's Ralph Russo said. "This is what the Super League looks like. It has been all about stopping upward mobility. If Iowa State can't play Texas, then Iowa State is sort of stuck in Iowa State Land. It doesn't get as much revenue, and it can't build itself up by saying 'We beat Texas,' right? I don't think [a breakaway] happens with a press release and a big announcement and just, like, a guillotine. I think it's brick by brick. We're gonna slowly build that wall, and all of a sudden we're on one side of the wall, and you're on the other side, and there's no ladder. We're practically there, and we are still like, 'Are they gonna leave?' They've left!" Without any reason for the Big Ten and SEC to share their riches or ensure good health for the rest of the sport, they have what they want, they're going to figure out how to take even more, and everyone else has to simply make the most of whatever they get.

▻

During the late 1800s and early 1900s, the relationship between the East and West—in a *world geopolitics* sense, not a "division winners playing in the SEC Championship" sense—was dictated primarily by what came to be called "unequal treaties," in which the winner of a skirmish like, say, the First Opium War, or the assumed winner of a *potential* skirmish would extract trade agreements far more favorable for themselves than their treaty "partners." Both sides got something out of the deal, but it was clear who got more. Over time, this would become a source of frustration for the side getting less, but it kept peace for quite a while. (Until it didn't.)

More than anyone else, California and Stanford accepted unequal treaties when they landed with the ACC. They were unwanted by the Big Ten—well, unwanted by the Big Ten's primary television partner, Fox, anyway—and unimpressed with the types of schools they might end up associated with, in terms of both academic and power-conference stature, if they stayed with Washington State and Oregon State and attempted to rebuild something out west. So they took a reduced media rights share to join the *Atlantic* Coast Conference. It was a short-term move designed as much to simply keep them on the power-conference roster as anything else. Cal's first ACC schedule included first-ever trips to Wake Forest (about 2,750 miles away), Florida State (~2,600), and SMU (~1,750); the first trip to Pitt (~2,600) in 61 years; and a prearranged nonconference visit to Auburn (~2,450). Stanford made first-ever trips to NC State (~2,850), Syracuse (~2,850), and Clemson (~2,600). SMU had volunteered to take no immediate media rights money in an effort to land a power-conference slot, but at least the Mustangs were only one time zone away from most of their conference opponents, not three.

This was far from optimal, but Cal fans tried to make the most of it. And for a moment, the "Calgorithm" took over the world. Following a Week 2 win at Auburn, a poster going by the handle @golDonbear on Twitter/X, responded to the official Auburn football account with a photoshopped collage including Vice President Kamala Harris, Oski (Cal's creepy mascot), Cal players, a rainbow, and the words, "You just lost to the woke agenda." For weeks, Cal fans leaned into Berkeley's left-leaning reputation, posting AI-generated or photoshopped images with jokes about wokeness, participation trophies, communism, et cetera. They joked their way right into a first-ever visit from ESPN's *College GameDay*. The team eventually couldn't match its fan base's performance. The Golden Bears built a massive 35–10 lead on No. 8 Miami in front of *GameDay* and the school's first non-Stanford sellout crowd (52,428) in 11 years, but the Hurricanes charged back to win 39–38. It was the story of the season for

Cal, which came achingly close to a huge year but lost five games by one score on the way to a 6–7 finish. Still, the Bears were ever-so-briefly the sport's main characters.

"I had a very hard time envisioning what my engagement and my investment in the program would be," said Nam Le of Cal's first ACC season. "I had no idea what my falls were going to look like. I didn't know how excited I was gonna be when it was North Carolina State, when it was Syracuse. And it's not any disrespect to those teams—it's just that we are Pac-12 fans, watching the traditional path and journey we would have through the fall splinter."

Every school either has or *could* have a 500-page football history book. Le could write Cal's. He's a teacher, a longtime blogger, and a mainstay on the Cal football Internet, and it's possible no one enjoyed the Calgorithm's moment more than he did. "My dad went to Cal, and he was a first-generation immigrant," he said, "so Cal had a lot of draw on me. I was also growing up during the peak [Jeff] Tedford years," as the Golden Bears spent parts of five seasons in the AP top 10 from 2004 to 2009. They would slip to a combined 12–13 in 2010 and 2011, then let Tedford go after a 3–9 campaign in 2012. "I would enter college on the downslope of that. But I was following this local program, and I expected success, not knowing any better." The Bears would bowl three times between 2012 and 2022, but they haven't topped eight wins since 2008. You don't really know the peak until you're well past it, but the journey remains the journey. "As I've continued since then," he said, "a lot [of my fandom] has been driven by following the story of the program and the journey, no matter how foolish that seems at times, and the ties I have in the community, and the investment in just watching this thing play out. I think that's the case for a lot of fan bases in college football."

Cal fans tried to make the absolute most of an unequal treaty. "Clearly losing the regionality is tragic and disappointing," Le said, "and yet we found a way to capitalize on that and, honestly, get excited about it. I am interacting with fan bases in ways that are more deeply interesting than normal. I think the Stanford aspect of it—your core, one-to-one rival—is very important, and we have UCLA back on the schedule [from 2026 to 2029] for alimony-related purposes." (The regents for the University of

California system ordered UCLA to pay Cal over $10 million per year in "Calimony" because of the damage caused by UCLA and USC moving to the Big Ten and the Big Ten eventually destroying the Pac-12.) "But I think what matters to most people is that we are still playing games of consequence that aren't significant drop-offs in prestige. If it still feels like there is an opportunity for success and that we're not in the lower class, that seems to be most important.

"What I worry about most is our ability to remain at the table," he continued. "We basically caught the last boat. We were deemed literally unviable by the Big Ten even though we offer a major media market and would've made a ton of sense in terms of scheduling. TV networks just decided that we don't matter enough. I think that's the worry of a lot of teams that are on the smaller side that would not necessarily get an invite immediately to that smaller superconference type thing. I know the only thing that can help in this regard is the continuation of a winning program. That is the thing I'm immediately concerned about."

Cal's *GameDay* spotlight didn't end as happily as it could have, but the game isn't really the important part of the *GameDay* experience. When the show sets up on your campus, you've already won. It is a nod to simply *mattering*. As one would expect, *GameDay* spends most fall Saturdays in the hometowns of college football's elite. In its three decades or so as a Saturday roadshow, it's been to Columbus 25 times, Tuscaloosa 19 times, Ann Arbor 15 times, Baton Rouge 14 times, et cetera. The crowds there are reliable but might sometimes take things for granted. The most magical moments tend to come when the show goes off-script. Sometimes that means visiting an exciting smaller-school game—Harvard-Penn in 2002, Division III's Amherst-Williams (aka "The Biggest Little Game in America") in 2007, Harvard-Yale in 2014, North Dakota State–South Dakota State in 2019, Montana–Montana State, or Jackson State–Southern in 2022. But it frequently means visiting an FBS non-heavyweight that is having a moment. Cal and Indiana both hosted *GameDay* in 2024, as did Duke and Colorado in 2023, Appalachian State and Kansas in 2022, Iowa State and Cincinnati in 2021, and Wake Forest and Coastal Carolina in 2020. App State was the story of early 2022, upsetting Texas A&M to bring *GameDay* to town, then beating Troy via Hail Mary on the day of the show. The Mountaineers faded from there, but there's always an upstart doing delightful things in September, and it adds a layer of depth and world-building that no other American sport can match. Both *GameDay* and college football itself are at their best when opening the tent as large as possible.

"What we love about the sport—and I'm not just talking about Cal fans—what's essential to the sport is the ability for non-traditional schools to jump into the picture," Le said. "The ability for TCU to make a run randomly [in 2022]. I think those things are important for creating the next generation of fans across the country because once you get down to this model of 'only a few,' when you are told that your school doesn't matter, and your community doesn't matter—and it's not even so much that you have to guarantee an opportunity in any given year. It's just important being told that you're still viable."

Almost as if I had cued him up, Le tied the idea to soccer. "When you root for a smaller school like us, I think the European football pipeline is very similar: You're a mid-table club a lot of the time, and you have to be able to extract joy in this sport from something else, rather than winning the big one." (California: the Crystal Palace of FBS.) "You have your rivalry game, your derby, and that's important, and then outside of that you are trying to construct an enjoyable experience however you can. And that sometimes means, as fans, injecting yourself into the picture and creating these kinds of memories and silly movements." Still, it's important that Cal's at the table. The Super League threatened to take away Crystal Palace's access to Arsenal and Chelsea, and English fans as a whole made sure everyone knew how they felt about that.

"I am very much a believer of the joy," Le continued. "The ultimate big one is not viable for most fan bases, and we're realistic enough about that. Success and enjoyment really has to be something that you figure out how to cultivate." Just because football passion doesn't exist in the same volume at Cal, or TCU, or App State, doesn't mean it doesn't exist. And our football season would be far less fun if *GameDay* was just bouncing between Columbus and Tuscaloosa. There are endless stories—and there is a lot of joy—under a big tent. Which brings us, finally, back to promotion and relegation. The *biggest* tent.

▻

"I hate to say it, but I think at this point we have gone so far that we need the Doctor Doom solution."

A lot of my best/worst ideas have come from speaking to The Athletic's Jason Kirk, the progenitor of the quote above, the author of *Hell Is a World Without You*, a cohost of "Shutdown Fullcast," and my editor at SB Nation for nearly a decade. When I had my own personal, *WE SHOULD HAVE PROMOTION AND RELEGATION IN COLLEGE FOOTBALL* epiphany, he was the first person I told.

I even know the date it happened: May 13, 2012. That's when Manchester City pulled off one of the greatest finishes in soccer's history. Needing to beat Queens Park Rangers to win their first top-division English title in 44 years (and fend off soccer royalty and rival Manchester United), they instead found themselves trailing 2–1 in the final minutes. But Edin Dzeko scored in the second minute of stoppage time, then Sergio Aguero scored on virtually the last kick of the match—announcer Martin Tyler's call of "AguerOHHHHHH!" is almost as famous as the goal itself at this point—and City were champions. The moment was magical for title-related reasons, especially when mixed with shots of Manchester United, awaiting word of the result and preparing to celebrate. But there was a completely different subplot going underneath all of this: with Bolton Wanderers leading Stoke City elsewhere, it appeared QPR needed to at least tie City to save themselves from relegation, too. The three teams at the bottom of the Premier League standings (sorry, *table*) get relegated to the second division. One match featured do-or-die stakes for both ends of the table.

In the end, despite the loss, QPR were saved by a late Stoke City goal. They were safe when Aguero's shot went into the net, even though they didn't know it. But the angst of the moment was overwhelming. Within days, Kirk, Spencer Hall, and I had whipped together a "Relegation for College Football!" series. "What relegation would allow," Hall wrote, "is the possibility that underperforming teams not living up to the aristocratic standard would be booted off into the mob to prove their worth anew, and perhaps lose their seat permanently to a hungrier, scrappier underling determined to bend the system and its rules to their advantage. If that and possibly screwing someone else out of a spot in the penthouse at the same time isn't the American dream, we don't know what is." Meanwhile, I put together an eight-year relegation simulation (2005–12) that ended up bumping Boise State and BYU into the Pac-10 (at the expense of UCLA and Washington, who were dumped into the Mountain West); UCF and Tulsa into the Big 12 (Iowa State and Kansas to Conference USA); Appalachian State into the SEC (Ole Miss to the Sun Belt); and Northern Illinois and Toledo to the Big Ten (Indiana and Minnesota to the MAC). Duke, meanwhile, was dropped all the way down to FCS's Colonial Athletic Association, Kent State landed in the Missouri Valley, et cetera. It was a fun exercise that we would return to in following years, roping in new converts along the way.

Plenty of people have had similar epiphanies through the years, and I'm guessing a lot of college football fans who fell in love with the popular *Welcome to Wrexham*—a TV show about the travails of the Welsh football club purchased by Hollywood stars Ryan Reynolds and Rob McElhenny—had similar revelations as Wrexham moved up the English football ladder. There's no American sport for which the concept of relegation would work like it could in college football, which has nearly 1,000 teams that have spent most of the last century moving slightly up or down the ladder as is. Not even American professional soccer is as well set-up for it thanks to the "You'll never be relegated if you start this franchise" agreements that Major League Soccer has seemingly baked into its expansion plans from the start to ensure the largest possible investments (and valuations). But college football teams, like European soccer teams, are civic entities of a sort. They don't have valuations and can't be sold or moved to other cities (beyond things like "Miami playing its home games 20-something miles away from Coral Gables at the Hard Rock Stadium," anyway). And the idea of introducing actual *merit* to college football—basing a program's status on what it has earned, not which schools it was friends with 90 years ago—will always be incredibly appealing.

It actually had the attention of the Mountain West for a moment. After the Pac-12 had effectively dissolved in 2023, its remaining schools

(Oregon State and Washington State and, briefly, Cal and Stanford) were looking into a strategic partnership with the MWC. Front Office Sports and other outlets reported on a proposal drafted by Boise State associate athletic director Michael Walsh. The 22-slide PowerPoint presentation was called "Control What You Can Control: An Opportunity to Create a Stable Future for College Athletics in the West," and it laid out a potential 24-school league—featuring the Pac-12's remainders, the MWC and, potentially, Central Time Zone members of the AAC, Conference USA, or the WAC—that could be split into three tiers of eight teams each. It would ensure that the league's best programs were playing each other more frequently, creating the best possible schedule strength for future College Football Playoff pushes. And hey, there was symbolism to this idea taking root in what was once the home of the too-early-for-its-time mega-WAC.

Since one of the scariest parts of a relegation structure is trying to plan a budget for future years when your revenue could shift massively based on success (or a lack thereof), Walsh devised it so that there wasn't a dramatic drop in media rights revenue from tier to tier. MWC commissioner Gloria Nevarez told Extra Points' Matt Brown that the idea had merit, and Washington State's athletic director at the time, Pat Chun, said, "The core concept itself is probably not practical today, but it could be tomorrow, simply because there is so much change coming in college athletics." Translation: *We're not brave enough to do it, but someone else might.*

They indeed weren't brave enough. Instead of embracing creativity and unknowns, the remaining Pac-12 schools followed a tried-and-true path instead: a raid. They took some of the Mountain West's bigger brands in an attempt to create a Mountain West Plus of sorts, a closed version of what might have become the MWC's top-tier division. We could have had three MWCs linked together, but instead we have two competing with each other. Zero-sum, everywhere, at all times.

We also saw the idea of relegation baked into some of 2024's Super League proposals, like CST's April 2024 pitch above. But it was only included as an option for mid-majors—the best schools that didn't get included in the Super League could get promoted into and relegated from one of eight divisions. If the power schools can't ever get sent down, and only one sliver of the teams is ever moving up and down, that only reinforces the gaps between both a) the powers and everyone else, and b) the most powerful mid-majors and everyone else at that level. It only works if the risk exists for everyone.

A few chapters ago, I called the idea of sharing revenue and resources "sports socialism," but what is the current closed system, which forever protects schools that don't earn their spot all that often, if not socialism for elites? As Alina Schwermer put it in *Futopia*, "Closed leagues are a type of elitist socialism in which there is division because there is no competition. More cumbersome, more solidarity, a promise that this world will stand still and that its inhabitants will be taken care of." To hell with that. Forcing schools to consistently earn their spots would raise intrigue across the board; it would also *improve* the top divisions of the sport. With the Boise States and Memphises of the world replacing power-conferences' dead-weight programs, every power conference would be populated primarily by top-40 programs within a few years. Plus, promotion and relegation are incredible storytelling devices. "People love the sense of the narrative journey," Kirk said. "It's not about just one season where you can progress. Boise State would've been progressing that entire time in the 2000s."

Regardless, as with any of the immediately doomed super league proposals above, If there's no reason for Greg Sankey, Tony Petitti, and their presidents to agree to it out of their own self-interest, then it's not going to happen.

But what if it *were* in their own self-interest? What if they were in charge of the entire enterprise? "The only real hope I have is if the SEC and the Big Ten literally just gobble up the entire rest of the country," Kirk said. "They need to realize that it is in their financial interest to be governors of more than just 16 to 32 schools each. It is in their interest to have pipelines of teams that can advance, each of them having their own relegation territory. It is in their financial interest to do that, because look at all those internal competitions you've just created—teams trying to play their way into the SEC—and establish it so that you're not doomed financially if you hire a bad coach and slip for a few years or whatever."

Doctor Doom is a classic Marvel Comics antihero. He serves as a villain most of the time but sees his own actions as benevolent—he thinks of himself as the smartest being in existence and believes the world would benefit from his conquering of it. He works with heroes at times if he believes his own goals are served from it. I'm not saying Greg Sankey would make for a solid Doctor Doom. But I guess I'm not *not* saying that either. "We have gone so far that the Big Ten and the SEC have the chance to install an actual system to a sport that has never had one," Kirk continued. "And it sucks that they're only getting there because of naked greed. But I keep coming back to the Doctor Doom metaphor where it's like, this guy's a sinister asshole, but he's the only one with the greed and the talent to install whatever he wants, and it's going to be a system that works well enough that people think, *Oh, great, we're so grateful for our tyrant overlord*. It's better than an incompetent dictatorship.

"The dream is that the Big Ten spans a part of the country where they have a Northeast division, a Midwest division, a Heartland division, and a West Division," he continued. "And we can just think of the Big Ten West as the Pac-12 rivals playing rivals. Volleyball teams are not traveling across the planet. They're all in the Big Ten, but it feels like they're in the Pac-12. We can recreate regionality in the aggregate. And games between 2–7 teams are more valuable and more watchable! They won't give you Ohio State–Alabama ratings, but it'll lift the floor of every single game."

By now, he was rolling. "This is a business idea! I see the financial incentives. Currently, that end-of-season game between two teams that aren't rivals, they're just playing after Thanksgiving, they're on interim coaches—okay, give that some actual stakes: they're trying to avoid being replaced by Tulane. We have a way for people to give a shit about games between 1–11 teams! And you are then guaranteeing that if a school decides to go all in and invest huge in sports, they're already in your pipeline. That's already your school. And if they decide not to invest, well, they'll slip down and you'll owe them less money."

Let's close our eyes and use our imaginations for a moment, then. Let's say that, at one of their upcoming power summits, Sankey and Petitti decide, "Actually, we *should* just try to rule all of college football!" They somehow convince the presidents of their less-football-hungry (and more likely to be relegated) schools, and they split up all of Division I between them. The ESPN-based SEC absorbs the ESPN-based ACC, while the Big Ten finally nabs Notre Dame and absorbs the Big 12, and having established loose geographic boundaries—the Big Ten takes the Northeast, Midwest, some of the plains and anything to the west, while the SEC is mostly based from Texas to Florida to Virginia-ish—they absorb all the other conferences that fit into these regions. The SEC takes the Sun Belt, AAC, and Conference USA, plus FCS conferences like the Southern, Southland, and the HBCU conferences (SWAC and MEAC). The Big Ten takes both the MWC and the Pac-12, plus the MAC and FCS conferences like the Missouri Valley, Big Sky, Ivy League, and Patriot League. We can even make some geographic corrections, like sending the ACC's Stanford and Cal (and, perhaps, the AAC's Army, Navy, and Temple) to the Big Ten and maybe sending the Big 12's UCF and West Virginia to the SEC.

Now the SEC has the Bayou Classic! And the Big Ten has Harvard-Yale! Both "conferences" end up with around 130 teams, and they split everyone into four tiers: a 24-team top tier, a 24-team second tier, a 40-team third tier, and a 40-ish-team fourth tier. Just think of the inventory! They'd have to create a second Big Ten Network! Call it B2N. At first, the top tier consists of everyone from the ruling conference, plus the best teams from elsewhere, and within these tiers, everyone is split into four divisions based on some combination of geography and rivalry history. Based on 2024 quality, that gives us something like this for the top tier:

SEC Tier 1

DIVISION 1A

Alabama, Arkansas, Auburn, LSU, Mississippi State, Ole Miss

DIVISION 1B

Florida, Georgia, Kentucky, South Carolina, Tennessee, Vanderbilt

DIVISION 1C

Louisville, Missouri, Oklahoma, SMU, Texas, Texas A&M

DIVISION 1D

Boston College, Clemson, Georgia Tech, Miami, Pittsburgh, Syracuse

Division 1A is the original SEC West, 1B is the original SEC East, 1C is a set of old Big 12 rivals (plus the most geographically convenient ACC schools), and 1D is the other ACC schools. From a quality standpoint, these divisions are at least relatively even.

Big Ten Tier 1

DIVISION 1A

Maryland, Michigan, Michigan State, Ohio State, Penn State, Rutgers

DIVISION 1B

Illinois, Indiana, Northwestern, Notre Dame, Purdue, Wisconsin

DIVISION 1C

Arizona State, Iowa, Iowa State, Kansas State, Minnesota, Nebraska

DIVISION 1D

Boise State, BYU, Oregon, UCLA, USC, Washington

Other than the fact that there were seven western schools, and one had to move to the mostly midwestern Division 1C (which will happen from time to time), these are pretty well distributed in terms of geography, rivalry history, and quality, at least aside from that Big Ten East–esque problem where Ohio State, Michigan, and Penn State are stuck together.

Each team plays everyone in its own division, at least one team from each other division, at least one team from a lower division, and at least one team from the same tier in the other conference. That should account for most necessary rivalry games, but that can be tweaked however it needs to be to get everyone to 12 games and get all the sport's most historically valuable games played. Each division champion in this tier qualifies for a 16-team CFP, along with the four highest-ranked division runners-up. Based loosely on 2024 quality and actual results, that gives us a CFP that looks something like this:

Hypothetical 16-Team Top Division CFP

Big Ten No. 8 Iowa at SEC No. 1 Georgia

SEC No. 5 Miami at Big Ten No. 4 Ohio State

Big Ten No. 6 Arizona State at SEC No. 3 Tennessee
SEC No. 7 Alabama at Big Ten No. 2 Penn State
SEC No. 8 Clemson at Big Ten No. 1 Oregon
Big Ten No. 5 Indiana at SEC No. 4 Ole Miss
SEC No. 6 SMU at Big Ten No. 3 Notre Dame
Big Ten No. 7 Illinois at SEC No. 2 Texas

Meanwhile, we've gotten rid of the need for conference championship games, but we're replacing them with something almost as gripping: promotion/relegation playoffs! The last-place team from each Tier 1 division is paired up against a Tier 2 champion (perhaps on the home field of the Tier 1 team?) to fight for a spot in Tier 1 the next season. Envision something like this:

SEC Tier 1 Promotion/Relegation Playoffs

Memphis at Mississippi State
Virginia Tech at Vanderbilt
Tulane at Pitt
UCF at Oklahoma

Big Ten Tier 1 Promotion/Relegation Playoffs

TCU at Purdue
Colorado at Michigan State
UNLV at UCLA
Army at Nebraska

You would have relegation playoffs for Tiers 2 and 3, as well. For Tier 2, they would look something like this:

SEC Tier 2 Promotion/Relegation Playoffs

North Texas at Arkansas State
Old Dominion at Wake Forest
Troy at Florida State
Appalachian State at Western Kentucky

Big Ten Tier 2 Promotion/Relegation Playoffs

Buffalo at Cincinnati
Bowling Green at Northern Illinois
Fresno State at Houston
South Dakota State at Stanford

Fans get to watch their schools playing the opponents they want to play, and we've added an extra layer of stakes to virtually everything. Never mind all the stuff about college football needing someone to say no to Sankey and Petitti. If the goal is to establish the largest possible tent instead of the smallest, maybe all we need is to convince them to unleash their inner Doom.

▻

Even if we don't do it much, I know sports protests work in this country because Tennessee didn't hire Greg Schiano.

In November 2017, Tennessee athletic director John Currie began to home in on Schiano, the architect of a rousing Rutgers revival, as his replacement for fired head coach Butch Jones. Schiano had indeed worked miracles at RU (and has done well again after returning there in 2020), but a brief stint as an NFL head coach had gone sideways quickly, and he spent the last two seasons as Urban Meyer's defensive coordinator at Ohio State. When news broke that Schiano had agreed to terms, Tennessee took to the streets in protest. Someone painted SCHIANO COVERED UP CHILD RAPE AT PENN STATE on The Rock, UT's famous and constantly vandalized campus landmark. (In a deposition in the aftermath of the Jerry Sandusky scandal at Penn State, a former PSU assistant basically testified that he had been told that Schiano had seen sexual abuse taking place. Schiano denied this, and no one else corroborated it.) Surely, plenty of irate Tennessee fans were indeed protesting Schiano's Penn State involvement, fairly or unfairly, but it sure seemed like a lot of them just wanted a coach with a better head coaching record. Regardless, the reaction was swift and massive, and Currie quickly moved on.

(Strangely, he eventually set his sights on pass-happy wild man and Washington State head coach Mike Leach; fans seemed to approve, but other, more powerful entities did not. Currie was fired before he could make the hire and was replaced by former head coach Phillip Fulmer, whose own coaching tenure had begun and ended via catty UT politics. Fulmer would hire former Alabama defensive coordinator Jeremy Pruitt, who would be fired within three years for ultra-sloppy recruiting violations. College football!)

Sadly, when it comes to American sports fans, and college football fans in particular, we don't have all that many other examples from the department of loud protest. What might fans actually fight for? "The depressing answer is, very little," Matt Brown said. "We occasionally will see fan protests over sports cuts. We occasionally will see fans protest over a very unpopular hire or very unpopular administrator. I mean, it was Astro Turfed to hell, but one of the rare examples where this worked was Tennessee and Greg Schiano. It was co-opted by people with money, but there were a lot of actual fans that would show up and yell, and that kind of pushed things. But even that is really rare.

"In this country, schools tend to respond more to capital strikes," he continued. "Florida Atlantic, for example, got rid of 'Owlcatraz'"—the school had signed a stadium naming rights deal with a particularly gross for-profit prison company—"but they didn't do it because of public outcry so much as donor outcry. They could have stomached faculty and students being angry for a little while."

"If there's a situation where it's personally inconveniencing people, it sucks to go to the games or whatever, that could be a bit of a revolt," Kirk said, "but we get used to it. We go along with it. The prices go up all the time. We grumble, but we pay. We have the stupidest conferences, and we're all going along with it. Maybe the bright side of it is we are very adaptable people"—Cal fans are certainly trying to prove that—"and we are good at finding the entertainment in the mess, but we ain't going to rise up about a damn thing."

These answers feel awfully true, which is what made visiting Germany in February 2024 such a jarring and incredible experience. I write quite a bit about the Bundesliga, especially during the (American) football off-season, and in my most recent visit, fans were taking matters into their own hands.

The Deutsche Fussball Liga (DFL), Germany's version of the English Football League, had come to an agreement with good old CVC Capital Partners, in which it would trade a 20-year chunk of Bundesliga (and 2. Bundesliga, the German second division) broadcasting and sponsorship revenues in exchange for a huge chunk of up-front cash—the exact kind of deal we're probably going to see struck by the Big 12 and/or other conferences soon—to be spent on marketing and infrastructure. But in Germany, fans wouldn't stand for it. For weeks, they unfurled huge, angry banners in the ultras sections (where the most intense and organized fans gather) and caused lengthy stoppages at matches by throwing tennis balls onto the pitch. In my favorite touch, a number of fans threw remote control cars (some with flares!) onto the pitch as well: as a steward came to collect it, the car would then drive off, and the crowd would cheer. Fans in the home and away sections unleashed coordinated call-and-response chants. Even during important matches, fans made their opinions clear and created stoppages.

In general, the spirit of the protest seemed to be asking, "How much money do you actually need?" German clubs are fan-owned in a sense—the country's 50+1 rule means that fans are assured a voting majority over club matters no matter who buys into the club—and even if it means that German clubs don't have as much money to work with as clubs in England, the fan-centric culture keeps ticket (and beer) prices down and keeps them loud and engaged. It creates the most incredible match environments imaginable. Fans rebel against anything that violates their habits and traditions, right down to kickoff days and times. (There's no equivalent to Tuesday night MACtion in Germany.) And throughout the country, certain clubs actively stand for something: in Hamburg, St. Pauli is an openly anti-fascist club. The club's decor is pirate-themed, right down to the skull-and-crossbones, and the team walks out onto the pitch as AC/DC's "Hells Bells" plays, but you walk into the stadium under signs that say things like, FOOTBALL HAS NO GENDER. By and large, German fans seem to genuinely want their clubs to reflect their communities and values in Germany. That's one of the major reasons why 2021's failed

Super League included no German clubs—even those who run ultra-rich and ambitious Bayern Munich knew their fans wouldn't stand for such a thing for even one second.

One more thing: the protests succeeded. By late February, the DFL had abandoned its plans. Fans won. They usually do when they fight for something. Chelsea fans wanted their team to keep playing Brighton instead of Atlético Madrid, and it happened. In this country, Oklahoma fans simply said, "Bye, we won," to Oklahoma State upon leaving for the SEC. So much for "You think long and hard before you leave your neighbors."

Could this ever change? "I don't think regular fans are good at really predicting their future behavior," Matt Brown said. "You had people saying NIL would be bad, and they would be less likely to watch their team if it happens, and then they still do it. We have people saying conference realignment is bad, and it is, but TV ratings are great. This is a passive group. They'll whine, but eventually consumers are trained to keep on taking it. It's difficult to get them to change that kind of behavior. This is true politically, too—we don't strike like our European or South American brethren do about non-sports stuff—but it's also true for sports.

"People are invested in college sports because of an emotional connection that they have with that particular institution," he continued. "It's a more personal kind of connection than it is with professional franchises. It's generally less transactional. But while people say that they care about rivalries and regionality, that they care about affordable experiences, their actions don't necessarily react to that. That's why I think there's a bunch of suits in Bristol and Chicago and New York that say, 'Well, they don't really care about that, and we can make more money by making this more accessible to casuals.' And in the short term, they may be right. Long-term, maybe not, but it's like Keynes said—in the long run, we're all dead."

It's hard to imagine what, if anything, might rally college football fans to protest nationwide. But they could still just choose to stop showing up.

10.

From Here to Utopia

My key worry about guys who cover a sport, whether it was football or golf, is you not only cover it, you have to be a caretaker.

—Dan Jenkins

If you were starting from scratch, you would never devise a system that relies on universities to serve as a feeder system for pro sports. It is not what universities were intended to do, and no other country in the world does it that way.

—Joe Nocera, *New York Times Magazine*

Whenever I'm done, I want college football to be great. I want people to want to watch it forever, and I don't want to lose the pageantry of it. We've lost some of it, but if smart people can make good decisions, we can regroup and rally and keep it running for a long time.

—Mike Gundy

It has been said that we all carry our own America with us. My own personal America comes with six seconds left and the home team—anybody's home team—with the ball and trailing by a point or a goal. There is barbecue at the concession stand, and there is beer in a paper cup, and a band is playing across the way. I can be happy there.

—Charles Pierce

> Football must become fairer, more beautiful, and freer. For example, by recognizing it as art, exempting it from the regulations of associations. By democratic production companies creating many parallel formats as cooperatives or foundations. With a financial 50+1 that takes away the dominance of corporations, *a global sports social fund that redistributes money*. Fines for boring competitions. And a system where the clubs that are best relative to their requirements get the most points.
>
> —Alina Schwermer, *Futopia*

> Nothing comes by itself. And little is permanent. Therefore, remember your strength and the fact that each time needs its own answers.
>
> —former West German chancellor Willy Brandt

> Let's start with a little history lesson: in the past, everything was worse.
>
> —Rutger Bregman, *Utopia for Realists*

I've always had a vision for a travel TV show that basically amounts to *Anthony Bourdain, But Sports*. (To any bosses reading this: Hello. Let's talk.)

The basis of Bourdain's shows—*No Reservations* on the Travel Channel, then *Parts Unknown* on CNN—was basically his getting to know a place and its culture through its food. It went far beyond that (especially *Parts Unknown*), but food was home base. Now replace the word "food" with "sports," *et voilà*. There have been a few sports-related travel shows here and there, but nothing quite Bourdain-like in the way that I have in my head. I want to travel across the country and the world, asking "What's it like to be a sports fan in [insert city here]?" But while there are certainly pockets of the United States that live through other sports—high school football in West Texas, college basketball in North Carolina, any number of pro sports in New York or L.A.—you could almost create an entire travel-and-culture show based around college football. Go to Berkeley, then Lubbock. Seattle, then small-school Wisconsin. Tuscaloosa, then

Bozeman. Texas–Rio Grande Valley, near the Mexican border, is getting its startup program going in 2025. Go there. Maybe hop south of the border to Monterrey, too; there's a pocket of college football passion there.

I often joke with my wife that, while we indeed still live in Columbia, our college town, I don't really *exist* here. I don't watch the local news. I'm not entirely sure I could tell you the mayor's name. My commute, into our living room, is about 10 seconds long. If I leave the house, it's probably to go to the grocery store or farmers market (there's a great farmers market here) or pick up a restaurant carry-out order, to be eaten at home. And the only time that really changes is on home-game Saturdays. If I'm going to talk to people in person, if I'm going to have a drink with a friend, if I'm going to meet somebody new, if I'm going to feel like an outgoing person at all, it's almost certainly going to be at a Mizzou tailgate. I share some laughs, I go into the game for a bit, and then I disappear back into my (glorious) hole. My 13-year-old daughter comes along with me, too. Wherever she attends college, she'll be a tailgater. She enjoys going from tent to tent, and she loves cheering and high-fiving with others. She loves college football in that sense and doesn't even like football. That's a pretty amazing thing. Our society has isolated itself from itself of late, and it feels like the list of things capable of actually uniting us, of getting us to actually *physically exist and bond with others*, is as small as it's ever been. But if all we have in common at this point is sports—and college football in particular—then we should lean into that. And if fall Saturdays in college towns are going to be so important to our overall ability to connect as humans, then colleges and college towns should be as well-supported and subsidized as possible. Whether we're talking about government funding of higher education or the financial consolidation of college sports, it feels like we're charging in the opposite direction instead

In the fall of 2023, Rodger Sherman quit his job and hit the road. His goal: to attend as many college football games as possible in a single season. Granted, it was a bit strange that he quit his job *as a college football writer* to do this, but there was method in the madness. "I've been writing about college football for about 10 years now," he said in a video on social media, "and in the Internet age that mainly means just sitting on the couch with my dogs...and blogging about the game I'm watching on

TV. But college football isn't about watching on TV—it's the sport you live, the sport you breathe, the fans and the tailgates and the traditions."

I met with him at a Barnes & Noble near the interstate at the start of his journey, when he was headed west for the first of what felt like about 50 times. During our conversation, he reinforced his main point. We both get paid to write about college football, but you can do that without actually experiencing any of it. Being that I still somehow live in my college town—don't know how I've pulled that one off, honestly—I can hop up to Memorial Stadium on Saturdays, see friends for a bit, and take in at least part of a given game (before I get antsy about all the games I'm missing and return to my sofa); Sherman, on the other hand, lives in New York and felt the need to make up for lost time.

Sherman ended up making it to 62 games. He attended huge rivalry games like the Backyard Brawl in Morgantown, West Virginia, and the final Bedlam Series battle between Oklahoma and Oklahoma State before OU's departure for the SEC. He attended totally random contests like Hawaii at Vanderbilt, Kansas at Illinois, Georgia State at Coastal Carolina, and even an Army vs. Navy sprint football game. He attended some of the biggest games in the small-school universe, like the Brawl of the Wild (Montana vs. Montana State) and an epic battle between NAIA heavyweights Morningside and Northwestern (Iowa) in a blizzard in Orange City, Iowa. He looked exhausted and haggard the whole time as he posted videos and photos of himself on the road and in random stadiums, and I couldn't have been more jealous.

(Okay, I was jealous of *some* of it. I didn't need a mid-August Hawaii-Vandy game in my life.)

One primary theme followed Sherman wherever his journeys took him: college football's superpower is community. "It's such a big undertaking," he said. "For there to be even a Division III football team, at the lowest level of the sport, you probably need at least 50 guys, jerseys, and weight room equipment...the game itself is going to have at least 20 people working it. And when another team comes in, it's gonna be another 50 guys. And to support it, just in the stands and financially, it requires a level of buy-in from the community. It's Division III, it doesn't really have an impact on the larger sport, but all the families are there, and they're out in the parking lot making food for each other, talking... if there wasn't a community around the team, they wouldn't be able to have a team."

There are two types of people in this world: the people to whom this all makes perfect sense and the people who cannot fathom caring so much about a sportsball team. As an esteemed member of *New Yorker* society, Roger Angell seemed to spend a lot of his time around the latter, but he understood and wrote about the former brilliantly. About the raucous celebrations during and after the famous 1975 World Series (Reds over Red Sox), he wrote, "This belonging and caring is what our games are all about; this is what we come for. It is foolish and childish, on the face of it, to affiliate ourselves with anything so insignificant and patently contrived and commercially exploitative as a professional sports team, and the amused superiority and icy scorn that the non-fan directs at the sports nut (I know this look—I know it by heart) is understandable and almost unanswerable. Almost. What is left out of this calculation, it seems to me, is the business of caring—caring deeply and passionately, really caring—which is a capacity or an emotion that has almost gone out of our lives. And so it seems possible that we have come to a time when it no longer matters so much what the caring is about, how frail or foolish is the object of that concern, as long as the feeling itself can be saved." College football combines that level of caring with a level of pure ownership and responsibility that a professional team cannot match.

Whether you're talking about Oklahoma, Georgia State, or Morningside, "There is a feeling of, the guys aren't going to be able to win games unless we get them better equipment, better facilities, or this, or that," Sherman said. "And it makes people feel like they're a part of it, whether it's just the families in the parking lot, or whether they're one of 100,000 people in the stadium, or whether they're one of several million people watching on TV. I don't think other sports necessarily have that."

I don't think it's a coincidence that the NFL fan base and stadium experience that seems most admired by casual fans is likely to be Green Bay's. A city of 100,000 can care about and support a name-brand team like that? Yep. Welcome to any of tens or hundreds of college towns in America. English actor and author Stephen Fry visited every U.S. state for his 2008 series *Stephen Fry in America*, and he attended the 2007 Iron Bowl while in Alabama. He summarized it as only an outsider could. "It's an indication of the size of the U.S. economy and their passion for sport that this is the stadium of Auburn, no more than a medium-sized college," he narrated, almost as if he was voicing a nature documentary, "and this is their annual game against another college within the same state, the University of Alabama, based in Tuscaloosa, a few hours' drive away. This fixture has the scale, intensity, and hoopla of a grand national final but is in reality no more than a local derby between amateur students. Only in America." After soaking in the bands, talking to fans, watching fighter jets flying overhead and taking in everything the event had to offer, he said, "I really don't know if anything sums up the United States better. It's simultaneously preposterous, incredibly laughable, impressive, charming, ridiculous, expensive, overpopulated, wonderful... American." In his corresponding book, *Stephen Fry in America: Fifty States and the Man Who Set Out to See Them All*, he wrote, "If I were asked to find one example of cultural life in the United States to use as proof of how different America is from Europe, I would choose college football. Until one can unravel all the signs and meanings, tribal codes, and weird social nuances behind this powerful and bewildering phenomenon I do not believe one can come close to approaching an understanding and penetration of American life.

College football's long tail—the sheer volume of venues herding in four, five, or six digits' worth of people on a given Saturday—makes it incomparable to anything other than European or South American soccer. And it all comes back to community. "There's a real desire to just be a part of this," Sherman said. "That comes about because football's such a big production. The bands! It requires a band to play a college football game, apparently! I don't know why we decided that! But the size and the grandiosity of it requires this commitment that no other sport asks of us."

No other sport so openly needs us as much as we need it. And it's indeed the only thing a lot of us can agree on at all. At a press conference in 2024, Senator Ted Cruz said, "We can disagree on a thousand different issues all day long, [then] we can come in here and 105,000 people can cheer like crazy at a football game that's about to happen. It brings us together in a way that there is nothing else.... There's nothing like the attachments of alums who went to A&M 60, 70 years ago and still come back to cheer on their team in a football game. That is an amazing thing." If Cruz listed out his 1,000 most strongly held opinions, this might be the only one with which I would agree. But I definitely agree.

Greed, self-interest, and power moves have both pushed the sport forward and held it back. As with seemingly every other industry in America, that dynamic might only multiply moving forward. But, even if the negative effects multiply, we're still probably going to see 50,000+ in the Superdome for the Bayou Classic, and 40,000+ for Farmageddon (Iowa State–Kansas State, one of the nation's underrated rivalries), and even 15,000+ for the Anchor-Bone Classic (Grand Valley State–Ferris State), and some small-school playoff games. "The games are what save us," Jason Kirk said. "Maybe that's the main thing. There's a lot of shit that's just going to get worse—I'm talking about a lot of things at once right now—and institutions do not change for the better unless they absolutely have to. But the thing we love, it can't change. There's nothing that could make a college football game worse. Maybe it's just the cool shit in the middle of the shit storm."

"Here's where my optimism comes: you cannot fuck up Saturdays," Ralph Russo said. "As much as we've tried, you cannot screw up the product. Everybody loves the product. Saturday is amazing. Just use that as the bar. 'As bad as you guys have been at this job, you cannot fuck up Saturdays.' That's the place to be optimistic: people really love this thing, and they really want this thing, and they want a lot of this thing."

We're starting from a place of strength, in other words. There's a lot I don't like about current forces impacting the sport, and the thought of President Trump inserting himself into matters is not reassuring, but this is a long game; each time needs its own answers; and things are still better than they once were. If you reminisce fondly about college football in the 1990s, or 1970s, or 1950s, you're reflecting on a time in which access to the national title was nonexistent for most, fewer games were available on television, and players were less protected and compensated. The haves lord too heavily over the have-nots now, but they always have. Athletes are safer and more well-paid (and have more rights), fans can watch almost any game they want, and the CFP gives us a genuinely national title. There's no curbing the SEC's or Big Ten's bloodlust anytime soon, and it's difficult to create an accurate vision of any sort of socialist, revenue-sharing utopia. But things change. After all, to whatever degree, we're actually paying athletes now. If that can change, anything can.

"When I started, that wasn't even a possibility," Sherman said. "It's hard to really avoid framing it this way, but while some [changes] have not made the competitive aspect of the sport better, you have to listen to the moral part first. I think people overstate how bad NIL and transfers have been for the sport because they don't like when their team loses a player. But it's led to better fits between quarterbacks and offenses, it's led to some great all-time stories. So that's a good thing. But even if it did make things slightly worse, we don't have a leg to stand on here. I can't argue morally that players should be subjected to working for free at the same school for five years because [changing that] will make my enjoyment of the sport slightly less. That's not a legitimate argument, and we framed it as one for far too long."

In the past, everything was worse.

Of course, none of that means we can't still hope for something better.

▻

When you enter Boone, North Carolina, from the east on U.S. 421, you pass a sign that says, WELCOME TO BOONE: HOME OF APPALACHIAN STATE UNIVERSITY, BACK TO BACK TO BACK FCS FOOTBALL NATIONAL CHAMPIONS. The Mountaineers were an early 2000s FCS dynasty, winning three straight national titles from 2005 to 2007 and shares of six straight Southern Conference titles from 2005 to 2010. They pulled the most famous FCS-over-FBS upset of all time against Michigan in 2007, and they were the collective face of the FCS experience. But in 2013, they moved to FBS, passing up potential future titles for the lure of Camellia Bowl appearances, a bit more money and random, attention-getting wins.

Despite a frustrating 2024 season, App State has adapted well to FBS life. The Mountaineers won or shared the Sun Belt title each year from

2016 to 2019, and in their first 11 seasons they've won at least nine games eight times. They've hosted ACC schools Miami, Wake Forest, and North Carolina—something that obviously wouldn't have happened in FCS—and they've held their own with heavyweights, scoring a thrilling win over No. 6 Texas A&M in 2022, nearly beating No. 9 Tennessee (2016) and No. 10 Penn State (2018), and playing a trio of down-to-the-wire thrillers against North Carolina in 2019 (win), 2022 (loss), and 2023 (loss). They've hosted *GameDay*, and they probably will again. Catching a game at Kidd Brewer Stadium, "The Rock," has become a rite of passage for experience collectors like Sherman. They are one of many Group of Five programs that can realistically hope to contend for bids in an expanded College Football Playoff.

They almost certainly won't ever *win* the CFP, however. There probably won't ever be an update to that road sign. Most years are likely to end with minor bowl appearances. App State might therefore be the best example of both the benefits of and shifted goal posts that come with choosing FBS life.

In general, sacrificing title chances for bowls and a far lower spot on the proverbial totem pole feels like a flawed goal structure—one that promotion and relegation would completely solve, by the way: an ambitious program can rise when it has the arrows pointed in the right direction, then sink back toward its natural level when things aren't quite as aligned. Regardless, the jumps continue. Since 2005, 19 programs have joined FBS, including 2003 FCS champion Delaware and Missouri State in 2025; in that same span, only one has left: Idaho rejoined FCS's Big Sky in 2018 after getting booted from the Sun Belt and failing to find a new FBS home. That's it. In 2023, the NCAA raised the application fee for joining FBS from $5,000 to $5 million in an attempt to create a higher barrier for entry, but teams are still migrating, and further dilution of the FCS pool might leave ambitious programs feeling like they have no choice but to do the same. "There's a continued movement of FCS programs to FBS," said Rob Ash, former Drake and Montana State head coach. "I mean, [2016 FCS champion] James Madison, now [2021 champion] Sam Houston—those are the teams we used to compete with on a national level, and they're not in it anymore. If the FCS gets increasingly diluted, I worry about the temptation becoming too much. There are people who'd rather be last in FBS than first in FCS. Having access is still the bottom line, just the opportunity to potentially make it."

"Is it also legitimacy?" Jason Kirk wondered. "Is it being able to say, 'We are a big-time college football school, we're on the same channel as the teams that matter'? Being a school that people know of as a college football school? It doesn't feel like it's about big, 'We're going to win a national title at Temple' ambition. It's almost like it's a research collective, or an AAU designation or whatever. You're technically in the club—you're not *really* in the club, but you can say you are—and people who don't even pay attention to football know that you're in the club." (That's especially true now that club membership includes a spot in EA Sports' college football game again.) "Everybody wants an in-group. The actual 'winning games' stuff, well, that's about how much money you've got."

"I think schools [like App State] would point to whatever fancy building they built on the money they have gotten," Ralph Russo said, "even though it's not SEC money or ACC money. They're still doing a lot better than what they were, money-wise, in the Southern Conference. I think they would say, 'Here's tangible evidence of why we're better where we are.' If you ask Appalachian State's head coach, he might say he'd rather they were just playing for championships. But if you talk to the administrators at that level, I think they're going to point to the tangible things that were bought by [FBS money]."

Don't underestimate the power of a single moment of glory either. It doesn't even have to be with *GameDay* in town. Kennesaw State, Kirk's alma mater, made a rather unsuccessful jump to FBS in 2024, going just 2–10 and firing Brian Bohannon, the only head coach in the history of the program. But one of those two wins came against an unbeaten Liberty team, which had played in the Fiesta Bowl the year before, on a Wednesday night on national television. "We beat Liberty, and we got more attention for that than the previous, however-many decades of the university itself," Kirk said. "We got more out of that than winning three conference titles in FCS, more than hosting FCS playoff games on ESPN.

One FBS win, and there are people across the country who know about the school now because of that."

More schools than ever want to join the party, but those who run the party seem to want to make it a far more exclusive affair. And while we can debate what's best for the East Carolinas and App States and Kennesaw States, there's another layer of larger schools—ones that have only known power conference life and have built sturdy and loyal fan bases—that, like Oregon State and Washington State, could see their major football status revoked or phased out because of a lack of either TV eyeballs or the right allies.

In 2011, as the second round of conference realignment in as many years was playing out, Iowa State faced a loaded Big 12 slate that would feature visits from four ranked opponents and trips to four more. Paul Rhoads' Cyclones would go just 3–6 in conference play with five losses by at least 16 points, but they knocked off Big Ten rival Iowa 44–41 early in the season, and they upset No. 2 Oklahoma State on national television, 37–31, on a Friday night in late November. Despite a mediocre 6–7 final record, attendance at Jack Trice Stadium surged by 18 percent to 53,646 per game, about 94 percent of stadium capacity. And the fans haven't stopped showing up since.

ISU averaged 98 percent capacity during a 3–9 season in 2013. Following a 2–10 campaign in 2014, the school finished a stadium expansion that pushed capacity to 61,500—and averaged 92 percent capacity while going just 3–9. The Cyclones averaged *99 percent* capacity while going 7–6 in 2021. Not including the attendance-capped COVID season, they have averaged under 91 percent capacity only once in the last 14 seasons despite tons of ups and downs on the field. Their 2024 average attendance, 57,884, was higher than that of two SEC schools (Mississippi State and Vanderbilt) and five Big Ten schools (Illinois, Indiana, Minnesota, Rutgers, and UCLA).

In so many ways, Iowa State represents what I feel is major college football's *other* superpower: depth. ISU has almost never threatened to upend the status quo or steal glory from those who love reminding you that they "subsidize the sport." Before this run of great attendance started, the Cyclones had never finished a season higher than 19th in the AP poll and had only ever finished ranked twice. (Matt Campbell's Cyclones have done so twice since: they were ranked No. 9 in 2020 and No. 15 in 2024.) But they're an undeniable part of big-time college football, and they bring color and depth and richness to the sport in droves. To the extent that the school has a lower football ceiling than other power programs, it comes from a lack of great football history, a rather shallow local recruiting footprint, and the fact that it's not as large a land-grant university as others in the Midwest (and therefore doesn't have as rich or large a donor base). But like NC State, Kansas State, and plenty of other schools outside of the SEC and Big Ten, it's a model of program stability and support. Iowa State makes the most of what it has and has built extreme loyalty and enthusiasm in the process.

And yet, through recent trends and power grabs, it sure feels like college football is trying as hard as it can to push Iowa State et al. out of the club. If the Big 12 had collapsed as forecasted during the 2010–11 realignment chaos, Iowa State and Kansas State would have been among those finding themselves with relegated status, perhaps in either a weirdly reconfigured Big East or in the Mountain West. And now, as the SEC and Big Ten look for more and more ways to hoard revenue and distance themselves from the rest of college sports, well-supported programs in the Big 12 and ACC will have to be even more effective and efficient in their actions to have any hope of keeping up.

"The greatest thing about college football is...man, you go to a game at Iowa State, it doesn't feel like going to a game anywhere else in the world," said ESPN's Ryan McGee. "You go to a game at Kansas State, it doesn't feel like anywhere else in the world. I was covering a [NASCAR] race at Kansas Speedway, and I drove all the way out to Manhattan to see Kansas State play Texas Tech on a Saturday night, and I have never had more fun at a football game because I had never experienced it there before.

"Everywhere you go is different," he continued. "If you immediately carve half of that away, that's losing the DNA. TCU made 700 moves and ended up making the right moves, but is there going to be a place for them? If you're Kansas State, if you're Iowa State, if you're NC State, if you're Wake Forest, and you're looking at Mississippi State—I love

Starkville, love it—but these schools are looking over there and thinking, *Now why the hell do Mississippi State and Vanderbilt get to be part of this? It's not fair.*"

"We made this a national sport," Russo said, "and now we're trying to choke off a whole bunch of what made it national. What happens when those 60,000 people who show up in Ames every weekend feel like they don't matter? 'We love our team, but we're not part of anything.' Greg Sankey and Tony Petitti should worry about Iowa State's attendance. I don't know if they completely understand that those people who aren't showing up to the Iowa State game [in this hypothetical future], how many of them are also saying, 'I don't want to watch the Playoff, this has nothing to do with me'? This isn't the NFL—they don't get 15 million people to watch Jags-Colts on Amazon on a Thursday night. The folks in Ames, if they stop showing up, are they also tuning out Michigan–Ohio State? Are they also tuning out Oregon-USC and all those 3:30 SEC games?

"No matter how great LSU-Alabama is," he continued, "it's still getting blown away by Cowboys-Packers. If you've done all this work to build up a national sport, the reason why you've been able to do it is because you have 130 teams—60 or so that are probably more important than the others, and 30 that are more important [from] those 60, but nonetheless, they all count, right? They're all coming through the turnstile in one way or the other. And I don't know if Greg Sankey or Tony Petitti care about the attendance in Ames, but they probably should."

"You know who agrees with us, by the way?" McGee asked. "Kirby Smart. And Nick Saban. And Jimbo Fisher. I remember at SEC media days one year, talking to these guys about all that's changed, and they all basically said, 'All of what's happening benefits us, but does it benefit college football?' Kirby Smart said, 'I'm not worried about Georgia. We're fine. All of this is great for Georgia. But can you really say college football is healthy?'... Those guys agree with us, but they're not gonna say no to any of this other stuff."

College football may be unkillable, but if goals are maximum engagement, maximum support, and maximum enjoyment—and good lord, those *should* be the goals—it seems like telling the Iowa States of the world that they don't matter, preventing any future Boise State–like rises and making 2007-like blip years either even less likely or outright impossible would be a pretty awful way to go about that. Ohio State doesn't need further fiscal advantages. Auburn doesn't need more money to put toward a couple more eight-digit head-coach buyouts. With the expanded CFP in place, college football is awash in cash even if schools finally have to share revenue with their athletes—and even while a healthy chunk of money goes toward settlements and lawsuits and payment for the NCAA's past intransigence in the "compensating athletes" department. Those debts will be paid, and college football's annual revenue will keep expanding deeper and deeper into the billions. That should create the healthiest possible sport. At the moment, it's hard to make the case that it will.

College football's superpower might be community, but that community needs belonging. Or, to quote Roger Angell once more, "The ability to find beauty and involvement in artificial commercial constructions is essential to most of us in the modern world; it is the life-giving naïveté. But naïveté is not gullibility, and those who persistently alter baseball for their quick and selfish purposes will find, I believe, that they are the owners of teams without a following and of a sport devoid of passion."

▻

Everyone has their own version of college football that they carry with them. Even Rece Davis. Before he came to ESPN in 1995, before he began hosting *College Football Final* or *College GameDay*, before he began voicing play-by-play for the EA Sports video game, before he began doing all the things that led to him becoming almost the face and *voice* of the sport, he was a kid growing up in Alabama, becoming totally obsessed with college football. "Probably the first football season I remember is 1971," Davis said. "Alabama was really good, and the high school team in my small town in Alabama won the first of three consecutive state championships. And it was right out of *Friday Night Lights*, where streets rolled up and you went to the playoff games and it was the greatest thing ever. A couple years later, my dad and mom took me to the Alabama–Virginia Tech game, where Alabama ran for like 800 yards and beat 'em 77–6. I mean, literally, they had over 800 yards of offense [828, to be exact]. Bear Bryant had, I don't know, about 140 players, and some people you'd never seen were coming out there and running for 50-yard touchdowns. But even in '71, '72, I listened to every game on the radio and watched the Bear Bryant show and the Shug Jordan show Sunday after church—you didn't get to see [the games] on TV and you watched both shows."

Davis's fixation only grew. "I was a first-generation college student. My parents were not able to go to college, but I did have a cousin who was at Alabama in '73, and he got us tickets in the student section. I was seven years old, and I thought that was the coolest thing ever. It was really great. I remember playing a Pee Wee football game on a Saturday morning, and my dad came to the game. He said, 'Hey, you want to go to Birmingham and see if we can get tickets outside and go to the Alabama–Ole Miss game?' And I was like, 'Yeah!' So we hopped in the car and made the two-hour drive and bought tickets and went in and sat in the nosebleeds. It's always been an important part of what I like to do." A few years later, when Davis inevitably attended 'Bama to earn bachelor's degrees in broadcast news and public affairs, he took in a few more memorable moments firsthand. "Even in those dire times for Alabama," he said, "I saw some extraordinarily memorable moments and games. The Van Tiffin kick was my sophomore year [Tiffin's 52-yard field goal beat Auburn at the buzzer in 1985], and they played Boston College first game [in 1984] and Doug Flutie made some of the most spectacular, amazing—they were down 31–14 and about to get blown out, but Flutie was just a magician. He ran back and forth across the field three times and threw a touchdown pass." BC came back to win 38–31. "He was mesmerizing and just spectacular. So I saw a couple of the more memorable moments of the 1980s there, and it pretty much solidified and cemented what I loved."

Davis is capable of making friends with virtually anyone the world puts in front of him. He can run a conversation between some of the biggest names in the sport on a Saturday morning on *College GameDay*—Nick Saban, Kirk Herbstreit, Pat McAfee—and then he can hop on a podcast from his home on a Wednesday morning to talk to an old nerd blogger like me. He's a positive-but-neutral force in regard to most of the sport's major issues, but he still has opinions.

On realignment and lost rivalries: "I love [Oklahoma athletic director] Joe Castiglione. I think he's one of the finest people in sports administration, but it's malarkey that they can't play Oklahoma State. Come on, man, we got a whole schedule in a week and a half during the [2020] lockdown stuff, and you can't figure out a way to play Oklahoma State? And Oklahoma State's complicit, too, because they're mad, but it was like Texas and A&M, they could have played. They could have played! You can play these games, and you need to. I'm glad Washington and Washington State are playing, Oregon and Oregon State are playing. It was unfortunate for the Cougs and Beavs, but at least they didn't cut off their nose to spite their face."

On player compensation: "I think that it's made it a more honest enterprise. It's not perfect, but it's more honest now. Players have always been compensated in some way, but it has made it more above-board. It's more commensurate with the value of the players. And you don't have these farcical things where you're saying that Reggie Bush and their titles shouldn't count, that Cam Newton shouldn't have been playing. I think putting that farce to bed is probably the most productive change in the enterprise."

On the need for a college football commissioner: "Human nature is not to willingly cede power, and in order to have a commissioner, you're going to have to go against human nature. You're also going to have to go against pride in that. Warring factions are going to believe that they have the best commissioner candidate, largely because that commissioner candidate would probably benefit them, which kind of goes back to the first point of not giving up power. So it's going to be like everything else has been in this sport. It's going to be forced upon it by something from the outside, some type of existential crisis. Maybe it's another lawsuit, maybe it's the next thing that just keeps draining the resources to the point that this can't go on for our own survival, our own good, and we're going have to coalesce under one umbrella."

Davis is bullish about the sport's future because nothing in his past as a fan or face of the sport has given him reason to think otherwise. "You won't lose the hardcores in this sport," he said, simply. "It's so far down the line, and this sport has moved at a glacial pace for more than a century. It recently has picked up a little pace, but it's hard for me to even envision losing the hardcore college football fans, particularly dedicated to the big power schools. I can't imagine what they could do. Maybe the one thing is if it got down to a small enough subset that it was basically the same size as the NFL, and then you still had the big, expanded playoff and therefore you lost all of the feel on Saturday, and everything was, 'Okay, well, so what, we're 7–5, we will get that last wild-card spot,' that kind of thing. I think with something like that, that maybe you lose some hardcores, but that is so far-fetched and so far down the line.

"Now, the casual is a different story," he continued. "I mean, there are probably a lot of things that boost television rating numbers—the people on the edges who are compelled by a storyline or team, whatever it might be, you could probably do something to lose them." He mentions baseball's slipping ratings as an example. "I would argue that baseball has in many ways become very local. People still like baseball. I'll never believe that they don't. I mean, my son's playing in the Frontier League, and I go to Frontier League stadiums, and there are 3,000 people there. People like baseball. It's what you do to get the casual to watch your version of it, that probably you run some risks there." He isn't incredibly worried about creating a split between the nation's powers and a lot of its mid-majors—"If there is another division for the Jacksonville States of the world, for some of the schools in the Mountain West, if there's another division between the ultra-elite and what is now FCS, I don't think that endangers much, just to be candid about it." But he thinks the further culling of the power conference ranks, or the further separation of haves from have-nots among those ranks, might eventually have some consequences. "I don't mean to cast aspersions on these schools, but it seems like Indiana, Minnesota, Mississippi State, Vanderbilt, South Carolina, teams like that, if you start trimming it down, do you reach a point with the bigger conferences where Ohio State and Michigan go, 'Wait a minute, Minnesota, you're pretty much getting equal share here. I'm not so sure about that'? And then to use your Iowa State example, when you start cutting off teams like the Iowa States, the Minnesotas, the Kansas States, I do think that is something that could really hurt the overall perception of the product and the overall interest."

This is also concerning to a football veteran who has witnessed recent separations up close. "So far, we haven't screwed it up, but the one thing I think we have to be careful of is the way we divide up the money," Oklahoma State's Mike Gundy said. "We know that the SEC and the Big Ten have a considerable financial advantage right now over other schools, and moving forward, if we want to do what's best for college football—which is *college athletics*, by the way, because if you don't have college football, you don't have college athletics at Oklahoma State; that's the only one team that makes any money. Basketball makes a little money, but their budget, what they spend is more than they make. And you don't have to be very good at math to realize that won't work [if football revenue shrinks]. So we have to be careful. But I've been in this game almost 40 years. Fans on the West Coast, the East Coast, the Midwest, the South, the North, I don't care where they are—they don't want to turn the TV on and know who's going to win the game. Just like when I watch the NBA playoffs, I just want the team that's behind two games to none, I want them to win so I have a reason to turn the fourth game on."

Even speaking before a 2024 season that would feature some mammoth upsets that altered the final CFP rankings—Northern Illinois (a 28.5-point underdog) over Notre Dame, Vanderbilt (+22.5) over Alabama, Michigan (+20.5) over Ohio State—Gundy thought the recent years had brought an uptick in parity to the sport, even if it didn't prevent bluebloods from winning the titles. "The tragedy would be if we took all the money and we put it in one area where we had 10 or 12 teams, 15 or whatever, that had way more money than everybody else, and you created the Yankees and the Oakland A's," he said. "Would that discourage people from turning the TV on and going to the games? I don't have an answer to that, but I'm concerned. Whenever I speak to the powers that be that have control of this, I tell 'em, don't get away from the parity that's been created in college football over the last six or eight years with conference realignment and especially the last couple with the portal. I'm not in a conference that has all the money, and I don't make the decisions, but I'm hoping that reasonable people that are making these decisions don't get selfish, and I'm hoping they understand that there needs to be parity all the way across college football. Why do people turn the TV on the first two days of March Madness? They love to see the upsets. Over a five-year period, we need 35 teams at some point, once we get going with revenue sharing, to have a chance to win a national championship."

Talking about this sport offers up endless opportunities to contradict yourself—college football is unkillable but vulnerable, it's great but it's terrible, et cetera—but again, if the goal is maximizing enjoyment and engagement, my own beliefs about where things should head are hopefully pretty clear by this point, and I feel I have at least a little bit of evidence on my side.

College football is better when teams are playing the opponents their fans want them to play. Rivalries, after all, are the greatest single marketing tool college football has.

College football is better when athletes are represented and well taken care of...and as many schools as possible can compensate them appropriately. (College football is also better when coaches can still plan their rosters and develop their players at least a little bit.)

College football is better when *GameDay* is in Boone, or Boulder, or Greenville, or Columbia Damn Missouri. And when Southern Miss has enough of what it needs to scare the hell out of Alabama or Mississippi State every now and then.

College football is better when we know that someone is looking out for the sport. Or at least, I *think* it is—I haven't gotten as much proof as I'd like in this regard.

One would never create a system like this from scratch, but we've got this strange, beautiful thing, and we've got all we need to make it as healthy as possible. College football is a mirror of America—far more than preferable sometimes—and, like America, it could become so much more beautiful, fairer, and freer than it has chosen to become. It is appallingly flawed and desperately in need of a caretaker. It is also the highlight of millions of lives. It is wearing its coaches out like never before, but it is also treating its players better than ever. Its future is forever bright and intriguing. But there's no reason not to pursue something even brighter. We are its owners, and it can become whatever we want it to become.

Acknowledgments

I thought about writing this book chronologically, maybe still starting with the Texas-USC rewatch but then jumping back to the Carnegie report and the SoCon's formation, then working through those dastardly Penn Quakers, the playoff proposals of the 1960s, and onward. I thought about being a real journalist and interviewing about 150 prominent people, including all the current-day characters, and telling this story through their words.

Instead, I decided to write this thing in the most *me* way possible. Beyond anything else, I feel like I'm a pretty decent observer. So I did that. I reread books I'd finished long ago. I read quite a few new ones that I'd intended to get to for a long time. I scoured the archives as a decade-long subscriber at Newspapers.com, maybe the single most valuable subscription I've ever purchased. (The site is also a constant reminder of how blurry our current news environment is becoming. It's almost easier to find what people were saying and thinking about developments in 1959 or 1989 than, say, 2009 or even 2019.) I challenged my own set of ideals for more than a year, and I tried as hard as I could to find new potential solutions for old problems that I hadn't yet considered. I wanted to write 10 essays on 10 topics that could almost stand alone if they needed to. And I talked to people who could help me get from point A to point B as this production rolled along.

There were the incredibly smart and insightful current and former coworkers who have long helped to mold my college football conscience—some of them former SB Nation coworkers (Matt Brown,

Jason Kirk, Rodger Sherman, Bud Elliott), some longtime ESPNers (Ryan McGee, Adam Rittenberg). (I don't think Bud actually ended up with any quotes in the book somehow, which is an absolute injustice considering his opinions are more valuable to me than those of almost anyone else I know.) There were people who do great work and brought specific subject-matter expertise and insight to the table (Andrew Carter, Ben Haumiller, Max Laughton, Nam Le). There were a couple of individuals whose work I've followed for a long time and who, along with Brown, bring extreme, NCAA-related subject matter expertise to the table (Dan Murphy, Andy Schwarz). And there were just the plain old awesome professionals, veterans from different parts of the football machine whom I just really enjoy talking to: Rob Ash, Nicole Auerbach, Rece Davis, Mike Gundy, Ralph Russo, Craig Thompson. Hopefully you found the historical aspects of the book unassailable, the opinions apt, and the occasional emotional appeals worthwhile.

Thank you to those who spoke to me for the book (I owe you all free copies). Thank you to my father, who put the first set of eyes on everything and said he needed some Dramamine after reading the twisty, turny realignment chapter. Permanent thank yous to my mother for making me an optimist, to Jamie for making the sacrifices that helped to create this writing universe of mine, and to the rest of our little family unit (Erin, Darlene, Suzan) for making it a pretty awesome little family unit. Thank you to my literary agent, Erik Hane, and anyone else at Headwater Literary Management who helped to arrange for this book's publication. Thank you to the fine folks at Triumph Books for publishing it. (The cover rules. Thanks for that, too.) Thank you to those at ESPN who encouraged and helped me through this process—especially to the bosses and editors who helped to make sure I wouldn't get myself into trouble! And thank you to those who have read this far.